ZEN ENTRY POINTS

Paul F. Schubert

SophiaOmni Press

Sumi-e Paintings by the author

The chop impression on each painting has the characters of the name given to the artist.

粘大
鋼勇

Dainen Goyu (*Greatly persevering, with indestructible courage*)

ISBN: 9798565859355

SophiaOmni Publishing

Visit our website at:
www.sophiaomni.org

To Peggy, With Gratitude

Love emanates from her like a bath of diffused white light. As with light, love can be experienced as visible, obscured, or missed. Just as white light is also exactly all of the colors of the rainbow, each one having a differentiated effect on the senses, love is similarly nuanced and can be experienced in both unified and differentiated forms. The capacity to experience both forms is one that can be taught and learned. For almost four decades, Peggy has taught me Love.

Know that in a remote place in a cloud covered valley,
There is a sacred pine that passes through the chill of the ages.

Denkoruku Case 2

Contents

issues surface together, making them difficult to sort out and bringing a sense of malaise to the practice. The table below can be used to assist in addressing such issues.

Many of the topics in the outline are unpacked further in subsequent sections. These topics are highlighted with an *. These points may help sustain the practice.

Intent	Individuals practice for different reasons and it is useful to have a clear intent. The Buddha's intent for teaching was to put an end to the suffering of all sentient beings. This is also referred to as the ***Bodhisattva's Vow**. However, there are other intents, perhaps to calm one's mind, which have their own validity. There are a number of different classifications of Zazen which have addressed this and one type is included here. (***Categories of Zen Practice**) An intent is a direction, not a goal. There are no real goals to be achieved in the practice. (***Progress in Zen Practice**)
Zazen/ Posture	Since meditation is the heart of the practice, take the time to establish confidence in the method. There are many places to have access to personal instruction for zazen, usually from a senior student or teacher at a Zendo. There are also web-based videos. If the opportunity is available, take beginning instruction at different places. Every instructor emphasizes aspects of the procedure and each individual also responds to them differently as time and conditions change. Usually, people begin with awareness of ***Following the Breath** and may use ***Shikantaza**. (Procedural outlines for periodic review of both of these methods are included in Appendix B.)
Questions	Questions almost always arise after sitting for a short while. Procedural questions can be addressed immediately. (For example, a common concern has to do with the eyes maintained slightly open.) Make getting the questions about the method resolved

your first priority so that you can gain confidence in what you are doing.

Different questions about topics of practice grow out of continued sitting. These arise as part of the experience. (***Sitting Still, Silence**, **Problem Solving, Mistakes**)

A caveat: During periods of instruction, it may appear that zazen is a tool in order to be used for a purpose, occasionally stated as calming or purifying the mind. This is a normal reaction, but as the practice develops, zazen can be experienced as life itself.

Attitude/ Awareness

The approach is to make a full effort—sitting with body and mind is the aim. This expression is often referred to as whole-heartedness. As a reminder, the original Pali term that was translated as Mind, does not fully capture the meaning in English—heart-mind is sometimes used. In simpler terms, just put everything into it. (***Mind**)

A point often missed: Making a full effort does not mean controlling the mind or tying it up in knots (***Not Controlling the Mind**). A knotted mind is seeking a goal. A relaxed mind is not a striving mind. Further, a relaxed mind is not the same as a calm mind; one can be relaxed, agitated, and intense at the same time. It may seem paradoxical that a full concentrated effort can be made with a relaxed mind. An analogous example is high performance athletics. Athletes train hard, but do their best, when they are relaxed.

There is often anxiety at beginning a practice, 'of doing it right,' 'of getting rid of thought' (***Thoughts as Opportunities**) or 'attaining calmness/nirvana' which adds to strain. Such anxiety is a perfectly normal starting position and will be worked through in time. The awareness of this condition is nothing other than practice itself.

Discouragement (***Discouraged in Many Ways)** is part of the practice. It is disconcerting at the beginning, but with experience, confidence develops and discouragement is seen as another phenomenon that comes and goes. Discouragement may reoccur periodically. The adage two steps forward, one step backward is a useful guide.

Persistence

Identify a time in your schedule when you can usually meditate. A regular time slot conserves the mental energy of making a new decision each day of the time to sit. A key word here is 'usually.' Situations will arise that upset the daily routine and prevent it. If some days are missed, just move on to the next day without recrimination. If you are sitting at home, it is more important to sit regularly than for a fixed overly long length of time. The time period will naturally expand with regular sitting.

Sitting with a group is a proven way to re-energize the practice. As mentioned earlier, it is especially useful to sit with different groups at the beginning. This has the added benefit that you will naturally find a place that is best for you.

There are additional comments about working with a teacher. (***Working with a Teacher)**

Provisional

All phenomena, including teachings, are provisional or impermanent. Everything comes and goes—the obligation is to make the effort in the present moment. **(*Provisional Nature of Teachings)**

Sitting Still

The body must be quiet and still in order to work with the mind. This requirement for stillness is the foundational basis for the posture. As always, different people have different interpretations on what it means to sit still. Each individual brings with them their unique physical history, strengths, limitations, and residues of injuries. These factors have to be considered when others give instruction about sitting.

The first point is to differentiate clearly between conditions that lead to discomfort from those that can exacerbate or lead to an injury. Some discomfort is inherent in the process, but any activity that leads to injury should just be avoided, no matter what anyone says. With this criterion as a guide, instructions can be interpreted wisely, not literally. As an example of discomfort, an itch may develop and the tendency is to scratch it. If it is scratched, it will subside, but will return at a later time. An alternate possibility is simply to be present to it. Initially, an itch arises as a sensation, followed by a perception, and then a story may develop as the discomfort becomes the biggest concern in the universe. Finally though, it may fade with no physical activity. This approach is using the sense phenomenon of the itch to develop awareness. The itch will subside almost fully with the passage of time.

Yamada suggests that one begins with a full-lotus posture that may initially cause discomfort and just grow into it. "Although it may be rather painful at first, if you persevere you will eventually be able to sit comfortably in this position."[1] In this culture, few are successful with this approach.

Suzuki provides a generous and realistic guide:

> Yesterday I said, 'However painful your legs are, you shouldn't move' and some people may have understood what I said literally. What I was really saying is that your determination to practice should be like that. If it is too painful, you can change your posture, but your determination should be like that. And 'should be' is also a good example. It is not necessarily so.[2]

In practice at a zendo, there are often calls from the monitor to sit more intently, not to move, to maintain a posture. The calls often come across with a harsh edge. The comments are generally not personal but directed at the group. The real intent is to get one's attention so that they can devote themselves to the task at hand. Some practitioners benefit from these calls, others tense up. View them as aids or admonitions rather than criticisms.

Initial Stages: Not Controlling and Finding the Mind

I often choose this story as a good entry point for considering ways to work with the mind during meditation:

> Two shepherds were given flocks of sheep to care for in open fields. The first shepherd kept them together in a close formation. Whenever one moved from the herd, he jumped up and prodded it back to the formation. The more the sheep strayed, the more he jumped up. The sheep became irritated by all the prodding and he exhausted both his patience and energy. The second shepherd mentally marked out a larger area, like a playground, to keep a watch from the top of a hill. The sheep were free to move any-

> where in the area. Mostly, they were content, but occasionally one moved toward the boundary. The shepherd walked over and gently guided the sheep back into the playground. Neither the sheep nor the shepherd exerted much energy to do this and at the end of the day, calmness prevailed for both the herd and shepherd.

Zen meditation is about growing awareness and emptying the mind. At the beginning, some discipline is given with the procedural instructions, for example, paying attention to the breath and becoming aware of thoughts and attachments. Watching the mind is not the same thing as controlling the mind. Sometimes, enthusiasm kicks in and there is an effort to control the breath and mind. This situation is analogous to the first shepherd's behavior in the story above. The ultimate direction is to let the mind be free. Actually, since the mind is not a substance or a thing, there is no mind to find or control.

Takuan Soho writes about the initial stages of meditation practice:

> When the mind is tied down, it tires, and is unable to function as it should. If the mind does not stop with [i.e. attach to] things, it will not be stained by them and will be used well. Let it alone to run off wherever it will. Because the mind is stained and stopped by things, we are warned against letting this happen, and are urged to seek after it and return it to ourselves. *This is the very first stage of training* .... He lets it go where it wishes.
>
> The effect of tightening up the mind is to make it unfree. Bringing the mind under control is a thing done only in the beginning. If one remains this way all through life, in the end he will … not rise above the lowest level.[3]

Ta Hui emphasizes this tendency to control as well, adding that the mind has no real substance:

> These days there's a kind of phony whose own standpoint is not genuine: they just teach people to control their minds and sit quietly, to the point where the breath ceases. I call this lot pitiable. I'm asking you to meditate in just this way, but though I instruct you like this, it's just that there's no other choice. If there were really something to work on in meditation this way, it would defile you. This mind has no real substance; how can you forcibly bring it under control? If you try to put it under control, where do you put it?[4]

Yamada comments further that not only is there no substantive mind to find, but when desires stop, the mind is free from unrest:

> Bodhidharma sat facing the wall. The second patriarch said, 'Your disciple's mind is not yet at peace. I beg you master, give it rest.' Bodhidharma said, 'Bring me your mind and I will put it to rest.' The patriarch replied, 'I have searched for my mind, but I have never been able to find it.' Bodhidharma said, 'I have finished putting it to rest for you.'
>
> We are all searching for peace of mind outside ourselves, which is like hunting for a man on an uninhabited island .... Once you have found out that the island is uninhabited, your desire to search there for a man will end. [Added note: Not only that, the island is yours and you are free on it.]
>
> When you stop desiring, your mind will come to rest. You will be at peace just as you are. Then you will find that your mind is completely free from unrest and uneasiness. Is there any happiness other than this?[5]

I close this topic with a few points that are emphasized by the different teachers and one point that is not. It is clear that the mind is not a thing and not to be confused with the brain. However, we are so accustomed to being under the impression that we are controlling our minds that it is a normal entry stage of practice. Ta Hui even adds that 'controlling the mind' is a common instruction at the beginning. Ultimately, trying to control the mind is a self-limiting exercise. It's especially important to make this point or one can just go on trying to control the mind. However, left unsaid in the above quotes, is that allowing the mind to be free is not an easy practice. It requires time and effort. And with this understanding, one can continue practicing without being discouraged.

'Mistakes' in Practice

There are many ups and downs in this practice. If you are aware of the possibility of a rollercoaster practice at the beginning, it won't disrupt or discourage you so much. Mistakes and errors are the coin of the realm. You can either get real benefit from them or become discouraged. Right at the beginning, you must be aware that the benefits of a meditation practice do not proceed in a prescribed path. Two steps forward, one step backward is an appropriate characterization. Sometimes, it seems to be the other way around, one step forward, two steps backward! Based on my own experience, that's just part of it.

The first category of errors to consider are systematic errors in the meditation procedure. At the very beginning, there is much information presented on posture, breathing, and working with thoughts and distractions. Although they are presented sequentially, each of these elements eventually becomes integrated. After several sitting periods, you have a much clearer idea of the meaning of the instructions. If there are any uncertainties about the instructions, it is important to check back for clarification. Get the enterprise off to a solid start. At some places, introductory instruction is occasionally given to the entire group present, both beginners and long-time sitters. People from both groups often report that they heard something to enhance their practice—either because their perspective had changed, or the instruction just came from a different person. There is always something new to learn.

It is sometimes reported that after a relatively calm period of sitting, a turbulent period follows, such that attention cannot be maintained for two breaths in succession. The conditioned ego has its own agenda and does not give ground easily. The ego can be compared to a bully, but like a bully, there is nothing substantive behind it, and with persistence and effort, the power of the conditioning diminishes.

Procedural mistakes are a different matter. When you go to different zendos, the overall practice is the same. However, it seems that every organization has its own specialized procedures, which of course, are the 'authentic' ones. There are variations of bowing, walking meditation, entering or exiting the zendo, greeting the teacher, and chanting, to name a few. It's almost inevitable that the visitor runs afoul of some of them and is corrected. Corrections are often not made in a pleasant tone.

Such corrections can be viewed as teaching/learning opportunities rather than as errors. In addition to making the procedural change, be aware of the reaction of the mind. It might be anger, embarrassment, no reaction at all—it really doesn't matter. It is the awareness that is the important factor. On occasion, a monitor may shout at someone. Later, the monitor may remark that they weren't angry, they were just trying to get that person's attention.

One thing to keep in mind—in a well-run practice center everyone is working to support each other in their practice.

Reflecting on Experience during Sitting and Problem Solving

Q: I have noticed myself thinking a great deal about my experiences sitting, often thinking about the contradictions that seem to be in our perceptions. Does thinking about your experiences while sitting form an important part of practicing Zen?

A: There is often a strong inclination to reflect on life situations during quiet periods. Zen sitting periods are no exception. Sometimes this activity takes the guise of thinking through or clarifying a problem. The aim in Zen meditation is to empty the mind. This aim is reinforced in the introductory instructions: Become aware when a thought arises, acknowledge it, then let the thought gently go, and return the attention to following the breath. The thought fades away since it had no independent life of its own. In this activity, we are working with the nature (there is no independent existence) of the thought rather than its story or content. The story of the thought may be entertaining or even fun, but it is experiencing the nature of the thought that is the direction of practice.

This activity of becoming aware of what is actually happening and returning to the breath is really the engine of meditation. It doesn't matter if the same thought reappears in a few minutes or seconds. The procedure is the same. In this perspective, thoughts are natural products of mind and what we have available to work with, so we use them.

The content of the thoughts is a different issue. On our everyday level, thoughts are useful to navigate in the world, plan activities, do calculations, etc. There is an appropriate time for these activities. However, that time is not during the zazen periods. So when you find yourself reflecting or solving problems during the sitting period, just acknowledge it when you become aware of it. I find a good analogy for letting a thought go is that of a released feather, dropping and floating downward. The thought fades and attention is returned to the breathing.

People often report that after they sit zazen for a while, working at full awareness with the distractions of the mind and returning attention to the moment, they have more insight into their issue than when they had reflected on it deliberately. Practice returning your attention and see for yourself if this is the case.

It is tempting to use this quiet time in order to examine or solve a problem, perhaps an issue at work or in a relationship. The time seems like a step removed from the ceaseless demands of everyday life. There is an appropriate time to explore these types of issues in a rational or conversational mode, but it is not during a meditation period. Such an exercise of problem solving is actually dissipating energy and reinforcing the closed system of rational thinking. At those times when problem solving seems attractive, it is important to be reminded of the aim of zazen.

Dogen, one of most prominent Zen teachers, has very definite opinions about where the focus should be placed:

> "Do not think good or bad. Do not judge right or wrong. Stop conscious endeavor and analytic introspection. Do not try to become a buddha."
>
> "You should stop searching for phrases and chasing after words. Take the backward step and turn the light inward."[6]
>
> "It is taught not to wait for enlightenment outside practice."[7]
>
> "Zazen is not learning to do concentration. It is the dharma gate of great ease and joy."[8]

In full effort of body and mind, there is no space for speech or intentional thought or ideas about conceptual problems. A good summary by Fujita:

> Since these capacities—moving, speaking, grasping, thinking—are the ones which human beings value the most, we might accurately say that 'entering zazen is going out of the business of being a human being' or that in zazen 'no human being business gets done.'[9]

These quotes have stuck with me for different reasons. Dogen gets at the idea of thinking and searching outside and beginning the practice where you are, not where you hope to be. Also, a point that he makes consistently is that zazen is not a tool, but is our life itself. The phrase from Fujita "no human business gets done" resonates at both the level of not working out a rational solution and that the direction of a Zen practice is to go beyond our idea of the experience of our life as a human being. At this level, the direction of Zen is not to become a 'better' person, but to experience who we are.

Still, there may have been a pressing problem that was in mind to solve. The direction is to put full mind and body into the zazen. 'Awareness and returning to the moment' is the engine of meditation. Put your trust in the practice. Allow yourself to put yourself aside and to be the practice. Later, when it is an appropriate time for problem-solving, you may have a different perspective and 'know' something new.

Why Are They Shouting at Me?

In many sitting groups, and especially at retreats, participants are encouraged to really make a full effort at each moment, for example being aware and paying attention to each breath. The experience is that attention and energy do ebb and flow during periods of sitting. Sometimes, time is just passing with low energy effort and it is difficult to bring awareness to the present. This is a normal occurrence:

> When you become sleepy during zazen, you must wake up by vitally putting your energy into your zazen with your flesh and bones, especially so that you don't chase thoughts. You must be wide awake and return to the reality of life. (Uchiyama)[10]

In order to help individuals maintain energy during sitting periods, monitors may be assigned to have responsibilities to help the participants. These responsibilities include assisting any individual who may be in distress. The monitors also offer reminders and encouragement to maintain attention by moving slowly throughout the room. They may adjust the physical posture of some people in order for them to be erect. On occasion, there may be energetic exhortations to sit still, which can be startling to the practitioners. Although this may be disconcerting and misinterpreted by some practitioners, the aim is to help everyone to be, as in the quote above, "wide awake and return to the reality of life."

The misinterpretation of the monitor's actions sometimes leads to the nagging thought that making the effort is still 'not doing it good enough.' Doubts arise. A tense mind replaces a relaxed mind and the effort becomes forced in order to achieve an outcome, which may be staying out of the line of fire of the monitor! The effort may devolve into achieving longer term goals such as 'getting rid of thoughts' or 'settling the mind.' Energy is redirected to meet these perceived goals or, at least, measure progress. After a while, people get tied up into knots.

These posture adjustments used to happen very often with me. It seemed that every time the monitor would come past, there was an adjustment. It was very disconcerting to my practice. Finally, I realized that I did not have very much awareness of my body in space. For myself, I couldn't distinguish whether I was sitting upright or leaning to one side. Consequently, the adjustments did not have a lasting effect. Finally, I did some body work and could distinguish for myself if I was upright.

The intended way to take the exhortation is simply as a reminder. If it comes at a high volume, in the ideal case it is to get one's attention, never to denigrate anyone. Received in this way, one can simply check the posture, check the mind, and go back to work at a higher level, maintaining the non-striving mind.

At virtually all zendos, people are very welcoming and accommodating to the disorientation of beginners. People are happy to guide beginners in the right procedures. The attitude may appear gruff, however that is just the style.

Time To Pay Attention

> A master gardener, famous for his skill in climbing and pruning the highest trees, tested his student by letting him climb a very high tree. Many people had come to watch. The master gardener stood quietly, carefully following every move, but not interfering with one word. Having pruned the top, the disciple climbed down and was only ten feet from the ground when the master suddenly yelled: 'Take care, take care!' When the student was safely down, an old man asked the master gardener: 'You did not let out one word when he was aloft in the most dangerous place. Why did you caution him when he was nearly down? Even if he had slipped then, he could not have greatly hurt himself.' 'But isn't it obvious?' replied the master gardener. 'Right at the top he is conscious of the danger, and of himself takes care. But near the end when one begins to feel safe, this is when accidents occur.'[11]

The gardener knew what every safety expert now teaches: Accidents occur more frequently at the end of the work day. The job is almost done, perhaps some fatigue has occurred, but primarily the attention is turning elsewhere to the next activity. It is much the same for meditation. As the sitting period moves along, some tiredness may set in. I sometimes wondered if perhaps the person keeping the time was not paying attention and forgot to strike the bell.

Occasionally, there can be a sense of satisfaction that a good job was done this period and it's time to ease off. Though the period may be nearing an end, making the effort right up to the closing bell is important. The mind may have settled during the period and continued effort can build on the earlier work. People are encouraged to take advantage of the full opportunity. In the Zen hall, the monitor is filling the role of the gardener in the story.

Keisaku: An Encouragement Stick

There is an optional method to help restore alertness during a long meditation retreat. The keisaku is a thin, flat, flexible wooden stick that can be used during periods of meditation to remedy sleepiness or lapses of concentration. The practitioner can request, through a series of silent bows, that the monitor use the keisaku stick to strike acupressure points in the region on the back near the shoulder. These blows release tension there, cause a momentary sting, and restore energy. The action also makes an unexpectedly loud sound that spreads throughout the room. The sound often awakens others.

The keisaku is used only upon request now. In earlier times, the monitors had the authority to use it at their discretion. The level of intensity of the strikes depends entirely upon the individual monitor and may range from soft to sharp.

People have widely divergent opinions about this method of encouragement ranging from enthusiasm for its effect to avoiding it completely. Some places do not use this method at all for a variety of reasons from philosophical issues to physical concerns about injury.

In the absence of a personal monitor, here is an example of a good self-reminder at the beginning of the period: Imagine that there is a lion prowling in the room. A hungry lion. Just waiting to see movement so that he could pounce. How still you would sit then! The stakes are high. But actually, the stakes are higher than being attacked by the lion. Making the effort is the difference between being asleep in life or having direct experience of life.

Remembering Silence During a Retreat

During a retreat (whether a day or a week) there is full silence until the end of the retreat. Maintaining silence is often presented as a rule to be followed, but that directive shortchanges the practice of silence. Another view is that being in silence is the opportunity to experience the vastness of our life.

There are levels in the admonition that can deepen the individual's own practice. Mental activity is a form of speech which can be seen as 'communication' with ourselves—in our thoughts, our likes and dislikes, or in rethinking events of the day at bedtime. As a form of thought, this 'communication' is conceptual and is dissipating energy and hindering the full experience of our life. The admonition is also intended to bring awareness to this activity.

Holding silence is important for reducing interference with the practice of others. For that reason, this instruction extends to eye contact and other courtesies. At first glance, such behavior may seem unfriendly or rude, yet it demonstrates a deep respect for another's practice by not distracting them. It is especially important not to interrupt another since the depth of their practice cannot be known to us.

Remembering silence is the experience of full being. It is the stillness of our nature. So, silence can be practiced rather than viewed as a burden:

> Cast away all speech.
> Our words may express it,
> But cannot hold it.
> The way of letters leaves no trace,
> Yet the teaching is revealed.
>
> (Dogen)[12]

2

Sustaining a Meditation Practice

It is a common occurrence for people to enthusiastically begin a sitting practice, maintain it for a few weeks or months, and then have it fade away, often with a feeling of incompleteness. After the first flush of energy that arises from a new experience wears off, the unexpected elements of a practice begin to surface. The expectations that have brought one to give Zen meditation a try may very well not have been met. One may have ideas of how a practice should proceed, how long it may take, how progress is measured, exactly what zazen is, what the larger body of teachings is about, or how teachers and others can help.

The following story, although it may appear harsh, is a reminder that these types of questions have long arisen when a new discipline is begun.

Trying Too Hard: A Different Way to Learn

Matajuro, in a desire to become a sword master while his aging father was still living, went to the hut of master Banzo:

> 'How long will it take me to become a master?' he asked. 'Suppose I become your servant, to be with you every minute, how long?'
>
> 'Ten years,' said Banzo.
>
> 'My father is getting old,' pleaded Matajura. 'Before ten years have passed, I will have to return home to take care of him. Suppose I work twice as hard. How long will it take me?'
>
> 'Thirty years,' said Banzo.
>
> 'How is that?' asked Matajura. 'When I offer to work twice

as hard, you say it will take three times as long. Let me make myself clear. I will work unceasingly. No hardship will be too much. How long will it take?'

'Seventy years,' said Banzo. 'A pupil in such a hurry seldom learns quickly.'

Matajura accepted but was forbidden to handle a sword or even speak of fencing. Instead he was put to work cutting firewood, working in the garden, and cooking.

Finally, after a year, Matajuro grew frustrated, suspecting that he had been tricked into becoming nothing more than a servant for Banzo. Angrily chopping at a log one day, he sank the blade of his axe into a log. He failed to notice that he was no longer alone until he was sent reeling into the woodpile by a vicious blow. Dazed, he looked up from the ground to find the master brandishing a length of hard green bamboo above him. Wordlessly, Banzo left as silently as he had come.

It was a couple of hours later, while the boy was cleaning, that Banzo struck again, harder this time. 'You expect to learn swordsmanship, but you cannot even dodge a stick!'

He began to concentrate, no matter what else he was doing, on keeping himself ready for an attack. Banzo struck at him five times a day, then ten, then twenty, always when his student was busy at his chores. Matajuro would be occupied with one task or another, to find himself suddenly jumping at the slightest unusual noise and missing some of the swipes aimed at him.

When Banzo failed to connect his stick to Matajuro's head or shoulders, he switched his strategy. In addition to the daytime assaults, he started slashing at Matajuro, when the boy slept. Matajuro was forced to teach himself to sleep lightly with his subconscious remaining alert. His instincts continued to sharpen.

One night as Matajuro was preparing dinner, Banzo struck from behind. Matajuro didn't move from his crouching position by the fire. With one hand, he snatched up a pot lid and fended off the blow, then returned to the cooking without a pause.

That night, Banzo presented his student with a certificate of full proficiency in the art of fencing and a fine old sword.[1]

Progress in Zen Practice

Progress is so ingrained in our culture that we are conditioned to think that the quality of life is improving; that we are going somewhere better. Another view is that life is just going on. Similarly, in Zen, progress can be discussed from the everyday perspective or from an ultimate perspective.

Western perceptions about progress are conditioned by the environment. A good example is the General Electric Company in the 20th century. The company began in 1892 (with Thomas Edison as one of the principals). Similar to technology today, electricity was disruptive to the established system. The first application was for lighting. However, consumers had no idea of the potential impacts on their lifestyle. GE understood that their success depended upon convincing consumers of their need for electricity. Electrical products followed (electric irons-1905, vacuum cleaners-1908, refrigerators-1927) with the message to create a need. The attitude at mid-century is epitomized by their slogan: "In engineering, in research, in manufacturing skill, in the values that bring a better, more satisfying life, at General Electric, progress is our most important product."

There is a range of contradictory statements about progress in Zen practice. Some of the ambiguity in interpretation of them stems from the perspective from which the comments arise, the intention of the teacher, and the nature of the audience. The starting point must come from a recognition of the conventional attitudes about practice.

For example:

> How should you check on your progress in Zen practice? Since the benefits of zazen are intangible, even though you may practice earnestly, you may be unaware of the benefits and feel that practice isn't having an effect ... after several months to a year, you should compare your physical and mental condition to what it was when you began ... you should realize what you notice is only a fraction of the actual effects. (Yamada)[2]

Yamada is recognizing the general attitude toward progress and is proactively addressing it to the beginner. His stated concern is that if the person is unaware of the benefits, their resolve will weaken to the point of abandoning zazen altogether. One can become aware of physical changes (for example a tendency to become less angry, better sleep habits, increased ability to concentrate). The admonition is not to actively look for changes on a daily basis, but to be aware of them when they occur, and use them to bolster resolve to continue. Yamada shows a bigger card—that there is more to it than consciously observed. This is developed by Deshimaru:

> If you practice zazen only once, that once is progress.
>
> But the progress I speak of has nothing to do with the steps of a stairway leading to satori (enlightenment) at the top. If you practice zazen, here and now, you can become like Buddha. There are no degrees. If you are truly without goal or desire for profit, then you realize Buddha.[3]

No breath of zazen is ever wasted. Practice takes us in the direction of experiencing our life.

There are certainly periods when it doesn't appear that way. When the mind does not settle, or physical conditions of the body or environment distract, the whole enterprise feels like wasted time. That could actually be the case. However, if one is present to the experience, the "here and now" as Deshimaru says, it is true practice. It is being present to the time and conditions of life as they are now. This is progress in that life is actually experienced. It is not progress in the sense of General Electric products.

On the other hand, the teachings of Dogen and others flat out state there is no such thing as progress. How can there be if practice and realization are one? This is the perspective of zazen as life itself:

> Don't stain your zazen by saying that you've progressed, feel better or have become more confident through zazen. (Sawaki)[4]

> No need for advancement. Any idea of wanting to make progress is already a regression from the place of the Unborn. A man of the Unborn has nothing to do with either advancing or backsliding. He's always beyond them both. (Bankei)[5]

> Thinking that practice and enlightenment are not one is no more than a view that is outside the Way [that is, deluded]. In the buddha-dharma, practice and enlightenment are one and the same. (Dogen)

> Because it is the practice of enlightenment, a beginner's wholehearted practice of the Way is exactly the totality of original enlightenment. For this reason, in conveying the essential attitude for practice, it is taught not to wait for enlightenment outside practice. (Dogen)[6]

The implications of this last statement are enormous to the beginner.

He says that the beginner in wholehearted practice is no less a Buddha than any 'advanced' student. There is emphasis on wholehearted. I don't think that Dogen's statement can be explained, but rather intuitively known. Nonetheless, there are any number of commentators who do make a distinction between practice and enlightenment. They are speaking from the everyday perspective.

Discouraged in Many Ways

Discouragement is an integral experience of a meditation practice. It happens at some point to most everyone. For some, it is the end of the line. For others, it is part of the deal and it can arise at any time. Discomfort can occur right from the beginning. Quite frankly, it is disconcerting for beginners coming into a Zen Hall for the first time. The whole physical set-up can be intimidating. The rows of cushions, the altar, the various musical instruments—all have functions that are not fully understood. Then there are the procedures for moving in the zendo, (bowing, walking) which even if explained in an introduction, seem different when you enter the meditation room. Later, one becomes aware of the dedication and sustained practice of the long-time members. Doubts often arise as to whether one belongs there and can lead to negative comparisons about one's ability or interest to practice with such sustained dedication. Such doubts are often magnified in subsequent conversations since some practitioners have the habit of discussing their longevity as if it were a badge.

Discouragement may arise during a sitting period which is riven with distractions. It could be that one cannot hold attention for two breaths in a row. It may be the inability to sit still. Despair can rear its head when it appears that the timekeeper has lost track and the period will never end. The mental story often goes in this direction: "After sitting for all of this time, if this is the best I can do, I quit." I was at a week-long retreat (sesshin) and had exactly that experience on the third day. As it turned out, I did not have my own transportation, so there was no choice but to sit through it.

Some people do walk out there and then. Others just try to keep going and experience that distractions do pass and give way to other experiences. Arising and fading are experienced. Impermanence is the nature of all things and the lesson can be allowed to flow into our flesh and bones.

After practicing for some time, one can 'be the discouragement' that arises when anticipated awakening experiences have not occurred.

Sometimes this feeling is accompanied with a sense of embarrassment. After all, this is the direction of practice. A paradox of practice is that there is a direction but no goal. It is crucial to remember that all that anyone can do is make their best effort. We are fully responsible for the effort. The individual has no control over the time and conditions that contribute to the manifestation of any sudden experience. Our original nature is us, whether we know it or not.

Discouragement can also be a tool when viewed through the lens of an attachment. We may have a cherished idea of how the practice should be going and then realize that the situation does not meet the expectation. From this perspective, discouragement can be treated in the same manner as attachments discussed in an earlier section; acknowledge the thought, let it go, and return attention to the breath.

There is an exchange attributed to Soen Nakagawa Roshi. This exchange is often quoted, but the original reference has not been located:

> Student: "Master, I am discouraged, what should I do?"
> Master: "Encourage others."

How this response is interpreted depends on the individual at the moment of hearing the words. For some, it may mean to leave your ego pursuits behind and put your energy to others, either by example in practice or direct action. The work of helping others and reducing suffering is not dependent upon the transient emotion or feeling. It is a constant teaching. However, at another level, if no separation is perceived between self and other, there are no others to encourage, and there is nothing to do but live fully in the moment, whatever it is. Helping others occurs as a spontaneous activity.

As this verse shows, one never can predict what becomes of seemingly futile effort:

> Three years of bitter suffering
> To finish planting the bamboo
> One more night of careful work,
> And it turns out plum trees.[7]

Categories of Zen Practice

People become interested in a practice for different reasons. Some have personal issues and have a desire to calm their mind or emotions. Others are dealing with problems of suffering and life and death, and their aim is to resolve them. At the beginning, students are encouraged to practice at the level of their energy and interest.

Based on the intent of practice, a classification of five styles of meditation was made by Kuei-feng Tsung-mi (780–841). The categories below are not fixed and may overlap. They reflect the fact that individuals have different motivations in practice. This is sometimes an issue since the aim of many experienced practitioners is to arouse 'bodhicitta,' the desire to save all sentient beings, and can marginalize the other categories of practices. Dogen reminds everyone: "A beginner's meditation is the complete expression of perfect enlightenment."[8]

These styles are summarized below:

Ordinary Zen (Bompu Zen)

Ordinary Zen does not contain religious or philosophical elements. It involves practice and experiencing the law of cause and effect. Typically, it is a person counting or following the breath. The objective of ordinary Zen is to increase happiness in the emotional sense. As concentration and insight develop, responses to everyday situations become more appropriate to oneself and others. It is a real practice, but does not have the direction of awakening. Ordinary Zen is a fine introduction and may (or may not) lead to the other categories.

Outside Zen (Gedo Zen)

'Outside' here refers to practice outside of the Buddhist framework. Practice might consist of prayer and devotional meditation. It is often associated with the cultivation of mystical powers (siddhis).

Theravada Zen (Shojo Zen)

The intent of this practice is to become free from attachments and suffering from the idea of a 'self.' The intent is to work with one's own suffering, not just to relieve the symptoms but also the cause. This leads to an experience of one's own life.

Mahayana Zen (Great Vehicle, Daijo Zen)

This practice has awakening as its aim—to experience the fact that self and things are both empty. The practice may be shikantaza or koan study. The practitioner directly confronts the problem of life and death, delusions, the suffering in the world, and the salvation of all sentient beings. An emphasized difference is that since all beings are interconnected and have one nature, our own liberation cannot be separated from all beings.

Supreme Vehicle Zen (Saijojo Zen)

There is no objective and the practice is shikantaza, just sitting, and being present to what is. The practice goes beyond distinctions, just life arising. It is the realization that all beings have the same nature, embodying our own, and living it out.

Can People Acquire Mystical Powers from Zen Meditation?

Experience in many cultures and religious traditions has demonstrated that psychic powers can be developed by spiritual practice and awakening. The manner in which these powers are employed has varied widely among religions and depends upon both the cultural and historical circumstances.

In the *Kevatta Sutra*, the role of miracles is discussed by the Buddha. The conversation begins with a suggestion by Kevatta to show a miracle for teaching purposes:

> It would be good if the Blessed One were to direct a monk to display a miracle of psychic power from his superior human state so that Nalanda would to an even greater extent have faith in the Blessed One.
>
> When this was said, the Blessed One said to Kevatta the householder, 'Kevatta, I don't teach the monks in this way: Come, monks, display a miracle of psychic power to the lay people clad in white.' (DN 11)

Edward Conze emphasizes the point that these phenomena exist, but historically were not central to the teaching of ending suffering:

> On the whole, the attitude of the Buddhist Church during the first millennium of its existence seems to have been that occult and the psychic are all right as long as one does not take too much notice of them as a kind of cheap stunt to the populace. One day the Buddha came across an ascetic who sat by the bank

> of a river, and who had practiced austerities for 25 years. The Buddha asked him what he had got out of all of his labor. The ascetic proudly replied that now at least he could cross the river by walking on the water. The Buddha tried to point out that this was little gain for so much labor, since for one penny the ferry would take him across.[9]

The anecdote above, taken from his 1951 book, is not in the current translations of the sutra and is apparently apocryphal. It has been cited innumerable times over the years in slightly different forms. In today's teachings, there are a number of different approaches to this question. The opinions below range from the everyday explanations to the teaching of emptiness.

Joko Beck:

> Practice is not about having or cultivating special powers. There are many of these and we all have some of them naturally; some people have them in extra measure .... I sometimes had the useful ability to see what was being served for dinner two doors away. If they were having something I didn't like, I didn't go. Such abilities are little oddities and again they are not what practice is about.[10]

Special powers in this view are not unusual at all. Each person has different native abilities, which may be particular to an individual. Examples are an enhanced sense of smell or the ability to memorize pi to a ridiculously large number of decimal places. The point here is that these are aspects of life and nothing to be sought after.

A famous saying of Layman P'ang.

> [My] supernatural power and marvelous activity—
> Drawing water and carrying firewood.[11]

These words are a reminder that what we see and hear and sense as 'normal' are actually miraculous in their own right. Although people may not appreciate it due to habit or conditioning, all of life is mystical. Every activity, such as eating, breathing, running, is beyond thought or rational understanding. Letting go of conditioning allows this magic to shine through.

Nagarjuna is credited with developing some of the core teachings of the Zen Mahayana School. A major focus was on emptiness: Phenomena do not have an inherent existence, they are 'empty' of independent existence. Further, even emptiness is empty:

> "All is possible when emptiness is possible.
> Nothing is possible when emptiness is impossible."[12]

From this perspective of no independent existence of phenomena, there is the possibility of anything manifesting. In the everyday world, there do seem to be limitations. However, the perception of the phenomenal world is constrained by what the senses can detect and experience. This constraint is a limitation that we have become so conditioned or accustomed to, that it is taken for reality. When there are no barriers, the infinite range of possibility can be appreciated. The question of special mystical powers then is irrelevant.

Is Zen a Religion?

It depends on who you ask.

There is some interesting background here. If the question was asked in early 19th century Japan, there would have been no response. There was no concept of Western religion at that time. In broad outline, the Japanese word 'shukyo' meant 'principles and teachings,' specifically of Buddhism. In the mid-19th century, when Japan began to open to the West, and 'modernize,' there were major changes in the lives of the people. During the Meiji Restoration (1868-1912), there was intense infighting between Shinto, Buddhism, and the government. The practices of Shinto and Buddhism were separated. Buddhism was suppressed and struggled to redefine its role in modern Japan. It was the result of the confluence of long tradition, politics, and some Western influence, that led to the reconception of religion in Japan and the adoption of the term 'shukyo' for this new situation. The role of the Western influence has generally been overstated and the process of how the idea of religion developed continues to be debated by scholars.[13] This background is a reminder though, that there is a tendency to interpret the past through our present cultural lens.

Obviously, there are many different ideas about the definition of religion, so that discussion is best left for the 'professionals.' For some, the question of religion is an important question to consider before they take up a Zen meditation practice. Below, three 20th century Japanese Buddhist teachers offer slightly different perspectives on the question. The intent is to provide some examples so that individuals can draw their own conclusions.

Yamada:

> "I often say Zen is not a religion. But if salvation is considered the task of religion it is. However, unlike faith-based religions, Zen rejects concepts and beliefs as a means of knowing the truth."

He has explained to Christians that zazen is not religion in the same sense as Christianity and in his view, anyone with a heart and mind can practice zazen in order to deepen their own experience in their native belief:

> However when seeking to produce the right conditions in the mind, ideas associated with one's religion can become obstacles for one to practice single-mindedly. The conditions that zazen requires of the mind are concentration of attention and forgetting oneself. If one is a Buddhist, one must put aside Buddha, if one is a Christian, one must put aside God.[14]

Uchiyama:

> Zazen is in no sense a sect or creed, nor should it be.
>
> If religion means teaching about the most refined attitudes towards life, then Buddhism is certainly pure religion. This basic Christian attitude towards life is also the basic Buddhist attitude towards life.[7]
>
> Behind zazen, there is the religion of Buddhism .... For zazen as religion it is of primary concern to cast out this ego-centered way of thinking which clings to body and mind.[16]

He states that in zazen we can see directly the "kingdom of God within us" and that the "pure content of prayer is all included in the zazen form of prayer."[9] Uchiyama uses the term religion here, but the description of zazen is a practice which takes one in the direction of full experience.

Deshimaru:

> Zen is beyond religions. Christians, nuns, and priests practice zazen.

> Zen is not philosophy, not psychology, not doctrine. It is beyond philosophies, concepts, forms. The essence of Zen is not expressed in words. Of course, there is Zen Buddhism which is a traditional framework with disciplines, rites, and rules. And there is Zen that is open to everybody in its teaching of the universality of consciousness, in the practice of meditation, in the perfect posture of zazen.[17]

Deshimaru adds that it is important to attach Zen to its origins in order to have a grounding to ensure that the true direction or intent of Zen is maintained going forward. In conclusion, Sokei-an sees religion as love:

> Zen makes a religion of tranquility. These days human beings have forgotten a peculiar love which unites their human nature to Great Nature. This love has nothing to do with human love. Standing in the midst of nature, you feel this love of Great Nature .... Zen students must experience this peculiar love. This is religion.[18]

There is no one answer to the question. The viewpoints express a wide range of opinions. Some teachers emphasize the practices of the religion, others the direction of the religion. The different responses are neither contradictory nor overlapping. It really does depend on whom you ask. One can consider the responses and decide for themselves. Many who practice Zen are not Buddhists. Some choose to have dual or no religious identity.

Four Practices: Bodhidharma

Bodhidharma was a Buddhist monk who lived during the 5th or 6th century. There are many legends about him, but little reliable information is available and there are many unverifiable details about his life story. He is traditionally credited with bringing Zen to China and is recognized as the first Chinese patriarch. It is said that he spent nine years in meditation facing a rock wall in a cave. Bodhidharma strongly encouraged that the practice of Zen extend into nature and everyday life. He instructed his students in the True Path—how to pacify the mind, develop practice, be in accord with all beings, and skillful teaching.

He said there were essentially two roads for entering the Path. One is to enter using the teachings to awaken the source and to realize that all living things have the same nature—a nature often clouded by delusion. It means abandoning the false and returning to the real, concentrating attention and gazing at a wall until there is no self or others, no differentiation. This road is called entering by inner truth

The other road to enter the Path is through practice. He refers to the Four Practices since all other practices are contained within these. Each of these are considered in more detail in later sections, indicated in brackets. The essential practices as adapted from different translations are:[19 20]

1. Repaying wrongs: When encountering suffering or injustice, accept it without complaint. This suffering is a manifestation of past actions which have now ripened and manifested. Just endure it without anger or complaint. When this attitude toward suffering arises, you are in accord with the inner truth, and advance on the path. The Sutras add: "Encountering suffering, one is not concerned, it makes sense if one is conscious of the basic cause." [***Karma**]

2. Adapting to conditions: As mortals, we're ruled by conditions, not by ourselves. All suffering and joy we experience depend on conditions ... When conditions change, it ends .... But while success and failure depend on conditions, the mind neither increases nor decreases. Those who remain unmoved by the winds of joy or suffering follow the Path. [***One Moment**]

3. Not seeking anything: The behavior of people is to crave things and become attached to them. These things contain nothing worth desiring. Wise ones use inner truth to experience the everyday world without attachment or seeking joy or avoiding suffering. Sutras: "To seek is to suffer. To seek nothing is bliss." When you seek nothing, you're on the Path. [***Attachments**]

4. Practicing in accordance with the Dharma (teachings of the Buddha): The body of the Dharma is not stingy with the physical body and life. This is practicing giving: Let there be no stinginess or holding back in the heart. Since there is nothing to be attached to, the wise give their body, life, and property in charity, without regret, without the vanity of giver, gift, or recipient, and without bias or attachment. This is the perfection of giving and is on the Path. [***Eightfold Path**]

These four practices can be incorporated into daily activities from the very beginning of one's practice. As noted above, the sections in brackets can be referenced for additional description and commentary by other teachers.

Zazen: Sawaki's Perspective

Kodo Sawaki (1880-1965) was a prominent Soto Zen teacher. He is considered to be one of the most significant Zen priests of his time for bringing Zen practice into the lives of lay people. There are many stand-alone quotes from his teachings and he did not mince words. He often called Zen "wonderfully useless," discouraging any gaining idea, or seeking after special experiences or states of consciousness.

Sawaki's emphasis on zazen and shikantaza coincides with this direction. However, his own style expresses it in different, memorable ways, which may resonate more strongly for some. He responds to the question "Why bother?":

> When somebody asks me what zazen is good for, I say that zazen isn't good for anything at all. And then some say that in that case they'd rather stop doing zazen. But what's running around satisfying your desires good for? What is gambling good for? And dancing? What is it good for to get worked up over winning or losing in baseball? It's all good for absolutely nothing! *That's why nothing is as sensible as sitting silently in zazen.*
>
> What's zazen good for? Absolutely nothing! This 'good for nothing' has got to sink into your flesh and bones until you're truly practicing what's good for nothing. Until then, your zazen is really good for nothing.

His comments on quality and persistence:

> Often people ask me how many years they have to practice zazen before it shows results. Zazen has no results. You won't get anything at all out of zazen.
>
> You say, 'When I do zazen, I get disturbing thoughts!' Foolish! The fact is that it's only in zazen that you're aware of your disturbing thoughts at all. When you dance around with your disturbing thoughts, you don't notice them at all. When a mosquito bites you during zazen, you notice it right away. But when you're dancing and a flea bites, you don't notice it at all.

> Don't whine. Don't stare into space. Just sit![21]

I have heard many long talks, but Sawaki gets right to the point. Without ever having heard his voice, it is easy to imagine the intensity and energy that came with the words; an intensity borne of a desire to encourage practitioners in their sitting.

3

Provisional Nature of Teachings

Buddhism has one direction—the awakening of all sentient beings. The teaching of the Buddha springs from the enlightened perspective, not from the everyday world of the senses, but has to be expressed to unenlightened people living in the world in a way that allows them to receive it and grow.

After the Buddha's awakening, ascetics who had practiced with him in the past, immediately recognized the profound change in him. They asked to be taught. The Buddha was reluctant because his experience could not be expressed in words. For example, what does it mean to be enlightened? People can give it a name or a definition, but that does not get directly at it. Even the sutras only point at it. The following passage from the Lotus Sutra is a reminder that it is not an enlightenment destination, nor can it be described:

> Liberation isn't merely about freeing your body or your mind;
> Liberation is to be free of all references, marks or signs.
> Enlightenment is having no references at all; it is beyond reference.
> Enlightenment cannot be defined by subjective mind.
> Enlightenment cannot be fabricated, contrived or made-up.
> Enlightenment is not make-believe.
> Enlightenment is not the by-product of hopes or wishes.
> Enlightenment is beyond all views.
> Enlightenment cannot be wished for – how can you wish for liberation?
> Enlightenment is neither abandoning, nor adopting; it is beyond grasping and beyond fixation. Enlightenment is none other than knowing everything is equal.[1,2]

The Buddha needed to invent a way so that words and other activities could be used to point to the 'experience beyond concepts' in such a way that the teaching would actually help people experience it on their own. The method of teaching that he developed was termed 'provisional teachings.'

There is the tendency to receive teachings as having a fixed meaning. This is not the teaching situation in Zen. The teachings are useful and essential but they do not have absolute meaning, hence the term 'provisional.' They are presented at a level to meet the capability of the practitioner to receive them. Thus, the teachings may change as time and conditions change—an answer of 'yes' today may very well become 'no' at some other time. This teaching style presents a conundrum at the beginning—since the content of the teachings is needed now, but ultimately cannot be treated as fixed dogma.

The approach taken in the discussion here is to first make clear the provisional nature and then present different perspectives of the content. This approach is intended to counteract the tendency to become attached to the words and ideas just as they are presented. The effectiveness of these provisional teachings has been demonstrated to have helped awaken people over the centuries. It is a skill of the practitioner to be able to both use the teachings with full effort in the present and still be aware of their provisional nature.

Yang-shan's Pop-Up Shop

Yang-shan opens up a temporary store. He knows that even though ultimately he has nothing to sell, he has to attract interest to get things going. This approach is a recognition of the provisional nature of the teachings:

> Illusions are deeply rooted and can hardly be extirpated at once. That is why we use, temporarily, expedient techniques to remove your coarse consciousness. This is like using yellow leaves to stop a child's crying by pretending they are gold; it is not actually true is it?[3]

> When a man cries out 'Things for sale!' he will do business; but when he does not call out, he will have no dealings. If I reveal Zen only in its genuine form, no one will be able to go along with me, not to speak of a group of five or seven hundred. But if I talk of Zen in this way or that, people will strive for it and collect

> whatever words I have left. This is just like fooling a child with an empty hand, for there is nothing real in it at all. Although I tell you that enlightenment abides, do not try to locate it with your conscious mind.[4]

The teachings are a balancing act. Initially people can only be helped through their senses, but ultimately that becomes an obstacle. There is a strong tendency to become attached to the media or objects of the teaching.

Provisional Teachings

After his enlightenment, the Buddha was confronted with a paradoxical situation. His friends recognized the significance of his awakening and began asking for instruction about it, despite the inexpressible nature of his experience. Out of compassion, he began to teach. The intent of the teachings to end suffering and to experience one's own nature was always clear. However, the presentation of the teachings changed over the years as the capacity for receptiveness of the followers grew.

The challenge to present the teaching at the appropriate level is the same today. More specifically, the pointers to reality itself can only be conveyed through everyday activities and experience. It is important to know that there is a difference between the two levels of truth. Ultimately, the teaching has to be understood at two levels, intellectually at a worldly level, and intuitively at the level of its ultimate meaning. If this difference is forgotten, it is easy to get stuck in the everyday language of the teachings, rather than the reality to which they point. The deeper meaning is going beyond the two levels, realizing that there is just one reality.

Each person who practices has their own experience and readiness to respond. Consequently, the teachings are provisional even at the individual level. They can be utilized fully at a particular time, but may not be effective at another time.

The most common analogy, which is frequently cited, is the use of a raft to cross to the other side of the river. When the river is crossed, there is no longer a need for the raft. A difficulty with the modern interpretation of the analogy is that the image of using a raft today is generally to go down the river, as a leisure activity. However, to go across the river, paddles and energy are needed. Real effort is required to benefit from the teachings.

Robert Pye has described the process of using the teachings:

> The expressions of Buddhism include words, stories and legends, political patronage, the language of rites and yoga, temple bells and cemetery stones; but all these expressions undergo shifts of meaning in the context of individual development.
>
> At first, they are not understood, but they are acceptably present in a world which seems more or less definitely existing. Later they come to be understood, but their disappearance, together with that of the transitory world, is anticipated. So it is that all religious language and symbolism comes to be de-literalized. This maturation can be understood in terms of skillful means, namely in a move from profligate differentiation towards an inward consistency.[5]

There is a process of understanding described here. As practice develops, a shift in perspective may occur so that the words have a different impact.

The invention of methods of provisional teaching from the discriminating (everyday) world to the essential requires skillful means. 'Skillful means' is the use of actions or teachings adjusted to the receiver's needs and capacity for understanding. Skillful means can apply to a teaching at a specific time and place. In a larger sense, all of Buddhism is a provisional practice with the direction to end suffering.

As a caveat which merits emphasis, not every activity of a specific practice or a teacher can automatically be regarded as skillful means.

Bowing as a Provisional Practice

Bowing has a long history in Buddhism and the Zen sect. Shortly after the Buddha's enlightenment, he saw five of the monks with whom he had previously practiced before he set off on his own. Upon approaching him, the monks were immediately aware of the change in their friend and quickly placed their hands together and greeted him with deep bows. Bowing continues to be an important activity of practice to this day. However, there are always concerns about the procedure and its meaning. For some, bowing is an act of devotion and remains as such. However, for others it may develop into a more provisional practice with a changed meaning and experience.

Viewed from the provisional perspective, the first step is the procedure itself. Some practice centers are very defined about the procedure, others less so. For example, Maezumi at ZCLA gives explicit instructions about both the procedure and the perspective.

First, he states that the attitude is to be humble in the mind. Then, he describes different types of gassho (holding the palms together), specifically the position of the palms, the location of the hands with regard to the eyes, the angle of the arms, and the appropriate time for each specific type of gassho to be used. Next, the full prostration bow requires kneeling, touching the knees and hands to the ground in the prescribed order, and touching the forehead to the ground and elevating the hands above the head. Finally, the order of movement is reversed to return back to the standing position. He emphasizes that all movement should be fluid. So at the beginning, there are many sequential actions to keep track of just in the mechanics themselves.

The question arises—what are we bowing to? It is not about worshiping a deity. For some people it is bowing out of respect to what the Buddha represented. For others it is bowing to ourselves, our buddha nature, and to all beings.

As practice progresses, the instructions and the attitude toward bowing may begin to drop off, so that there is just the activity of bowing. As activity is continued, there may be an intuitive awareness that this activity is a transitory stage. One becomes aware, at some level, that there is an experience beyond the physical activity. That experience may be the giving up of self for the moment. When there is full intimacy with the bow, there is no self or other. There is only the manifestation of emptiness and oneness in the activity of the moment. This represents the next stage of the practice. Maezumi said: "So, joining our hands palm to palm, we simultaneously create and express the oneness of the absolute and the relative, beyond all dualities."[6]

This stage is summarized by an exchange between Master Obaku and his student:

> Student: "You always tell us not to expect anything from the three treasures (Buddha, Dharma, Sangha). Yet, you have been making deep bows."
>
> Master Obaku: "I don't expect. I just bow."[7]

Uchiyama's final poem, written on the last day of his life, expresses bowing as a realized practice:

> Just Bow
>
> Putting my right and left hands together as one, I just bow.
> Just bow to become one with Buddha and God.

> Just bow to become one with everything I encounter.
> Just bow to become one with all the myriad things.
> Just bow as life becomes life.[8]

These expressions put a different direction on bowing and allow the discussions about the physical procedures of the activity to fade into the background. Reconsideration of bowing is just the beginning of what Yang-shan's pop-up shop is offering as 'things for sale.' What appears to be for sale is beyond the physical representation.

Mistaking Practice Metaphors for Reality

The Buddha often spoke in metaphors or parables and these words eventually took on an absolute meaning of their own and found their way into practices. On some occasions, the original intent was forgotten. Metaphors are often thought of as teaching stories and the literature abounds with them. However, that these metaphors can be seen from two perspectives is not always emphasized. These metaphors have a dual role both as everyday practices as well as pointing to the absolute. Bassui expresses the situation:

> Ordinary people, being rather dull witted, delude themselves and mistake these metaphors for facts. When you truly understand your own mind, you realize for the first time that the sermons of all the Buddhas are nothing more than metaphors to point to the minds of ordinary people.[9]

Bodhidharma was very stern and austere and his comments are quite pointed and direct. The instruction is refreshing since nothing is held back. He exhorts:

> The sutras of the Buddha contain countless metaphors. Because mortals have shallow minds and don't understand anything deep, the Buddha used the tangible to represent the sublime. People who seek blessings by concentrating on external works instead of internal cultivation are attempting the impossible.[10]

Bodhidharma followed this tirade by providing examples of ways to use the tangible to experience the intangible. The point of all these examples is to reconnect awareness to the original intent and to harmonize the essence of the teachings with the form of the practice. By using the external form and cultivating the internal meaning, the teachings can be fully engaged.

Incense:	Burning incense doesn't mean ordinary material incense, but the incense of the intangible Dharma, which drives away filth, ignorance, and evil deeds with its perfume.
Fire:	When Buddha was in the world, he told his disciples to light such precious incense with the fire of awareness as an offering to the buddhas of the ten directions. But people today don't understand the Tathagata's real meaning. They use an ordinary flame to light material incense and pray for some future blessing that never comes.
Flowers:	This holds true for scattering flowers. This refers to speaking the Dharma, scattering flowers of virtue in order to benefit others and glorify the real self .... They last forever and never fade. If you think the Tathagata meant for people to harm plants by cutting off their flowers, you're wrong. Those who observe the precepts don't injure any of the myriad life forms.
Lamp:	The eternal lamp represents pure awareness. Persisting in delusions and clinging to the tangible, they light lamps of everyday vegetable oil and think that by illuminating the interiors of buildings, they're following the Buddha's teaching. How foolish.
Fast:	The same holds true for observing a fast. It's useless unless you understand what this really means. To fast means to regulate, to regulate your body and mind so that they're not distracted or disturbed. And to observe means to uphold, to uphold the rules of discipline according to the Dharma .... The world is full of deluded people who don't see this.

Bodhidharma's admonition is also the foundation and direction of liturgical practices. Among all major Buddhist traditions, there are some forms of liturgy. In some traditions it is a focus of daily practice, in others there is less emphasis on it. These ceremonies include morning and evening chanting services, weddings, memorial services, repentance services, and taking the precepts, as well as other rituals. The intent of liturgy can also be stated as 'making the invisible visible.' It is a matter of growing attention and awareness of the activity. We all begin with the physical practice. For some, the activities remain at the physical level and there is benefit in that. For others, the awareness does not stop there and the practices become internalized at a deeper level.

4

Zen Teaching Methods

Most people have more exposure to teaching and teachers than they care to remember. They have experience with both effective and ineffective methods. So, when it comes to interactions with Zen teachings and teachers, there may be expectations that the experience proceeds along the same lines as earlier encountered. Certainly, on one level, it does appear to do so. But there is also a different method of teaching that is intended to help one go beyond past experience.

The intent of all teachings is to help one move in the direction of awakening and the end of suffering. But it is more than becoming acquainted with unfamiliar methods and words. In Zen teaching, words may be used differently or the meanings may change with the circumstance. Teachers and sutras may appear to contradict each other or even themselves. Some teachings may make no sense and simply be confounding. In order to use the teachings effectively, it is helpful to have some background about the methods used and compare them to conventional teaching methods in order to see how they are both similar and different.

As noted earlier, the Buddha recognized that teaching the path to an awakening experience required several different methods. He recognized the difficulty of the task and explained this to his disciple Ananda:

> It's not easy to teach the Dhamma (Dharma) to others, Ananda. The Dhamma should be taught to others only when five qualities are established within the person teaching. Which five? The Dhamma should be taught with the thought:

1. "I will speak step-by-step."

This quality is sometimes referred to as the gradual method. To the best of the teacher's ability, it means addressing an audience at their level of comprehension and receptivity. The approach requires adapting the teaching to the time and conditions in a skillful way. In order to help individuals develop their spiritual potential sometimes the teaching may be modified. The modifications may take the form of analogies, parables, questions, or dialogues. From the student's perspective, the instruction is to begin to practice 'where one is at.' So, the first step may be different for different people. The beginning place does not matter. Start there.

2. "I will speak explaining the sequence [of cause and effect]."

This statement refers to the Law of Karma which is created by our actions on a moment to moment basis. The Law of Karma has many ramifications and is often misunderstood. It is discussed in Chapter 12.

3. "I will speak out of compassion."

4. "I will not speak for the purpose of material reward."

5. "I will speak without exalting myself [hurting myself] or putting others down. (AN 5.159 Udayi Sutta)

These last three statements apply both to formal teachers and to all who speak to others about the Dharma. The first of these is based on motivation; the only reason to speak is to help others. The comment about material reward is open to interpretation. There are Zen teachers living in poverty and those who have made a fortune from their work. The comment about material reward is about purpose and refers back to the motivation. The last refers to the manner in which teachers and students interact.

Skillful Means

'Skillful means' is the ability of teachers to adjust or modify their statements or actions to balance the students' own openness to receive instruction with the level of teaching. Consequently, there was sometimes confusion or apparent contradiction in the Buddha's words, but his teaching was attuned to the time, conditions, and receptive capacity of the listeners. From the Buddha's perspective, the teachings are fully consistent. In the Lotus Sutra, the Buddha states that his earlier words (about different paths to enlightenment) were superseded because people were now ready to hear them:

> I know that living beings have various desires, attachments that are deeply implanted in their minds. Taking cognizance of this basic nature of theirs, I will therefore use various causes and conditions, words of simile and parable, and the power of expedient means and expound the Law for them. I do this so that all of them may attain the one Buddha vehicle and wisdom embracing all species.[1]

However, learning through skillful teaching is not a passive activity. There is a real responsibility of the recipient to actively employ the teaching. Without the effort of practice, the listener will stay with the provisional meaning. The teaching must be taken as presented and then seen or experienced in the deeper sense. This process, where the teaching is seen from a different perspective, may initially cause confusion or discomfort. Still, at times it will be successful. On other occasions, time and conditions are not aligned and the provisional teaching is not transcended. In that situation, one just has to move on with their practice.

Example: Teachings of Nirvana

Nirvana is a term that seems to have entered into mainstream conversation. The word 'nirvana' comes from the root meaning 'to blow out' and refers to the extinguishing of the fires of greed, hatred, and delusion. It has had other interpretations such as the extinction of desires or the cessation of suffering. Over the centuries, different types of nirvana have been described.

Before reading the discussion of teaching about nirvana, it may be helpful to take a moment and see what comes to mind from the term 'nirvana.' A Buddhist metaphor for entering nirvana is that of a fire going out because its fuel has been consumed. For people, the fire is fueled by desires and attachments. A Zen practice offers the opportunity to allow desires and attachments to fade causing the fire to go out. What is meant by nirvana? Is it a place or a state of mind, or neither, or both? Is it a fabrication? In any group of people there may be many different responses.

The direction of all of Buddhist teaching is to end suffering and experience nirvana. Because of the familiarity of the term, the teaching of nirvana provides an excellent example of the provisional methods used. There are two steps. First is the recognition that teaching the inexpressible experience can only be done by the skillful use of discriminating words. Then, when the inexpressible has been experienced, the provisional teaching is rejected. This teaching method (using skillful means) is illustrated by the narrative adapted from Michael Pye. His comments are indented:

> The term nirvana needs special consideration because it is used on both sides of the fence.
>
> Two different terms seem to distinguish . . . *Nirvana* as a cypher (code word) for the inexpressible, valuable meaning, and *nirvana* as that provisionally taught for the ending of ill.

It is recognized here that nirvana is an experience that cannot be expressed in words (awakened perspective). However, a discriminating concept of nirvana as the ending of suffering and distress has been formulated. This concept is used as an appropriate starting point for leading people to the experience.

When the Buddha is said to 'enter' nirvana, this is an example of a use of a conceptual understanding. Although nirvana is not a place that can be entered, the concept is used as a point in teaching progression. Pye then addresses the skillful use of the discriminating perspective to allow the hearers to move beyond it to the awakened perspective:

> It must be admitted that the reference to the possibility of the Buddha himself 'entering' nirvana instead of preaching makes use of the term for the discriminated nirvana.
>
> Yet the two steps of the teaching represent a real enough progression on the part of the hearers, for they must move from an acceptance of the Buddha's teaching on the basis of ignorance to a rejection of it on the basis of enlightenment.
>
> Recognising the 'nirvana-nature of all dharmas' ultimately subverts (eliminates) the necessity for teaching nirvana as an end to distress and suffering, but the latter (discriminating perspective) was first necessary and continues to be so for the benefit of living beings still 'sunk in suffering.'

However, this experience of the 'nirvana nature of all beings' is only taught through the Buddha's power of skillful means using a discriminating perspective. It must be taught from this perspective since people can only begin to hear and benefit from it at this level. Then the discriminating teaching can be discarded. Pye concludes by stating that the skillful use of provisional method is the basis of Buddhist teaching:

> Yet by so preaching on the discriminated side he can eventually bring others to the pure, balanced Buddhahood which carries the same rejection of the discriminated nirvana and the same compassion for beings still 'sunk in suffering.'

> The benefit which they reap from the discriminated teachings enables them to move forward to the undiscriminated. This move also involves perplexity and doubt, giving way to recognition and joy.
>
> The teaching of the discriminated perspective of nirvana is rejected. If the provisional teaching is taken as fact, the meaning will not be transcended. The teaching … characterizes the operation of the Buddhist religion.
>
> Almost anything in the whole range of Buddhist teaching and practice can be described … skilful means. [2]

Once experienced, the provisional, conceptual teaching is no longer needed and is discarded. The important point is that holding on to the concept of nirvana is to become stuck in the discriminating perspective

All teachings of Buddhism are intended to be used skillfully and provisionally and not be taken as fixed dogma.

Teaching Using Words

Words are a currency for exchanging information and energy. When using language to teach, the thoughts presented often appear as conceptual ideas, especially at the beginning of learning and to those inclined to intellectual interpretation. So, it is sometimes difficult to realize that they are provisional and being used to point to the reality beyond the intellectual idea. When 'Dharma' language is used, the words sound the same to those present, but they may mean something different to each listener. For example, one individual may experience the words as conveying emotional or spiritual energy to be interpreted and used in a way that another person hearing the same words does not experience. It is important to have an understanding of the difference in meanings and use.

Rely on the spirit, rather than the literal meaning. The spirit should have priority over the letter.

Words: Fluid or Frozen

A fiord in the Arctic in summer is all liquid; there is one body of water emptying into the sea and whales are free to come and go. As winter comes, a band of ice can form quickly at the mouth of the fiord, separating it from the open sea and, at least temporarily, trapping the whales in a small area of open water called a 'savssat.' This creates a real problem for air breathing mammals. If the entire body of water freezes before the ice melts or the whales cannot break out, they are doomed. Fortunately for whales, they have developed a sense of when this sudden freezing will occur and they are rarely trapped.

Words can be like the freezing water at the mouth of the fiord. We swim in a sea of words if they are seen as fluid. However, although the words of a teaching may have both a literal meaning and also may point beyond meanings or concepts, one can become artificially trapped in the literal meaning only.

For example, I have often heard the expression in one form or another: "I have a problem with this person."

Do the words of this phrase have meaning in themselves? That is, does a problem with this person exist in everyday experience or can the words be used to point in the direction of reality? What happens if this phrase is taken as having meaning in itself? In an everyday situation, a problem may involve people at work or with another person in a relationship. Perhaps the problem can be defined and the needed adjustments to resolve it can be made. Perhaps not. But whatever is accomplished is all based on the words "I have a problem with this person" having a fixed meaning.

In Buddhist teaching, there is one reality. Boundaries and meanings are arbitrary and impermanent, like the ice near the shore that sometimes forms and then breaks up. A change in conditions does not change the one reality. If a boundary becomes rigid, it can readily be forgotten that the division is arbitrary. Importantly though, the words can also be an entry point to explore a deeper truth. Then they become an opportunity to practice and grow awareness. But the words are only vehicles and are aids to point to the actual reality.

Reconsidering the above statement: "I have a problem with this person."

The 'I' sets a boundary.

The 'I and this person' makes a separation.

The 'problem' characterizes an attached opinion to a situation.

The use of the word 'I' freezes the boundary like ice because it is easy to forget that the idea of a self is an arbitrary, temporary, fluid designation.

'I and this person' results in separation. Is the separation illusory or real? Once there is a subject and an object, a separation follows.

The word 'problem' describes an attached opinion or judgment of the situation. 'Problem' indicates that the present moment is in some way unsatisfactory. There is an idea or mental image of how the moment should be and an attachment to that idea. Is there any real difference between the actual situation and my opinion of what it should be?

The words in this discussion may identify areas for productive practice. One approach that may be helpful is to let these words, questions, and meanings go and use the energy generated from them to experience what comes up from paying attention to the energy. In this sense, the words can also have a use as a vehicle to communicate that energy.

The Taoist View: Words, Useless or Useful

Zuangzi (~360 BC) was an influential thinker in the early period of Taoism in China, although his exact role is not known. Zuangzi emphasized the provisional nature of words when he was challenged with the statement: "Your words are useless!"

He replied:

> A man has to understand the useless before you can talk to him about the useful. The earth is certainly vast and broad, though a man uses no more of it than the area he puts his feet on. (*i.e. The rest of the land is not useful because it is not being occupied by the person.*)
>
> If, however, you were to dig away all the earth from around his feet until you reached the underworld, then would the man be able to make use of the vastness of the earth?
>
> No, it would be useless. (*There would be no place for the man to step off.*)
>
> It is obvious, then, that the useless has its use.[3]

When the man was standing still, the vast ground had no use to him and digging it away had no consequence. However, when it was time to move, that vast ground now became important. The usefulness of the ground was fully dependent upon the situation. By analogy, words can have their use. They are means of communication that can affect our practice. But when the words are no longer needed, they can be discarded and deemed no longer useful. They did not have a fixed meaning; rather the utility of the words was dependent upon the situation. Moving beyond this example and extending it, all phenomena have such a provisional nature. They can mistakenly be taken as fixed, or more appropriately used provisionally to experience the one reality.

In order to complete the contribution of Zuangzi here, his most famous quote is included:

> The fish trap exists because of the fish; once you've gotten the fish, you can forget the trap. The rabbit snare exists because of the rabbit; once you've gotten the rabbit, you can forget the snare.
>
> Words exist because of meaning, once you've gotten the

meaning, you can forget the words. Where can I find a man who has forgotten words so I can have a word with him?[4]

The "man who has forgotten words" refers to an enlightened person. The experience is not dependent on words.

A summary verse:

Words cannot express things;
Speech does not convey the spirit.
Swayed by words, one is lost;
Blocked by phrases, one is bewildered.
(*Gateless Gate* # 37)[5]

Four Types of Questions

Questions have long been used in teaching settings. When I was teaching engineering, the students had all kinds of questions. Some were about the clarification of technical subjects, others about insight into the scientific principles. There was always a student who would like to ask questions geared to getting the lecture off-track. The adage "There is no such thing as a stupid question" may be true, but certainly some questions are more useful in a discussion than others.

The Buddha was quite focused on his intent to end suffering. The conversations with disciples were often in question and answer style. The responses were not merely factual, but were presented to questioners as an aid to shift their understanding. Again, the responses were ideally framed at the appropriate level of the audience receptivity. A skillful response can activate motivation to help individuals frame their own questions more appropriately and develop the skill to discover answers for themselves.

There was quite a systematic approach to the questions and the Buddha enumerated four ways of responding:

"There are these four ways of answering questions. Which four?" "There are questions that should be answered categorically" (straightforwardly yes or no; this or that).

The answers to the categorical question speak directly to the point of attention.

"There are questions that should be answered with an analytical answer" (qualified; defining or redefining the terms).

The purpose of the analytical answer is to reframe the question—either by adding an extra statement or by reframing the question itself. The reframing may aid the questioner's understanding. It also allows for a clear response.

> "There are questions that should be answered with a counter question."

The counter-questions provide an opportunity for the questioner to clarify his own position.

> "There are questions that should be put aside. These are the four ways of answering questions." (AN 4.42 Pañha Sutta)[6]

Questions deserving to be put aside are those that are wrongly framed and dealing with topics that distract attention from the intent.

In Chapter 6, there are a number of passages designed in the question/response format. With some understanding of these 'Four Types of Questions,' the responses in those passages can be better interpreted and the teachings more effectively incorporated into one's practice.

Unanswered Questions

As noted above, there are some questions the Buddha put aside. To stay on the point, the intention of Zen and each of its practices is to help beings awaken and experience each moment of life fully. Still questions often arise. These questions may arise from individuals seeking instruction or clarification about practices. However, the Buddhist teaching below is also a reminder that not all questions and discussions are helpful. Some well-intentioned questions may actually be distractions and if answered in the expected verbal way, would not have benefit to practice.

Many meditation groups have a discussion component in which participants share their practice, experiences, and concerns. People often have much to say about these topics from their perspective of life and such meetings can be supportive of practice. However, it is not always recognized or acknowledged that some discussions lose direction and may inadvertently reinforce separation, dualism, or speculation.

Take for instance, The Parable of the Poisoned Arrow (The Shorter Instructions to Malunkya):

> It's just as if a man were wounded with an arrow thickly smeared with poison. His friends and companions, kinsmen and relatives would provide him with a surgeon, and the man would say, 'I won't have this arrow removed until I know whether the man who wounded me was a noble warrior, a brahman, a merchant, or a worker.' He would say, 'I won't have this arrow removed until I know the given name and clan name of the man who wounded me … until I know whether he was tall, medium, or short … until I know whether he was dark, ruddy-brown, or golden-colored … until I know his home village, town, or city … until I know whether the bow with which I was wounded was a long bow or a crossbow … until I know whether the bowstring with which I was wounded was fiber, bamboo threads, sinew, hemp, or bark … until I know whether the shaft with which I was wounded was wild or cultivated … until I know whether the feathers of the shaft with which I was wounded were those of a vulture, a stork, a hawk, a peacock, or another bird … until I know whether the shaft with which I was wounded was bound with the sinew of an ox, a water buffalo, a langur, or a monkey.' He would say, 'I won't have this arrow removed until I know whether the shaft with which I was wounded was that of a common arrow, a curved arrow, a barbed, a calf-toothed, or an oleander arrow.' The man would die and those things would still remain unknown to him.

This parable was precipitated when a monk asked questions to the Buddha. The monk's questions have been translated in different ways and cover the topics:

> Is the cosmos finite in space?
> Is the universe finite in time?
> Is the self the same or different from the body?
> Does the Buddha exist after death?

The Buddha did not respond in words. Questions of this type were a distraction from the intent of ending suffering. As in the case of the poisoned arrow, the time taken for a discussion would not have been helpful to the intent.

The monk demanded that the Buddha answer directly or admit that he did not know the answer. He was up for the discussion. The Buddha replied:

> So, Malunkyaputta, remember what is undeclared by me as undeclared, and what is declared by me as declared …. And why

> are they undeclared by me? Because they are not connected with the goal, are not fundamental to the holy life. They do not lead to disenchantment, dispassion, cessation, calming, direct knowledge, self-awakening, Unbinding. That's why they are undeclared by me. (MN 63)

The Buddha is addressing the question of ending suffering and some types of discussions would not be helpful. That is one lesson. However, Katagiri and others have considered that the Buddha's silence itself also has underlying teachings which can be guides in practice. Summarizing two main points:

> Since there is no response made, there is no concept to grasp. In this sense, no verbal response becomes an expression of emptiness and impermanence. A reminder that life is activity.
>
> Silence is vast. Normally perspectives are limited to a familiar view. Silence is a space where all views can be considered.[7]

Not answering some types of question shows a compassionate dedication to end the suffering. Because the questions were not allied with the intent of the Buddha's teaching—to end suffering, the focus is maintained on the intent of the teaching. Such a silence can be understood as practice. In zazen, there is just silence and practicing it. The silence animates our life. It can be used to express our nature in the world.

It is an interesting and ironic aside that scholars have spent a great deal of effort analyzing this response of not answering questions. Many approaches have been used: examining the nature and structure of the questions, seeking different motivations for the Buddha's response, and viewing them from different historical perspectives. The voluminous scholarship on this subject is truly astounding.

Parables as Skillful Means

When Buddha began his teaching, he said that there were three paths to awakening. In the Lotus Sutra, he proclaims that there is only one path, and all living beings can attain it. This was a change from his previous teaching and he understood that people may have been disconcerted by it. The Buddha stated that people were not previously ready to hear the full truth, that it would have discouraged them. He told the following parable to illustrate the point and provide an interpretation:

(In this translation, Buddha is translated as Tathagata. Other clarifying terms are in Appendix A.)

The Apparitional City

You should know, O monks, that the Tathagata through skillful means deeply penetrates the dispositions of sentient beings. Knowing their inclination toward the inferior teachings and that they are deeply attached to the desires of the five senses, he teaches nirvana for their sake. If they listen, they will accept it.

Suppose in a desolate, fearful place there was a dangerous road five hundred yojanas long. There is a large group that wants to travel along this road to reach a place where there is great treasure. They have a leader who is wise and penetrating and who knows the passable and impassable parts of this dangerous road very well.

Although he wants to guide these people past the danger, they become exhausted along the way. Addressing the leader they say: 'We are extremely tired and frightened. We cannot go any further. We are still far away from our destination, and we want to turn back.'

The leader, knowing many skillful means, thinks: 'These people are to be pitied. How could they want to turn back and abandon the great treasure?' After thinking this the leader, through his skillful means, magically creates a city three hundred yojanas away along the dangerous road. He addresses the people, saying: 'Do not be frightened. Do not turn back! You may now stay in this great city and be at your leisure. If you enter this city, you can be comfortable and at ease. Once you are able to go on and reach the treasure site, then you can depart once more.'

Then the exhausted people rejoice greatly and praise this unprecedented experience, saying: 'We are now free of this evil road and will be comfortable and at ease.' Then they proceed to the apparitional city and enter it. They believe that their hardships are over and feel at ease. Then the leader realizes that they are rested and their fatigue has gone. He immediately makes the apparitional city vanish and says to the people: 'All of you, come along! The treasure site is near. I made that great apparitional city only in order to let you rest.'

O monks! The Tathagata is exactly like this. Now for your sake he has become a great leader who knows the long, dangerous, and evil road of birth, death, and desire's confusion. You should leave it and be saved.

If sentient beings hear only about the single buddha vehicle they will then want neither to see nor approach a buddha. They will think that the buddha path is long and attainable only after

> enduring severe and protracted suffering.
>
> The Buddha, knowing their minds, knowing that they are weak-willed and of lowly aspiration, teaches them the two nirvanas through skillful means in order to let them rest halfway to the goal. If there are sentient beings who abide in either of these two stages, the Tathagata immediately teaches: 'What you have accomplished is not complete. The stage you abide in is close to the wisdom of the buddhas. You should observe and consider that the nirvana you have obtained is not the true one. It is only through the power of the Tathagata's skillful means that the single buddha vehicle is explained as three.' The Buddha is just like that leader who conjured a great apparitional city to let the people rest. Knowing that they were rested, he addressed them, saying: 'The treasure site is near. This city is not real. It is only my invention.'[8 9]

"It is only my invention." The invention serves the purpose at hand. The parable is reminiscent of Yun-shan's earlier "Things for Sale." In that example, the yellow leaves may not have been gold, but they did stop the child from crying. Here, the City may not be real, but its appearance keeps the pilgrims on the road. The teachings may be impermanent and provisional, but they keep people in the direction of awakening.

This is a guiding parable for anyone beginning a meditation practice. The road of practice may appear to be long, but there are many ways to rejuvenate oneself. It is the responsibility of listeners to see beyond the literal meaning and realize the parable is guidance and encouragement directly for them. Just as the travelers on the road received unexpected help to allow them to sustain their journey, so also assistance becomes available to the discouraged practitioner, often in unexpected forms.

Dialectics: Teaching Method in the Diamond Sutra

The Diamond Sutra is one of the most important teachings concerning the nature of reality. The commonly referenced title itself, "Diamond Sutra," steers some people in the wrong direction. Other more complete translations of the Sutra are "The Diamond that Cuts Through Illusion" or "The Perfection of Wisdom That Cuts Like a Diamond." The emphasis is on the hardness of the diamond which has the capability of cutting off or disrupting conceptual thought and illusions. There have been many translations and commentaries of differing quality. The text is not included here but several printed and online translations and commentaries are readily available.[10 11 12]

The Diamond Sutra is a teaching to undermine and break through our conceptual understanding and open to us a deeper intimacy with our own life and reality. Consequently, many passages do not make intellectual sense. Nonetheless, these sections are important in the process of intuitive understanding. As such, it is a difficult teaching with a paradoxical and elusive style. In the discussion below, the dialectic method is outlined. This method of teaching is used frequently in the Diamond Sutra. Being aware of how it is structured opens the opportunity for deeper study.

Everyday Example of Dialectics

This example illustrates the method in the sensory world. There are three propositions:

Thesis → Antithesis → Synthesis

Thesis may be the color white. Antithesis, the color black. The two elements are dualistic opposites.

White → Black → Synthesis

What are the possibilities for a synthesis? The candidate that most commonly comes to mind first is 'gray.' Gray is more of a combination or blend of the two and doesn't quite make it.

'Color' contains both the characteristics of black and white, yet extends beyond each of them.

However, the analogy is not exact since the synthesis step in this example remains in the conceptual world. For the example below, the synthesis is on the level of experience, beyond rational or conceptual expression.

Truth resides, according to Buddhist belief, somewhere between affirmation and negation, between 'is' and 'is not,' in a realm that cannot be adequately expressed in words. Each element is important, but analogous to the example above, the truth is not a combination, but an experience beyond them.[13]

The dialectic method has three elements:

First statement (Thesis):	x
Second Statement (Antithesis):	Not x
Third Statement (Synthesis):	And so it is called x

Example from the Diamond Sutra

"All bodhisattvas ... should realize as they vow to save all sentient beings that in truth there are no sentient beings to be saved."

The first truth (x):	"Sentient Beings"
The second truth (not x):	"No Sentient Beings"
The third truth (the union of these):	"Vow to save them anyway"[14]

Thich Nhat Hanh's commentary on the "Diamond Sutra" points out that when a practitioner helps living beings in a natural and spontaneous way, there is no distinguishing between the one who is helping and the one who is helped. There are neither sentient beings nor no sentient beings. This is an example of the synthesis of two truths. The activity occurs in a formless way. The analogy is when one hand is burned, the other grabs it in an immediate way. Although there is a right and left hand, there is no distinction in that moment, just activity.

Mountains are Mountains

There is a famous verse attributed to Seigen Ishin (Ch'ing-yuan Weihsin) in the 9th century. It has since been translated and interpreted by many authors. This one is by Alan Watts:

> Before I had studied Zen for thirty years, I saw mountains as mountains, and waters as waters. When I arrived at a more intimate knowledge, I came to the point where I saw that mountains are not mountains, and waters are not waters. But now that I have got its very substance I am at rest. For it's just that I see mountains once again as mountains, and waters once again as waters.[15]

This verse follows the same pattern as the earlier example of the dialectic method. First, there is a conceptual perception which can be incomplete or inaccurate. Looking at a mountain, it is a mountain separate and distinct from other objects. However, with practice there can then be the perception that a mountain is not a mountain because it is composed of other elements, with the arbitrary distinction between the 'mountain' and the other non-mountain elements. Finally, the interconnected experience that the mountain, just as it is, is already luminous and magnificent. The mountain is experienced as a reflection of our own minds and there is nothing to add.

Such mountains and waters of themselves become wise persons and sages. (Dogen)[16]

5

Working with a Teacher

Zen training can be extraordinarily frustrating. One role of teaching is exactly that—to frustrate the calculating mind so that one can go beyond ideas. Often, a teacher is fully supportive at the beginning of practice until students get their footing. At some point though, the teacher appears to withdraw the support, behavior that may baffle, confuse, or frustrate the student. This change in behavior is normal and intended to be beneficial. A caveat here: The teacher must be interacting from a skillful, non-ego perspective. This is an important point and is discussed below. However, even when the teachings are appropriate, they may not be welcomed by the recipient. Discomfort is not the issue. Teaching and advice can be difficult for both the teacher and the student. We are studying how to express our true nature.

'Skillful means' (also referred to 'upaya') is the term frequently used in connection to the effectiveness of teaching. Skillful means covers a lot of ground and in itself can be used to justify actions or methods in dealing with a student. In the majority of interactions, the actions are intended to benefit the student. The declaration by the teacher that it is a benefit is not necessarily a sufficient judgment. Unfortunately, Zen teachers do make mistakes (although it is an unusual occurrence for some teachers to admit an error). Errors may be rooted in arrogance, personal opinions, or financial consideration. This caution is emphasized in Suzuki's comments below.

The criteria of the teacher in teaching or correcting a student's practice should be clear to both participants. Clarity is not a simple matter and there are a number of elements in the interaction of teachers and students. As noted in the discussion below, the student has an integral, necessary role in this teaching. Teachings received on the individual level, in order to be skillful, must involve the participation of the student. The teaching is not 'received wisdom' from one person; both have responsibilities in the interaction.

Below is a composite of effective teaching methods compiled from different talks and sources. The indented sections are additional comments from Shunryu Suzuki.

1. The teacher must be connected to the Way.

> If a teacher thinks that what his student did is a mistake, he is not a true teacher. It may be a mistake, but on the other hand it is an expression of the student's true nature. When we understand this, we have respect for our student's true nature, and we will be careful how we point out mistakes.[1]

As an observable matter, this means that the ego and attachments of the teacher are not involved. In other words, if their self-desires, attachments, or ego emerge in the interaction, this criterion is not met.

2. The teaching must be true to the Dharma.

> "The teaching does not violate the precepts."

> "The teacher is reminded to be truthful, which means the teacher does not point out his disciple's mistake just because he thinks it is a mistake."

3. The teaching must benefit the student.

> "The teacher gives advice or points out the student's mistake solely for the sake of helping him, and does not do this just to get something off his chest."

4. The teaching must be delivered at a time and manner when the student is receptive.

> "The teacher is reminded to be gentle and calm, and speak in a low voice rather than shouting."

> "And puts emphasis on having a calm gentle attitude when talking about someone's mistake."

> "And not point out the student's mistake in front of many people."

> "Points out the student's mistake with compassion, which means that the teacher is not just the teacher, but also the disciple's friend."

Sheng-Yen independently reinforces these points:

> The teacher has a correct view of the dharma.
>
> Their actions reveal no attachment.
>
> Shows a clear sense of responsibility.[2]

Oral Teachings

Teachings can be in words, acts, or presence. Their effect on an individual depends upon time, conditions, and receptivity. Unlike a podcast, it is not just information transmitted in conceptual form; the teachings may have a spirit or energy that can have an effect beyond the rational mind.

Teachers may also give oral teachings referred to as 'Dharma Talks' or 'Teishos.' Such talks may be non-discursive, that is, they may not progress in narrative style with beginning, middle, or end. The talk may or may not make points. One approach to interact with these types of talks is simply to listen as an enlightened person, with full attention of mind and body, and without opinions or mental effort to figure it out. When something is heard that resonates with energy or spirit, this energy can be used in sitting. On the other hand, if something just goes by, simply let it go and do not chase after it. If the attention leaves the talk and goes in some other direction, when you become aware of the distraction, just pick the talk up in the present without going back. It is not uncommon for listeners to report hearing words not recalled being spoken by the teacher. The talks may help shift perspectives.

These talks are differentiated from instructions, for example meditation postures, the procedures to enter the hall, or walking meditation (kinhin). These instructions are essential and need to be understood both intellectually and physically. However, as noted earlier with bowing, they do not have to be maintained at the conceptual level but can really be opportunities to express our original nature.

Role of Reading

As with everything else, there are divergent views about the value of reading. Reading is a conceptual activity, but the effect of reading can transcend concepts. There are several occasions when reading for concepts is not appropriate. One example is if it is done in place of sitting. Another is during a retreat of a day, weekend, or five-day sesshin. Reading for concepts at this time interjects (conceptual) thinking and disrupts intuitive processes. During periods of intense sitting, the energy is directed toward stillness and not toward conceptual thought.

Seung Sahn is particularly adamant about this. He distinguishes two different types of reading:

> Anything that can be written in a book, anything that can be said—all this is thinking. If you are thinking, then all Zen books, all Buddhist sutras, all Bibles are demons' words. But if you read with a mind that has cut off all thinking, then Zen books, sutras, and Bibles are all the truth.
>
> So is the barking of a dog or the crowing of a rooster: all things are teaching you at every moment, and these sounds are even better teaching than Zen books. So Zen is keeping the mind which is before thinking. Sciences and academic studies are after thinking. We must return to before thinking.[3]

Seung Sahn's comments are an admonition not to emphasize reading and study at the expense of meditation. There are many appropriate times to read for concepts, and the study of the teachings is an integral part of practice. These include the very basic instructions for meditation. Study progresses to the foundations of Buddhism such as the Buddha's initial sermons, the Bodhisattva Vows, the precepts, and the chanted sutras. These teachings are augmented by commentaries and spoken words of a teacher. A number of the Japanese teachers (Yasutani, D.K. Suzuki, Sheng-Yen, to name three) developed a series of talks and literature to provide Westerners with a framework for understanding the concepts of the practice.

Much of the Buddhist literature consists of sutras, commentaries, and elaborations of the basic teachings. The connections to the foundations are difficult to assimilate if the basics are unfamiliar. As with oral talks, there are different ways of using the written works and commentaries. They can be read as narratives, or for intellectual understanding. Reading for insight is a fully conceptual activity and the insights will be conceptual.

A real value of the secondary literature (or a talk for that matter) is to provide an opportunity to change one's perspective and take that change into the sitting practice. The works can be read for spirit or energy, in which case a line or phrase may jump off the page with resonant non-conceptual energy. That energy can then be used in practice. Then whatever manifests from the practice is a surprise. The response to any teaching depends upon time and conditions so that a reading at one time may resonate differently than at another time.

It is an interesting irony that some authors, in their own publications, rail against reading.

Dharma (Teacher) Transmission

The decision to transmit teaching authority to a student is at the sole discretion of the teacher. Generally, but not always, it may occur after a long period of study with the teacher. The authority given is to teach the dharma, conduct individual interviews, and transmit authority to future teachers.

There are several stages. The first is a probationary period, in some places called a dharma holder. The next step is the ceremony with specified documents to install the student as a sensei. After an indeterminate period of time, the teacher can give their final seal of approval as a successor, known as inka, and confer the honorific 'roshi.'

Direct transmission refers to the practice of having an authentic, unbroken line of succession traced back to the Buddha. It is also referred to as a 'special transmission outside the teachings.' This practice has traditionally been considered essential to preserving the authenticity of the teaching. The unbroken lineage explicitly imparts an authority fully endorsed by the institution. The traditional rituals contribute to this endorsement. Extensive lineage charts are available which detail successive generations of teachers.

However, in a tradition that spans centuries and cultures, there have been and continue to be different interpretations of what dharma transmission means. Bodiford ("Dharma Transmission in Theory") places it in an historical and cultural context, from Dogen in the 9th century to current practices in the West. He states, "One of the reasons that dharma transmission has proved to be such a powerful source of Zen's success is because of its inherent flexibility."[4] For example at Soto institutions in Japan, transmission is the first step, without teaching authority. At other places, particularly in the West, the transmission allows full teaching authority.

On this subject, the point is often raised that the idealized concept of Zen teachers is promoted. There is often the encouraged perception that roshis are deeply or fully enlightened beings. Such a perception is often used to justify their actions so they cannot be evaluated or understood by lay people. Experience has shown that this may not always be the situation. Hagiographic accounts of life activities are often employed by both followers and teachers themselves.[5][6] Some are blatantly self-serving. This idealization could be interpreted either as skillful teaching for inspiration or as ego manipulation by the teacher. These ambiguities serve as a reminder that the truth of the teaching of the Buddha is transmitted by real humans and it serves everyone's purpose to be aware of and responsive to this fact.

Perspective from a 'Mandated Reporter'

There have been instances of teachers misusing their position and authority to take advantage of students. A new student may have difficulty in recognizing such a situation. This section provides some background perspective for awareness and appropriate responses.

As noted in the introduction, this project originated as a college level practice/seminar for students in a public school. One of my job requirements was immediate mandated reporting of any suspected abuse in or out of the school setting. The initial report had to be made to a state agency outside of the school. This directive increased my responsibility for the well-being of the students. The situation is different in a Zen teacher and student relationship, but these comments flow from that experience.

When a beginner, especially a younger person, comes to practice, the implicit understanding is that the teacher has the insight and maturity to act in their best interests. Many adults begin practice from a vulnerable situation and are entitled to that same understanding. There is no question that the overwhelming number of teachers make their best effort in their work with students to end suffering. As noted earlier, the effort at times will be challenging to students rather than providing encouragement to them. At this point, it is important to distinguish occasional human mistakes from patterns of a serious breach. When a normal mistake is recognized, the teacher can take responsibility by initiating the same procedure they teach—confession and repentance—and then moving on. This action is an appropriate response.

Experience has shown that some Zen teachers have exhibited behavior that is not consistent with the intent to end all suffering. In some cases their behavior has added to suffering. It is not always clear what appropriate behavior is. In a review of published comments by current teachers, there is a wide divergence of opinions about appropriate behavior ranging from nostalgia for 'anything goes Zen' to formal codes of conduct. As with anything else, 'appropriate' is a provisional term. One teacher even stated that there is a shared responsibility of the student to avoid inappropriate behavior with the teacher. In practice, this statement is problematic due to the inherent power differential of the situation.

An occupational hazard for idealized teachers and the hierarchy is that patterns of behavior are not to be questioned and may be kept secret. Inappropriate behaviors can manifest to the sangha (community) in different ways such as sexual, psychological, substance abuse, or financial impropriety. People have been hurt by these behaviors. The situation may be reinforced by complicity of assistants. The board members, dharma descendants, and senior students may have a deep investment with the teacher, individual ambitions, or face the threat of termination. Consequently, their responses may simply excuse or tolerate the behavior.

Even if inappropriate behavior is rare, it has to be effectively addressed. On one hand, it is important to be able to question what the teacher does. However, this is a difficult thing for a student to do and most in authority do not appreciate being questioned or called out, especially by a new student. Sometimes this approach works. However, there are also examples in which the behavior is explained away. In any case, if there are unresolved doubts and questions about the activities, the student should always consider seeking perspective and advice from practitioners and teachers both inside and especially, outside the sangha.

Additional Comment: The *Denkoroku* is a koan collection which traces the conditions of awakening of each successive lineage teacher. Each chapter also includes instruction (Teisho) by Keizan, written in the 14th century. One sentence in the case of Rahula has particular resonance for meeting a true teacher:

> "You have been fortunate to encounter the true Dharma,
> This is rarer than encountering a tiger in the city."[7]

Paraphrasing this in light of the above discussion:

> To encounter a teacher who recognizes their lapses,
> Is as rare as encountering a tiger in the city.

Priest Ordination

In Buddhism, the ceremony of ordination marks the passage from layperson to a monk or priest. The history and current practice of ordination have many cultural and geographical influences. The Buddha ordained monks and nuns. He presented an oral set of rules (vinaya) that laid out a framework in order for groups of people to function in community. Over time, different sets of rules (approximately 250-350 directives) arose. Some groups took them literally and were extremely strict. For example, celibacy was required, and outside work was forbidden since begging was common in the culture. Some schools continue to follow these rules today. However, other groups emphasized the spirit of the rules and modified the practices.

Geography and culture also impacted the monastic practice. In China, begging was not so integral to the culture. During some periods there was state support, at other times, persecution. The monasteries there became as self-sufficient as possible, and working to support the institution became a regular part of the day. There was also more emphasis on the precepts. Similarly, in Japan, the rules were condensed and emphasis was on the Bodhisattva Precepts. Later, some restrictions were relaxed further (by the influence or command of the Emperor) to allow monks to marry and have families. Changes continue to the present in the West.

Current Practices

Ordination is at the sole discretion of individual teachers and priests. There is no school or curriculum, and selection and preparatory practices vary over a wide spectrum. The criteria may be spiritual accomplishment, service, or just a personal affinity. The training requirements vary. Some organizations require a residency of five or more years following prescribed training rules and practices. Others have shorter residencies. Some have no residency or training sessions. Finally, there are some who choose to ordain their trusted friends.

Zen priests may perform many liturgical services including the daily liturgy and special services such as marriage and memorials for the dead. Priests are expected to be dedicated to the service of the community. Part of the practice is to be aware of the occupational hazard of hierarchical clericalism. There is much discussion about the role, responsibilities, and privileges on this topic. An insightful comment was made by Soyen Shaku, one of the first Zen teachers to tour the West in 1893. When asked about such a thing as a religious life, he replied:

> Attend to your daily business, do all you can for the promotion of good in the world, and out of fullness of your heart, help your fellow beings to gain the path of enlightenment. Outside of this, there cannot be anything to be specially called a religious life.[8]

That comment gets to the crux of the matter.

Different Ways to Become a Buddhist

People ask about procedures and study required to become a Buddhist. It is a serious commitment to take the precepts, the ethical code of Buddhism. Different schools have their own preparatory and ceremonial procedures. Each of them includes taking refuge in the Buddha, Dharma, and Sangha (the community) and then receiving the Five Lay Precepts. Some others may also include an additional Five Monastic Precepts as well as the Three Pure Precepts. The formal ceremony is sometimes referred to as lay ordination or Jukai (giving and receiving the precepts).

Taking the precepts expresses a commitment to ethical practices following the teaching of the Buddha in the direction leading to awakening to one's own nature. These precepts are viewed as either ethical guides or rules of conduct which the individual voluntarily accepts and strives to keep.

Some Zen Centers require the practitioner to be a formal student of the teacher for a minimum time of two years before they can petition to take the precepts. If accepted, there is a week-long training retreat followed by the ceremony. In the Soto sect of the Zen school, candidates also sew a rakusu, a multi-patched small garment symbolizing the robe of the Buddha, that is inscribed by the teacher and worn around the neck.

Other Zen sects allow the individual to study on their own and make the individual decision when to participate in the ceremony. Some schools (such as Theravada) provide an option for the individual to take the precepts by themselves, by taking 'Refuge in the Three Treasures' at a Stupa. Finally, many people believe in Buddhism or were born into a Buddhist family, but do not go through any initiation ceremonies. Such Buddhists make up the overwhelming majority. Similarly, there are self-declared Buddhists. It is a choice.

6

Teachings from the Pali Canon and the Sutras

Interlude: Employing Instructions and Teachings

As the emphasis shifts in the following chapters from procedural instructions to the teachings and commentaries based on the Pali Canon, it is an appropriate time to consider the different ways that these can be used. There is no real boundary between instruction and the teachings, rather they overlap depending on the emphasis on how they are used. Especially at the beginning, it is important to have a good foundation of the meditation practice procedures. The early emphasis is on meditation methods (Introduction, Appendix B), common difficulties encountered (Chapters 1,2), and teaching methods and working with teachers (Chapters 3,4,5). These can be used immediately. However, as we have already seen, even these instructions have a level beyond the procedures, for example practice metaphors and bowing (Chapter 3). So both instructions and the teaching commentaries can be used interchangeably.

All teachings not only emphasize understanding, but also point in the direction of aiding awakening. A common symbol is that of a finger pointing to the moon. In that representation, the moon stands for enlightenment and the pointing finger is the teaching. However, the admonition is strongly made to look in the direction that the finger is pointing and not become focused on the finger. The warning is that it is too easy to put attention on the finger itself and lose track of the intent. The finger itself may represent the teaching or the teachers.

As an example, a well-known line in the Heart Sutra[1]:

"Form is exactly emptiness, emptiness exactly form."

On the instructional level, it is essential to know the meaning of emptiness in the Buddhist context in order to proceed. On the teaching level, this phrase is a guide pointing to experiencing our nature, which cannot be experienced by rational analysis no matter how hard one tries. Though rational analysis is a natural starting point, this is where a meditation practice is crucial. The role of meditation is to settle the mind so that one can go beyond the rational understanding and intuitively understand the essential meaning.

Further, no teaching is definitive. The same teaching in the phrase from the Heart Sutra above may be expressed in different words, actions, or observations of nature. At any given time, one presentation may resonate with us more than another. One cannot rationally seek such resonance, such an occurrence depends on time and conditions. All teachings are incomplete in the sense that they do not satisfy the need for rational understanding. This book provides introductory explanations, but there are numerous books devoted to each topic here. These books address the teachings in more detail; they cannot capture the essence fully because that is impossible.

In order to be useful, the teaching must be actively employed both in meditation practice and daily activity. In meditation, energy arises and is the driving force for transformation. Sometimes, it arises during a sitting period. However, when resonant energy arises spontaneously during the study of a teaching, it can be especially valuable in meditation. One can sit with that energy, perhaps allowing the words of the story to drop away, and just be that energy.

Similarly, in daily activities, the teachings of the precepts are a valuable practice for growing awareness. The discussion of precepts in this chapter can be used as both a guide in everyday activity and an opportunity to realize the precepts in their essential meaning. It is again emphasized that there is no need to differentiate instructions from teachings, but to approach each with an open attitude.

Context of Written Teachings

Any discussion of Buddhist literature should keep in mind the concept of 'Buddhavacana,' which literally means 'the Word of Buddha' or 'words of enlightenment.' This term refers to works accepted as the authentic teaching of the historical Buddha. Some schools of Buddhism maintain that the Sutras are the actual words of the Buddha, others disagree. A tradition may recognize texts which are not acknowledged as the actual words of the historical Buddha but are regarded as authoritatively consistent with the teachings. Over the centuries, experience has demonstrated that these texts are teachings of the Buddha and can aid one on the path of liberation. The background of the teachings is not in question because they have been proven to be guides on the path of liberation. The basis of the acceptance of a particular work is the wisdom of Buddha rather than the documented historicity.

Buddhism has a long and complicated history reflected in its foundational documents. Scholars argue with scholars and different schools of Buddhism feud with each other about authenticity. It is easy to become entangled in such arguments and lose sight of the aim of the teachings. Some argue that some historical accounts may be myths, but even myths have truth. Karen Armstrong points out that "traditionally, a myth expressed a timeless truth that *in some sense happened once but which also happens all the time.*"[2] It is important to keep in mind that the teaching traditions are effective and are 'the Word of the Buddha' (Buddhavacana). However, there is no need to be ignorant of the history, or to gloss over or idealize it.

It is generally accepted that the Buddha taught for 45 years. Shortly after the Buddha's passing, the First Council (~ 483 BCE) was called. The purpose was to agree upon and preserve the accurate teachings. One disciple, Ananda, was renowned for his perfect recollection of the Buddha's talks. He had just qualified the evening before as an Arhat (one who has attained liberation) and had thus became eligible to attend the Council at the last minute. He was the star of the show! The monks agreed on the teachings and the rules of monastic discipline. His followers memorized the teachings and maintained their integrity by group recitations.

During the next 100 years, rifts developed in the interpretation and use of the teachings. The differences centered on monastic discipline and authority for interpretation, but these differences were not resolved by the 2nd Council in about 386 BCE. As time went on, there were other councils, and more significant divisions developed between the original Theravada school and the forerunner of what was to become the Mahayana sect or school.

Theravada school is more conservative, adhering closely to the teachings and rules of the Pali Canon. The school is most active today in parts of Asia (e.g. Cambodia, Thailand, Laos).

Mahayana (Mahasanghika) developed the ideas of the transcendent nature of a Buddha, the ideal of the bodhisattva, and the doctrine of 'emptiness.' This school advocated a somewhat more liberal approach to the monastic rules. As noted earlier, Zen is in the Mahayana school (active in China, Japan, Korea, Vietnam).

There continue to be differences in emphasis between the two schools.[3] Since Zen is in the Mahayana, the discussions here follow the Mahayana emphasis.

At the 4th council (~ 25 BCE) the monks realized that memorization was becoming fragmented. The practice of writing had advanced and so the work was inscribed on palm leaves. This effort became the Theravadin Pali Sutra, also referred to as the Tipitaka since it has three major sections. Obviously, the original palm leaves have not survived, but over the centuries many subsequent translations have circulated in different geographical locations and languages. The resulting ambiguities are grist for the scholars. They compare translations, match, and date passages, publish articles, and get graduate degrees or tenure.

At approximately the same period that the Pali Canon was being converted to written form (~25 BCE), additions were made to the core literature by the Mahayana school. The Mahayana practitioners continued to study the Pali Canon but added over 2,000 sutras written between 200 BCE and 200 CE. Examples of these additions are the Lotus Sutra, Heart Sutra, and the Vimalakirti Sutra. The Theravadins though, were not enamored of these additions. The word sutra means 'thread' in Sanskrit and the original sutras attempted to weave knowledge, thread-like, into a few simple words. Since some of the sutras are hundreds of pages, the brevity aspect has not been emphasized.

These newer sutras address some issues which arose with the Mahayana teachings. Though they were often written in the speaking voice of the Buddha, some appear to reference situations that happened at a later time. In a sense, these works also provided guidance for the later situations that arose. People disagree and argue about whether the Buddha actually uttered the words in these sutras, but the principle of Buddhavacana, which stresses the wisdom of the Buddha, can still be seen to operate in them. Much of the Pali Canon has been translated into English and is available in 33 volumes.

As an interesting aside: At the 5th council in 1871, the entire work was examined to make certain that no errors or discrepancies had crept in. After approval, and in a massive effort by craftsmen, the entire Canon was then inscribed on 729 marble slabs and each slab installed in a pagoda. This 'world's largest book' is still maintained in Myanmar.

Caveats: Sources and Translations

Generally speaking, most documents do not have an unbroken history because many of the works were often held and maintained as fragments in geographically isolated locations. Over the centuries, copying and random transcription errors were introduced. It's a formidable task to reconcile these documents and identify later additions. Different interpretations also come into play. Even now, some scholars assert that the most accurate renditions of some works of Dogen were not used as the basis for most translations of his work into English.

Many texts have been translated multiple times and on occasion, with almost contradictory interpretations. Translations are attempted by both practitioners and scholars with widely different backgrounds in context, usage, agenda, and practice experience.

We are fully dependent on these translators and, in the age of Google Translate, it is easy to disregard the fact that translation is an art and a science. Pajin states the issues clearly:

> In translating ancient religious and philosophical texts, one of the major problems is to decide whether a certain word is used colloquially or terminus technicus (technically). On such a decision sometimes depends not only the appropriate **translation** of a particular word, but the proper **understanding of the whole passage.**
>
> To decide, we should know the tradition of the text and have in mind the context, as well as previous commentaries, if such exist. The second problem is that the translator uses a language the words of which have the same ambiguity (colloquial/technical) as the original language, or a vocabulary which (itself) lacks the necessary technical terms.[4]

There are many excellent translations of the different sutras, but no 'definitive' translation that makes others obsolete. It is fair to say that there are some that miss the mark. It's clear that different translations will speak to individuals differently. As recently as 20 years ago, there was much less access to information and practitioners really had to rely on few sources. Even with multiple sources there continues to be a cognitive tendency to place more weight on the first information received (anchor bias). In the past, it was more difficult to evaluate context or to recognize idiosyncratic teachings. Now, of course, there is an abundance of information available. Individuals can take advantage of these choices and identify the versions that speak more directly to them. There are several passages in the following sections that contrast two different translations.

For example, Hsin-hsin Ming (Trust in Mind) by Sozan (C: Seng-can) has been translated numerous times. The Chinese word 'Hsin' in the title does not have an exact equivalent in English. It has been rendered as heart, mind, spirit, feeling, but has the nuances of each of them. The seven title translations below are all by well-known authors using the three Chinese characters in the title. The divergences continue for 36 stanzas!

- On Trust in the Heart (Christmas Humphreys)
- Inscribed on the Believing Mind (D. T. Suzuki)
- Words Inscribed on the Believing Mind (Heinrich Dumoulin)
- Faith in Mind (Sheng-yen)
- A Poetical Manuscript on Belief in the Mind (Katsuki Sekida)
- Poem on the Trust in the Heart (Thomas Cleary)
- Inscription on Trust in the Mind (Burton Watson)

A Sense of Suffering

> "In the past, monks, and also now, I teach suffering and the cessation of suffering." (SN 22.86 Anuradha Sutra)[5]

As noted in the earlier section about sources, original intents and meanings can change with both the passage of time and with translations into different languages. Also, the original expression may not have a direct counterpart in either the language or the cultural experience, so substitutions are made and nuances may be lost.

The term 'suffering' is an example. Physical pain often comes to mind first with this word, then mental distress. The Pali Canon uses the term 'dukkha,' and translators, linguists, Buddhists, and scholars have interpreted the meaning of that word for years. Literally, the meaning seems to be dissatisfaction, suffering, discontent —but with what?

Dissatisfaction, suffering, and discontent can appear in different contexts. Buddhist literature is nothing if not systematic. The categories quoted below are drawn from the Princeton Dictionary of Buddhism.[6] In the most common differentiation describing suffering, there are three categories:

(i) Misery caused by physical and mental suffering.
(ii) Misery caused by change, such that even when things are going well, they will eventually fade.
(iii) Misery caused by conditioning—all sensations are undependable and there is an underlying dissatisfaction that there is no solid ground on which to stake our life.

The exploration of suffering is central to the 1st Noble Truth. However, meaning is obscured when it is shortened to: " Life is suffering."

Suffering includes the physical pain of ordinary life, and also the mental, emotional, and spiritual dissatisfactions which appear to be inherent in life.

The short formulation reads more like a simple statement of one fact of life. A fuller description:

> Birth is suffering, aging is suffering, sickness is suffering, death is suffering. To be conjoined with what one dislikes is suffering and to be separated from what one likes is suffering. Not to get what one wants is suffering. In short grasping at the five aggregates (*skandhas*) is suffering. (SN 56.11 Dhammacakkappavattana Sutta)

Through investigating this passage, suffering takes on a more profound and actionable meaning. 'Grasping is suffering.' Life is always changing, yet the grasping at what cannot be held can only lead to problems. Inherently, impermanence is just the way it is, but it is the conditioned attitude toward impermanence that leads to suffering. Suffering is not external and hence is within our potential to end. The intent or motivation to put an end to suffering comes from within by turning one's attention to the pursuit of non-grasping, also called non-attachment. Viewed from a larger perspective, this formulation of suffering is an invitation, even a call, to action. This is the intent of practice, to live life fully without the added burden of attachments.

The Four Noble Truths

The Four Noble truths can be seen as the Buddha relating what he learned from his experiences. As straightforward facts they resemble a recipe, but exploring the depth reveals much more.

The 1st Noble Truth acknowledges this sense of suffering and impermanence.

The 1st Noble Truth: Life is suffering.

The appearances arising in this present moment are the consequence of past causes and conditions throughout the universe. Although the actions of each individual contribute to them, the result is a consequence of many activities and cannot be traced back to one's individual action. This is the law of karma.

This principle is expressed in the 2nd and 3rd of the Four Noble Truths

The 2nd Noble Truth: The cause of suffering is desire and ignorance.

When these appearances are viewed as independent or permanent, rather than arising and fading, the idea of self (ego) and other appears; attachments can take hold and suffering results. In short, suffering is the direct result of an incorrect view of the nature of reality.

The 3rd Noble Truth: There can be an end to suffering.

The great teaching of the Buddha is that the cause of suffering can be eliminated, leading to the end of suffering and the freedom of all beings. The practices are outlined in the 4th Noble Truth.

The 4th Noble Truth: The Eightfold Path leads to the end of suffering.

These four truths are intended to provide the opportunity to lead beings to a correct view of reality. This is a path to experience life beyond conditioning.

This is just the beginning of this teaching. Both in the Pali Canon and later commentaries, these statements are elaborated upon and include topics such as karma, dependent origination, and the steps in causation (Chapters 9 and 12).

Eightfold Path

The Eightfold Path is the 4th Noble Truth presented by the Buddha in his first sermon. The Eightfold path is the means to bring an end to the causes of suffering. There are countless written translations, oral commentaries, amplifications, and re-imaginations which interpret meaning and application of the Eightfold Path. Many of these commentaries are readily accessible and one can identify a version that resonates. The explanatory statements following the list of the Eightfold Path below are among the most literal.

In one sense, the Eightfold Path provides a practical guideline to maintain a practice to end suffering. This path allows intentional living between the poles of asceticism and sensual indulgence. Although they seem to appear as a list of rules which follow a prescription, that is a limited view. Sometimes commentaries are interpreted (citing the Buddha for authority) as telling people what they should not do. They are not a list of rules, but outlines of (or guides to) ethical conduct.

Consequently, the guidelines can be encountered and practiced at different levels. On the everyday level, they can be viewed as ethical instruction practiced intentionally as a discipline, with ups and downs. The individual will benefit with enhanced ethical living from following the path at this level. From the awakened perspective of a buddha, these practices are virtues that are the natural, spontaneous expression of an inner realization. Consequently, external actions taken by different people may appear the same, but the mental awareness and the state which motivates the actions may be quite different. In other words, you can't tell by looking!

Some clarifications generally not discussed in many commentaries on the Eightfold Path are useful in the initial reading of the Eight Truths:

The word 'Right' is used as a modifier for each of the truths. Although in English the first meaning of right is often taken as the opposite of wrong, this would be a limiting, prescriptive view. The original Sanskrit word was not used with this meaning. In this context 'right' is the sense of being consistent with the teachings of the Buddha to end suffering. A more accurate, expansive meaning of the term is 'complete' or 'perfect.' Similarly, the term 'Noble' was originally referencing those who have realized the path. Noble did not modify the statements of the truths themselves. By now, that distinction has been forgotten, without consequence.

The Eightfold Path is:

1. Right View—accurate understanding of the true nature of things.

2. Right Intention—avoiding thoughts of attachment, hatred, and harmful intent, promoting loving kindness and non-violence.

3. Right Speech—avoiding harmful speech such as lying, harsh speech, abusive language, slander, frivolous speech, and gossip.

4. Right Action—avoiding killing, stealing, and misconduct.
5. Right Livelihood—avoiding livelihoods which directly or indirectly harm others—selling slaves, animals for slaughter, or weapons, dealing in intoxicants or poisons.
6. Right Effort—abandoning unwholesome states of mind that have arisen, preventing them from arising, and developing wholesome thoughts that have yet to arise.
7. Right Mindfulness—maintaining awareness of the foundations of mindfulness: awareness of body, physical sensations, the mind, and phenomena.
8. Right Concentration—one-pointedness of mind.

Beginning from the everyday perspective, the individual components of the Eightfold Path can be used for practical training. They can be divided into three themes as shown in the classification system below.

Wisdom	**Morality**	**Concentration**
1. View	3. Speech	6. Effort
2. Intention	4. Action	7. Mindfulness
	5. Livelihood	8. Concentration

Two Perspectives of the Middle Way

The Middle Way (the avoidance of extremes), which was taught by the Buddha, can be experienced at different levels:

> There are these two extremes that are not to be indulged in by one who has gone forth. Which two? That which is devoted to sensual pleasure with reference to sensual objects: base, vulgar, common, ignoble, unprofitable; and that which is devoted to self-affliction: painful, ignoble, unprofitable.
>
> Avoiding both of these extremes, the middle way realized by the Tathagata—producing vision, producing knowledge—leads to calm, to direct knowledge, to self-awakening, to Unbinding. (SN 56.11 Dhammacakkappavattana Sutta)

The above passage is followed by a description of the Eightfold Path.

The activities of the Eightfold Path are the means to avoid extremes and intended to be active guides toward experiencing life as it is. The admonition is that one should be neither too strict nor too lax in both spiritual practice and daily living.

The passage below refers to the essential and the relative aspects of existence:

> But when one sees the origination of the world as it actually is with right discernment, 'non-existence' with reference to the world does not occur to one. When one sees the cessation of the world as it actually is with right discernment, 'existence' with reference to the world does not occur to one.
>
> 'Everything exists': That is one extreme. 'Everything doesn't exist': That is a second extreme. Avoiding these two extremes, the Tathagata teaches the Dhamma (Dharma) via the middle. (SN Kaccayanagotta Sutta)

The method of dialectics presented in Chapter 4 can be used to frame this passage.

As noted earlier in the Buddhist view, truth resides somewhere between affirmation and negation, in this case, between "Everything exists" and "Everything does not exist."

> "Everything exists" stands for the phenomenal world of senses.
>
> "Everything does not exist" refers to the absolute.
>
> The synthesis of the two: Neither existence, nor non-existence is Right View. It is the experience of the union of the two, in a realm beyond words.

Taken together, the progression of these three statements describes a whole that is beyond the sum of the parts. The experience of the Middle Way is neither existence nor non-existence. There is a moment to moment balance between practice and understanding, between wisdom and activity. For example, if there is too much emphasis on phenomena, there is suffering. Conversely, if there is excessive emphasis on the absolute, there is inactivity. If there is too much emphasis on the synthesis, the importance of each can be missed.

The two discussions above on the relative and awakened view are both about avoiding extremes. The Buddha taught at the level of his audience's receptivity. The first provides a method of practice guided by the Four Noble Truths and the Eightfold Path and the second is at a level that goes beyond them. Thanissaro Bhikku, the translator of the passage, actually goes a little further. In the last sentence of his comment below, he emphasizes that the Path itself is a provisional teaching and when fully realized, it also has to be abandoned:

> (The) level of right view that apparently lies beyond the four noble truths, and applies to the point in the practice where the path has been fully developed, has done its work, and now has to be abandoned .... It is in this way that all fabricated dhammas are abandoned and unbinding can be fully realized.[7]

Training with the Lay Precepts

The Five Lay Precepts constitute the basic Buddhist code of ethics and are an integral part of Buddhist practice. Together with meditation, they constitute a synergistic practice which takes the practitioner in the direction of awareness, wisdom, and compassion. However, to refer to the Five Lay Precepts as 'ethics' requires additional clarification. Here the word 'ethics' is not interpreted as a strict set of rules of behavior, but rather as guides and reference points which can lead to beneficial actions, with the realization that some actions lead to happiness and others to suffering.

In an historical context, similar oral training rules predate Buddhism and are considered by many scholars to have evolved from earlier Indian religious traditions. The precepts also differ from commandments in the Christian sense since they are not issued from a higher authority, as in many religious traditions, and there is no emphasis on guilt. Instead value is placed on making forward looking changes.

Further, the precepts can work on different levels. For example, they can be applied to the everyday level guiding one's behavior, which is an essential starting point. However, the precepts have meaning beyond this and they can be interpreted and practiced in the spirit of their ultimate meaning. This is the practice of the buddhas.

Consequently, there are many different interpretations and commentaries regarding the precepts. The practice of keeping the precepts has been emphasized differently by both the different schools of Buddhism as well as by individual practitioners depending on tradition, history, or personal preference. Although there are many people who are eager to have their perspective and teaching become the practice of others, it is each individual who has the responsibility to use an interpretation that is appropriate for their own life. For some, the precepts are a traditional code of ethics. They are taken as behaviors to avoid or as prescribed prohibitions. From this perspective, the literal meaning is scrutinized closely. However, for others they are seen as guides of intentions, aims, or aspirations for growing awareness.

As with everything else, the application of precepts is not fixed, but depends upon time and conditions. It is the responsibility of the practitioner to decide when and under what conditions the action is appropriate. For the individual, the reconciliation of actions in a specific situation with a particular precept leads to a higher degree of awareness.

One of the more focused comments which helps maintain the perspective of the role of the precepts is from the mid-20th century scholar Edward Conze:

> "One takes responsibility for one's actions because, behind the respect for the moral rules, lies the respect for the inexorable Law of Karma, which rewards good deeds and punishes misdeeds."[8]

Precepts are often broken. The role of 'confession and repentance' is to take responsibility for the actions which break the precept with an intention to try again. It is a stage of growth and a reminder of the direction of practice.

There are many translations from the Pali, as well as re-interpretations of those translations in both positive and negative tones. This translation is by Piyadassi Thera. There are many others that could have been selected (Panca-sila, for example).

Five Precepts for Lay People

1. I undertake to abide by the precept to abstain from killing.
2. I undertake to abide by the precept to abstain from stealing.
3. I undertake to abide by the precept to abstain from sexual misconduct.
4. I undertake to abide by the precept to abstain from lying.
5. I undertake to abide by the precept to abstain from liquor that causes intoxication and heedlessness. (Khp 1-6 The Khuddakapatha)

In addition to these, there are many other precepts and rules. For example, novice monks observe 10 precepts, ordained monks, 227, and ordained nuns, 311.

Renunciation or Opportunity: The 5th Precept about Intoxication

The 5th Precept sparks animated discussion concerning its literal application to alcohol, often at the expense of the overall direction of the precept. Respected contemporary teachers have addressed this precept quite differently and these views are often stated in a dogmatic way. A commonly referenced literal translation from the Pali Canon of the 5th Precept is: "I undertake the training precept to abstain from alcohol, liquor, or spirits that are a cause for heedlessness." (Vin I.83-84)

Drawing from a study of different commentaries which were influenced by history and traditions, individuals can begin to develop their own balanced perspective to form their own interpretation. When upholding a precept, it is important for one's decision to be motivated by belief and conviction rather than by a fear of violating an external rule. As an entry point, the episode from the Vinaya that brought this precept into the canon involves a disciple becoming inebriated:

> The account begins with six monks asked by lay people what might be a rare offering, to which they reply 'white spirits.' When Venerable Sagata subsequently goes on an alms round, he receives and consumes this drink in several homes. He then collapses at the town gate and has to be carried back to the Buddha, to whom he points his feet disrespectfully.

The Buddha picks up three changes in behavior, beginning with the impaired conduct:

> Monks, formerly was not Sagata respectful, deferential towards the Tathagata, second, the loss of capacity and thirdly, perhaps most significantly, the loss of consciousness: But, monks, could he become unconscious, having drunk that which may be drunk?

The Buddha declares:

> Monks, it is not fitting for Sagata, it is not becoming, it is not suitable, it is not worthy of a recluse, it is not allowable, it is not to be done. How, monks, can Sagata drink strong drink. It is not, monks, for pleasing those who are not (yet) pleased .... And thus, monks, this rule of training should be set forth: In drinking fermented liquor and spirits there is an offence of expiation. (Monks' Expiation, Pacittiya 51)[9]

This account is clear about the intentions, but almost immediately the translators, commentators, and early traditions make distinctions. (Expiation is defined as the act of making atonement.) The following discussions contrast two approaches to the 5th Precept.

Emphasis on Intoxicating Agents

In considering the use of intoxicating agents, the teachings and practices have not been uniform. For example, within China, some geographical areas observed complete abstention and others 'moderation.' Today, some teachers instruct their students to avoid any intoxicating or mind-altering substances, while others regard the taking of a small quantity of alcohol as acceptable since it is not intoxication. A debated question is whether any alcohol has a beneficial effect or muddles the mind.

This precept is sometimes viewed as different from the others since intoxication leads to carelessness and the breaking of other precepts. Arguments arose about what constitutes 'heedless' behavior. Heedlessness means being inattentive to how the student is affecting others and circumstances around them because they are incapable of seeing the results of their actions.

Today one can further consider the question of other agents of intoxication. For example, coffee is often consumed in large quantities which can affect behavior, but often gets a free pass. In this extension of the precept, anything used in excess can become an intoxicating agent—TV, internet, video, books.

Emphasis on Opportunity

The 5th Precept can also be used as a positive motivation which can provide opportunities for growth. Times change. Restatements of the precepts are common and may have different emphases. The two restatements below have the same direction as the original, but do not mention agents at all:

> "A disciple of Buddha does not intoxicate self or others but rather cultivates and encourages clarity." (SF Zen Center)

> "To the best of my ability, I will maintain a clear and alert mind that is aware of its motivations, moment to moment, such that it can discern between what is the cause of suffering and what is not the cause of suffering." (Marin Sangha)

There is a shift in emphasis here. The second statement focuses on becoming aware of the motivation that leads to the desire for an intoxicating agent. For example, a particular moment may not be satisfying enough, or there may be suffering, and the desire to turn away from it may arise.[10] Keeping the 5th Precept in mind, one becomes aware of this desire to change or control the present situation rather than fully experiencing it as it is. A person can be aware of what is happening and choose whether or not to continue. Using an agent to change the situation could also be an intoxication and the agent may be unique to the individual and not on any common list.

In either approach, there are real challenges to maintaining the discipline. Precepts are broken and as discussed in another section, the practice of confession and repentance is then appropriate. Guided by teachings, individuals are ultimately responsible to make different decisions on how to practice this precept. The important point here is restated from above: One's decision is best motivated by belief and conviction rather than fear of an external rule.

Confession and Repentance

It is an expected and normal part of practice that the precepts will be broken. 'Confession and Repentance' is a practice that offers the opportunity to let go of the past and move forward in the moment without attachments.

Hui-neng explicitly describes repentance as an activity that both looks back and forward:

> Repentance means repenting of former errors, previous bad actions, faults like stupidity, delusion, conceit, deceit, jealousy, and envy, repenting of them so that they don't ever recur. That is being penitent. Repentance further means regretting later mistakes, from now on aware of bad behaviors and faults like stupidity and delusion, conceit and deceit, jealousy and envy, and stopping them forever, not acting on them anymore. This is called repentance.[11]

Using the precepts as working guides, confession is taking responsibility for an action that is not in accordance with practice. It is an act of awareness of our lives as they are right now. There may be regret, but there is no guilt or punishment associated with this practice. This aspect represents a significant difference from confession in other spiritual traditions. For some, it is used as a method to bring responsibility and awareness to their lives. If another is negatively impacted by the breaking of a precept, an apology or asking for forgiveness may be a beneficial step in the process. In some cases direct contact may not be feasible or appropriate. As always, the time and conditions are a factor in determining the course of action.

Repentance is the resolve to do better going forward. Real repentance is not simply an apology and it does not necessarily require words. From this vantage, repentance means to return to the source of emptiness, the source of karma, and to live life fresh in the moment. It is the recognition that faults come from our mind. Zazen, as formless repentance, is being awake to reality as it is without subject or object.

The crux of true repentance is contained in these verses:

> The ocean of impediment of all karma
> Is produced from one's false imagination.
>
> Should one wish to repent of it
> Let him sit upright and meditate on the true aspect of reality.
>
> All sins are just as frost and dew,
> So wisdom's sun can disperse them.
> (Samantabhadra Meditation Sutra) [12]

There is a service of repentance, Fusatu, which is practiced as a communal service at some sanghas, often near the time of the full moon. Its direction is to take responsibility for our actions and to become more aware of the suffering caused by our actions and decisions based on our distorted view of the world. Chanting, bowing, and recitation of the precepts are included in the ceremony. True liturgy, which makes the invisible visible, can be an opportunity to interact with requests and responses in community between oneself and others. The experience can then expand, beyond normal limiting irritations and attachments, to encompass and hear the universe. Sometimes the intent of confession and repentance is not fully understood and consequently is underutilized as a practice. Many Zen groups begin their first sitting period of the day with this chant. It brings awareness to the intention of practice at the start of day.

Gatha Of Repentance

> All evil karma ever created by me of old
> On account of my beginning-less greed, hatred, and ignorance

Born of my conduct, speech and thought
I repent of it now.

Generosity and Patience: Companion Paramitas

Paramitas, which translates as 'perfections,' are virtues or qualities cultivated to strengthen practice and lead one toward awakening. As it is used here perfection means completeness or wholeness. There is a close relationship between paramitas and the Eightfold Path. Some even consider them as functionally equivalent. Others maintain that the paramitas place more emphasis on specific practices.

There are several different lists of these virtues. The best known is a group of six generally translated as generosity, discipline, patience, diligence, meditative concentration, and wisdom. Some lists enumerate ten paramitas; the additional four are skillful means, strength, aspiration, and primordial wisdom.

The direction of the practice with paramitas is that the actions or activities are done without ego attachment. For some, the activity or action is only considered to be a virtue when practiced in this way. The intent behind the practice is what is emphasized rather than the action itself or the result.

The virtues of generosity and patience are often considered to be companion paramitas. Generosity is the desire to help others while patience is the restraint needed to deal with others. From the perspective of the Eightfold Path, they are both in the category Right Intention.

Generosity (Dana)

Dana is the virtue of generosity or giving. Of the six perfections on the bodhisattva path, Dana has first ranking. The attitudes associated with giving are spelled out in the Sappurisadana Sutta:

> These five are a person of integrity's gifts. Which five? A person of integrity gives a gift with a sense of conviction. A person of integrity gives a gift attentively. A person of integrity gives a gift in season. A person of integrity gives a gift with an empathetic heart. A person of integrity gives a gift without adversely affecting himself or others. (AN 5.148 Sappurisadana Sutta)

Dana is an important preliminary step in the path of awakening. When the Buddha spoke to new people, he began the sermon with a discussion of the significance of the virtue of generosity. Generosity in giving reduces the attachment to the object and the act. It also helps develop practices on the Eightfold Path—morality, concentration, and wisdom. The offerings themselves are often listed in three categories: (i) gift of material goods, (ii) gift of fearlessness (giving protection to the frightened, or offering friendliness), and (iii) gift of spreading the Dharma.

In the practice of Dana, the awareness with which the gift is given is also considered. To give a gift carelessly is not the practice of this paramita. The understanding that the gift, the giver, and the recipient are impermanent is an example of awareness within the practice of Dana. At this level of egolessness, there is no giver or receiver.

In the examples below, Dana refers to everyday activities. At another level, bodhisattvas study the paramitas so they can carry out these practices completely in all their activities. Thus, giving becomes the practice of renunciation and complete letting go of attachments.

Dana as Solicited Donations

Dana in material goods has been a foundational practice of the Buddhist laity, presumably because of its value in weaning the layperson from attachment to material possessions, while also providing essential material support to monastic sanghas. There are chants which proclaim that the merit gained by such gifts to a monastic sangha is unequaled.

In 17th century Japan, every family was required to register and support (Dana) a local temple. This giving was a form of control over the people. But if there is coercion, as there was in Japan, the coercion deprives the giver of the opportunity to perform the intended practice.

The Dana tradition is actively practiced to support many Zen halls today such that the term is sometimes used synonymously with donations. There are often guidelines for donation and reminders about tax deductibility. Some groups advise their students to give more than they may be comfortable offering. Others stress that one should never give more than their comfort level. People who are not aware of the intent and scope of Dana will legitimately associate the practice of generosity with a transactional activity, quite the opposite of the intent.

Patience Under Insult (Ksanti)

Generally, this paramita is simply called patience. Patience is often referred to as forbearance, restraint as in accepting a burden, or tolerance for a hardship, either with ourselves or others. It is often equated with willpower. Hsing Yun considers the use of 'patience' an abbreviation or shortening of 'patience under insult':

The Buddha was asked:

> 'What is the greatest strength? What is the utmost brilliance?' The Buddha said, 'Patience under insult is the greatest strength, because people who are patient do not harbor hatred, and they gradually grow more peaceful and strong. Patient people, since they are not evil, will surely gain the respect of others.' (Sutra in 42 Sections)[13]

There have been many discussions and commentaries about patience, but this modifier of 'under insult' adds another flavor. Hsing Yun's comment here shows that this paramita is both a practice and also a recognition of delusion.

> You cannot feel insulted unless you are deluded. All anger is an illusion. To understand this is to understand the highest form of patience. At its highest level, patience is just another word for wisdom.[14]

He adds that 'patience under insult' is one of the most difficult assaults most people face, since social beings feel insult so acutely. The reaction to insults and disgrace are a consequence of the illusion of a self, which then has to be defended. With the realization of no-self, a defense is not needed and in fact is irrelevant. One cannot feel insulted if they are not deluded and anger does not arise.

True patience requires no energy since if energy has to be expended, it will ultimately be exhausted and the patience will not last. The practice is to find patience in the resting place between thoughts. This is the method to develop awareness and promote its growth.

Beyond Everyday Gratitude

The entry point for the understanding of gratitude is from the Katannu Sutra:

> A person of integrity is grateful and thankful.
> This gratitude, this thankfulness, is advocated by civil people.
> It is entirely on the level of people of integrity.
> (AN 2.31-32 Katannu Sutra)

When a scripture teaching is fully integrated into a life, it is a great inspiration to others. The Dalai Lama has written of the influence on him of Shantidevas's *The Way of the Bodhisattva*:

> "If I have any understanding of compassion and the practice of the bodhisattva path, it is entirely on the basis of this text that I possess it."[15]

The Dalai Lama has said that he is grateful to the Chinese for giving him the opportunity to love his enemies " 'as our most precious spiritual teachers' as they are often called because they help us to develop our spiritual practice to cultivate equanimity even in the face of adversity."[16] He states: "We need enemies and should be grateful to them .... Only an enemy can teach you tolerance. An enemy is the greatest teacher of altruism, and for that reason, instead of hating, we must respect him."[17]

For most of us, an expression of gratitude at this level is beyond the pale, but he is genuine about it. Perhaps he was born with it, but according to Eckel, this expression of gratitude has deep roots in the "exchange of self and other" from Shantideva's *The Way of the Bodhisattva*:[18]

> All the joy the world contains
> Has come through wishing happiness for others.
> All the misery the world contains
> Has come through wanting pleasure for oneself.
>
> Is there need for lengthy explanations?
> Childish beings look out for themselves,
> While Buddhas labor for the good of others:
> See the difference that divides them.
>
> If I do not give away
> My happiness for others' pain,
> Enlightenment will never be attained,
> And even in samsara, joy will fly from me.[19]

The practice of exchanging self and others is to regard the suffering of others exactly as our own suffering and to help others as if they were ourselves. This meditation exercise puts oneself in another's place in order to gain an appreciation of how and why others feel as they do, and how one's self appears from their viewpoint.

More generally, the Pali word 'katannu,' translated as gratefulness (actually grateful), has the element of 'acknowledging what has been done to us.' This introduces a sense of awareness in the response of gratefulness rather than the more common English connotation of an emotional response.

The awareness here is of the interconnectedness of all phenomena. It is a meditation practice that allows the experience of the interconnectedness of life to grow. This experience of an interconnected life is a gift without cause or doing which, by becoming aware of it, leads spontaneously to its expansion to all manifestations as they appear. And it all comes from this miraculous discovery and experience of the interconnectedness of life. There is gratitude simply for the opportunity to experience the unique unfolding of life with all of its possibilities.

Finally, there are many essays describing methods of cultivating gratitude in daily behavior. This cultivation is a continuous practice of growing awareness. Dogen summarizes:

> Continuous practice, day after day, is the most appropriate way of expressing gratitude. This means that you practice continuously, without wasting a single day of your life, without using it for your own sake. Why is it so? Your life is a fortunate outcome of the continuous practice of the past. You should express your gratitude immediately.[20]

This expression of gratitude is fully integrated with the daily practice to end suffering, informed by the interconnectedness of all beings, including the practice of those in the past.

Bounded and Unbounded Compassion

As with generosity, the term compassion can be applied to both everyday acts as well as acts from an awakened perspective. Compassion that is bound to self and other stems from the recognition of the suffering of sentient beings. More generally, it is compassion toward all things that we experience. It is activity in the world of forms. Katagiri adds that when compassion takes a form, it is just our idea of compassion and it takes a form that is limited by ideas and desires and hence, bounded.

Great Compassion (Unbounded Compassion) arises without the delusion of self and other. Without subject or object, actions naturally flow. The gift is just given and received back simultaneously. It has no form. Sak elaborates on the liberation of Great Compassion:

> Great Compassion has the prominent feature of not only giving

> rise to sympathy for the act of liberating others, but it also accomplishes the act of liberating … (the giver).
>
> The salient features of Great Compassion appear to me as not merely 'alleviating the suffering of others,' but doing so without the separation of others and accompanied by no distinction between living beings.
>
> Lastly, Great Compassion is not turned towards some beings—those who suffer—but towards all beings equally. It is activity in the world.[21]

There is often confusion or misunderstanding in making the distinction between bounded and unbounded compassion. Considering them properly is not a matter of comparison—that one is inferior to the other. The relationship is different. Compassionate activities in the world that can be seen as bounded are crucial, both to alleviate suffering now and to provide a practice component to move beyond all activities based on the separation of self and other.

Beyond Bounded Compassion

One begins with compassionate actions in the time and conditions where each individual is at that particular moment. Compassionate activities are not supplemental or additional to the everyday activity of the world. They are integral to the affairs of the world.

Dogen emphasizes that they are the practice of buddha dharma:

> Those who regard worldly affairs as a hindrance to buddha dharma think only that there is no buddha dharma in the secular world; they do not understand that there is no secular world in buddha dharma.[22]

The situation described below occurs so regularly that the response often becomes reflexive. It provides an opportunity to both act and grow awareness.

One is walking down the street and suddenly there is someone in front of you asking for money.

Some responses may include:

> Regret that this situation exists and that it is in front of me.
>
> Ignore it.

> Decide to contribute and do a mental calculation for an amount to be offered.
>
> Not have a rational reaction and just respond to the situation.

From the relative perspective, compassion is 'bounded' to the concept of self and other. In this example, there appears to be another person right in front of me asking for my help and there is the recognition of the suffering of others. It appears as physical suffering and the response to it may flow from an idea or emotion. Responding to the situation on this everyday level is an example of bounded compassion.

From the essential or wisdom perspective, unbounded compassion spontaneously arises without the delusion of self and other. Compassionate acts are not tied to an idea of what should be done, but to the experience from which it arises. Without subject or object, actions naturally flow. The gift is just given and received back simultaneously. The activity is appropriate, but may not necessarily respond to a particular stated request. The mind of wisdom grows from a meditation practice. In this example, the response may be something different from offering money, while still appropriate from the awakened perspective.

Sheng-yen relates an incident which reinforces the distinction of compassion based on emotion or wisdom:

> During this retreat, one student came to me in a very emotional state saying that her compassion had been moved powerfully, that she felt pity for suffering people and wanted to help them. From her point of view, this seemed like a very good experience to have, but I scolded her saying, 'You're just fooling around in sentimentality. This is not wisdom. In the mind of wisdom, there is no such thing as people needing to be pitied.' Compassion is not simple sentimentality; it is just a natural response to help people.[23]

Yamada describes a path that begins with bounded compassion and moves to unbounded compassion. He points out that we begin the practice of compassionate activity in our world and allow the compassionate experience to grow. It may begin as compassion that is bound to the suffering of sentient beings, and then expand to everything that is affected by the senses. With practice, it becomes unbounded and it just flows:

> As we gradually clarify the heart's eye—the eye that sees the ab-

solute—we more and more clearly experience this unbound compassion and come to fully understand that we love everything with an infinitely deep love, and that all things love us. What discontent could there be?[24]

Playing Chess, Experiencing Compassion

There are many versions of this well-known story which illustrate an experience of developing compassion:

> A young man who had a bitter disappointment in life went to a remote monastery and said to the Master: 'I am disillusioned with life and wish to attain enlightenment and be freed from these sufferings. But I have no capacity for sticking long at anything. I could never do long years of meditation and study and austerity. Is there any short way for people like me?' 'There is' said the Master, 'if you are really determined. Tell me, what have you studied, what have you concentrated most on in your life?' 'Why nothing really. We were rich and I did not have to work. I suppose the thing that I was really interested in was chess.'
>
> The Master immediately called his attendant and told him to bring a designated monk and a game board. The monk appeared. He was old and had lived in the monastery for many years. The Master sent the attendant for a sword. He showed it to the young man and the old monk, 'You two will now play a game of chess. Whoever loses, I will cut off his head with this sword!' They looked at him, and they saw that he was serious.
>
> The young man made his first move, and the old monk followed. After a few moves, the young man felt the sweat pouring down his back. He concentrated and put everything he had into that game and managed to gain an advantage. He looked up at the old monk and saw a face of intelligence and sincerity, worn with years of austerity and effort. He thought of his own worthless life and a wave of compassion came over him. He deliberately made a blunder and then another, putting himself into a losing position. But suddenly the master upset the board, saying, 'No one has won, and no one has lost.' Then to the young man he said, 'You have learned two things today: concentration and compassion. You were completely concentrated on the game, but then in that concentration, you could feel compassion and were willing to act on it. Now you can stay and train in this spirit.'[25]

Nothing in life is better than being free
But getting free is not luck.

(Stonehouse)[26]

7
Attachments and Freedom

The origin and consequences of attachments have been succinctly stated by the Dalai Lama:

> "Most of our troubles are due to our passionate desire for and attachment to things that we misapprehend as enduring entities." He adds: "These mental processes easily translate into actions, breeding belligerence as an obvious effect."[1]

The second vow in the Four Great Vows of the Bodhisattva (Chapter 11):

> Desires are inexhaustible, I vow to put an end to them.

Desires reflect how one wants a situation to be, and then how one responds to that desire rather than responding to the situation as it arises. Actions that arise without the filter of desires are a manifestation of our original nature. Actions that arise from desire reflect the ego.

Putting an end to desires does not mean getting rid of them by will power or conscious effort. Rather putting an end to desires can be viewed as doing the work of a meditation practice in order to become intimately aware of the nature of desires. Then their attraction fades and they are no longer relevant to our actions. Ending desires really means that the reaction to desire does not arise; it simply does not enter the conscious mind. This is what is meant by 'dropping attachments.'

There is a misconception that the absence of desires is a form of passivity. Almost the opposite is the case. Reactions to conditions can still arise, but the difference is in the response to them or the effect they have on oneself. Freed from energy sapping expectations, one can put full effort and creativity into the task and the moment at hand. Though expectations and emotions still naturally arise and fade, the experience of life becomes intimate and intense.

The absence of desires and attachment is non-attachment, not detachment. This is an important distinction. Detachment is commonly used in the sense of distancing oneself from the activity, but it is really a separation from the moment at hand. (However there can be some ambiguity with the term 'detachment' since in the Buddhist literature, that word is sometimes encountered in the sense of not being attached to the outcome of an event or action.)

The ideas or opinions which form the basis for attachments to objects have no intrinsic value. In the everyday world some ideas and opinions may even lead to or guide beneficial action which would seem to accord them intrinsic value. But here there is an important point to recall—even if the outcome appears to be a beneficial action in the sensory world, the intent of Zen practice is to go beyond the day-to-day world and experience one's original nature.

The Paradox of Attachment and Achievement

A question that naturally arises is how to balance the desire to go beyond our attachments to goals and desires in order to experience our original nature. The Dalai Lama has directly addressed this question:

> One of the key paradoxes in Buddhism is that we need goals to be inspired, to grow, and to develop, even to become enlightened, but at the same time we must not get overly fixated or attached to these aspirations. If the goal is noble, your commitment to the goal should not be contingent on your ability to attain it, and in pursuit of our goal, we must release our rigid assumptions about how we must achieve it. Peace and equanimity come from letting go of our attachment to the goal and the method. That is the essence of acceptance.[2]

The Monks' Breakfast

Preparing a meal is a routine activity. In the past, the last task of the monks for the evening was to prepare breakfast for the next day. This involved hulling the rice, cooking it into gruel, putting it into jars, storing it on the shelves, and cleaning up. Each effort to fulfill the task of preparing breakfast was made with full attention on the step at hand. There was no further expectation. After all, during the night they may die, an earthquake could knock the jars from the shelves, a thief may come and steal it, or animals could break in and spoil it. Such imagined scenarios were of no concern to them. The preparation of the breakfast was the task at hand. Thoughts of the future did not arise.[3]

As Bodhidharma said:

> Sages don't consider the past. And they don't worry about the future. Nor do they cling to the moment. And from moment to moment they follow the way.[4]

The word 'clinging' in the above passage can be viewed from different perspectives. It can refer to the timing of the activity. If there is joy in doing the cooking, it is just for that moment. To hold onto the idea of the joy of that moment is an attachment. In another direction, when most people prepare a meal, they have the expectation of sitting down and enjoying it. The clinging may be to the expectation of eating the food which is an attachment to the idea of a future activity. The Monk's Breakfast is also a reminder that tasks can be done fully in the moment with no attachment to an outcome.

All of us can act with direction and non-attachment. This short verse summarizes direction and non-attachment of a rice farmer in Japan:

> I don't know if the autumn will bring rain or storm,
> Still, I shall pull the weeds in the rice paddy.[5]

Working with Attachments

Why work with attachments at all? To understand a response to this question, it's important to keep in mind that the direction of Buddhism is not to make one a 'better' person, but to free oneself of barriers which keep us from experiencing life just as it is. Attachments are a hindrance in the mind which obstruct the full experience of the moment. Desires and attachments come in many different flavors, but all have the same effect—acting as a filter to the experience of reality.

Attachments may take many forms. Although one can generalize about them, specific attachments really are an individual issue. Often, a starting point may be obvious. For example, for some people, attachments may take the form of desires, opinions, cultures, or bodily features. For other people, these may not be important, but others such as wealth, relationships, or prestige may be significant. As practice develops and awareness grows, previously unrecognized attachments may emerge into consciousness as conditioned habitual responses, or ideas about how the present or future 'should' be. Finally, on a more subtle level, there can be attachments to the teachings of Zen, Buddhism, or any moral standard. As each desire or opinion comes into view and arises into awareness, there is no need to judge it, but to take note of it, and recognize that there is a choice in how to respond.

Frustration is a consequence of desires that are not realized. In many cases, frustration is the first step in developing anger and negative energy. However, viewed through the lens of attachments, frustration becomes a signal that there may be an unrecognized expectation lurking behind the frustration. The frustration becomes a useful tool to grow awareness of the mind. In many cases the recognition of frustration in an early stage allows the situation to be more clearly understood and defused in a natural way.

For example, although anger may appear to arise in a moment, there is a sequence of progressive steps beginning with irritation or anxiety and growing from there. The intermediate steps may progress so quickly that they may be unnoticed. An increased awareness of the situation as it develops can allow one to interrupt the cycle and take a different course of action in order to defuse our own behavior. Another example may be a negative reaction to someone else's good fortune. Such a reaction may be a consequence of a desire for wealth or prestige. If there is no attachment to what is seen, there is no such reaction.

Attachments are active in the present and have no independent existence, so there is no need to demonize them. They can be used as tools in the practice and then allowed to fade. A classic example is the analogy of the raft which is discarded when the other shore is reached. Just as the raft is necessary to make a river crossing, so all desires and attachments are initially useful in the practice. Zen practices are intended to make the time and conditions favorable for the exploration of attachments. Both meditation and ethical guidelines, such as the precepts, can be used for this investigation. It should be noted though, there can be a tendency for some teachers to prescribe specific precept practices. These can be viewed as provisional suggestions that have worked for many people in the past. However, the individual has to be open and willing to experiment and to make errors in order to find their own way here as well.

Questions that arise for exploration, that do not require a rational response, but can encourage insight:

Who is having these desires?

What is really happening right now? Is it objective or subjective?

Is there some aspect of the present moment that does not meet expectations of what it should be?

Are thoughts or desires permanent or just arising and fading, without independent substance?

Are situations being seen just as they are, or how they 'should be'?

Can the past be changed or accepted?

The Farmer

The following story illustrates how life can unfold without being attached to outcomes. It begins in the everyday world of happiness and disappointment. The calm actions of the farmer point to the experience of being open to the unfolding of the moment.

> There lived an old farmer who had worked on his fields for many, many years. One day, his horse ran away. His neighbors dropped in to commiserate with him. 'What awful luck,' they said sympathetically, to which the farmer only replied, 'We'll see.'
>
> Next morning, to everyone's surprise, the horse returned, bringing with it three other wild horses. 'How amazing is that!' the neighbors exclaimed in excitement. The old man replied, 'We'll see.'
>
> A day later, the farmer's son tried to ride one of the wild horses. He was thrown to the ground and broke his leg. Once more, the neighbors came by to express their sympathies for this stroke of bad luck. 'We'll see,' said the farmer politely.
>
> The next day, the village had some visitors—military officers who had come with the purpose of drafting young men into the army. They passed over the farmer's son, thanks to his broken leg. The neighbors patted the farmer on his back—how lucky he was to not have his son join the army! 'We'll see,' was all that the farmer said! (Attributed as Taoist story)

The horses, the injury, and the military draft were all events that unfolded in front of the farmer. Each event was related to previous causes and effects. The situations kept changing and were neither good nor bad, although the neighbors had opinions about them. The farmer had to face each event as it occurred. Nothing is permanent. With no expectations or attachments to ideas about how the future should unfold, he experienced each event without judgment. The farmer trusted life to take care of itself. On the other hand, the neighbors had definite opinions about each event and were attached to them. Their perspectives took them from unhappiness to happiness several times. Each event roiled their emotions. They were swept up by time and conditions.

This story is a good illustration of the different ways that most people react to situations as they arise. Each individual has a conditioned way to respond. These reactions can lead to a personal roller coaster of emotions and behavior. But even as attachments fade through practice, they still unfold and have to be dealt with. However, with diminished attachment, there is more space or freedom to respond in a natural and appropriate way.

As Bodhidharma put it:

> As mortals, we are ruled by conditions, not by ourselves. All the suffering and joy we experience depend on conditions. If we should be blessed by some great reward, such as fame or fortune, it's the fruit of a seed planted by us in the past. When conditions change, it ends. Why delight in its existence? But while success and failure depend on conditions, the mind neither waxes nor wanes. Those who remain unmoved by the wind of joy silently follow the Path.[6]
>
> Those who perceive the existence and nature of phenomena and remain unattached are liberated. Those who perceive the external appearance of phenomena are at their mercy.[7]

Zazen is crucial in order to move in the direction of non-attachment and calm acceptance. In zazen, there is no judging; sensory perceptions arise and fade. The comings and goings are seen as comings and goings. The practice is to grow awareness of the nature of phenomena. The power of the impermanent, conditioned phenomena fades and the mind begins to calm. When the mind is clear, obstacles become interesting playthings and life can be appreciated and enjoyed fully.

Freedom

Seung Sahn distinguishes between true freedom and the idea of freedom:

> Freedom means no hindrance. If your parents tell you to do something and you think that you are a free person so you will

> not listen to them, this is not true freedom. True freedom is freedom from thinking, freedom from all attachments, freedom even from life and death.[8]

Our original nature is free without conditioning, and silent, yet moving in full harmony with the cosmic energy of the universe. It's a tempting idea to search for freedom, as if it were something to be sought outside. However acting on this idea takes one in an unproductive direction. A search based on the idea is a hindrance, just as the child's concept of freedom was in the quote above. However, virtually everyone wanders off in the direction of seeking an idea of freedom now and then. As with any other distraction that arises during meditation, when you become aware of it, simply return attention to the moment, without judgment or recrimination. This practice is the direction of becoming free of attachments and hindrances.

Freedom can only be experienced, not defined or fabricated as a concept. Mind is always naturally functioning, but freedom is the functioning without filters or obstructions. When this occurs, our whole life manifests and acts appropriately and spontaneously in the phenomenal world.

Attachments, desires, and ideas are obstructions to that natural functioning. These hindrances may be obvious or so subtle that they are below the current level of awareness. Examples of those which are not so obvious range from ideas about our self to the desire for freedom. Although habits can be changed or broken, the root of desires cannot be released by willpower. The method which allows us to become intimately aware of attachments so they lose energy and dissipate in a natural way is zazen.

Freedom is having nothing to cling to and the key to it is practice. This essential direction has been expressed in many different terms. In addition to Seung Sahn, the two teachers below gave essentially the same direction, though each expressed it a little differently, so an individual might find one that resonates more strongly.

According to Taisen Deshimaru:

> True freedom also means being satisfied with one's lot. One can always try to improve it, to go further, to carry it beyond. But not to complain, because that is another self-indulgence, an attachment.
>
> A person who knows freedom cannot be attacked by anyone or disturbed by anything because that person is following the

cosmic force, like a great elephant that does not try to play on a rabbit's path.[9]

And, as Shunryu Suzuki wrote:

> Usually you have no freedom from things you have or see, you know. But if you experience or understand the experience of shikantaza, you will have freedom from things. And you will enjoy, you know, your life in its true sense because you are not attached to anything.[10]
>
> We feel free to express our self because we are ready to fade into emptiness. When we are trying to be active and special and accomplish something, we cannot express ourselves. Small self will be expressed, but big self will not appear from the emptiness. From the emptiness, only great self appears.[11]

To summarize: When attached to nothing, everything can be freely appreciated.

Freedom within Limitation

In 1973, Peter Matthiessen trekked with George Schaller and a Sherpa guide, Jang-bu, deep into Dopo, an isolated section of Nepal, and the home of the Crystal Monastery. He had a meeting with the Lama, an old and partially crippled man. He relates this passage in his book *The Snow Leopard*:

> The Lama of the Crystal Monastery appears to be a very happy man, and yet I wonder how he feels about his isolation in the silences of Tsakang, which he has not left in eight years now and, because of his legs, may never leave again. Since Jang-bu seems uncomfortable with the Lama or with himself or perhaps with us, I tell him not to inquire on this point if it seems to him impertinent, but after a moment Jang-bu does so. And this holy man of great directness and simplicity, big white teeth shining, laughs out loud in an infectious way at Jang-bu's question. Indicating his twisted legs without a trace of self-pity or bitterness, as if they belonged to all of us, he casts his arms wide to the sky and the snow mountains, the high sun and dancing sheep, and cries, 'Of course I am happy here! It's wonderful! Especially when I have no choice!'[12]

Life is as it is. The joy of life in intimate moments—in this passage, the sky, the snow, the mountains, the sun, and the sheep. The Lama has freedom within limitations of time and conditions. Without arising opinions, likes/dislikes, fair/unfair, right/wrong, there are no restrictions. What else is there to do but appreciate the moment of life fully and without attachments, which is what the Lama is expressing in his response. The seeming ordinary is quite extraordinary for him.

The Lama of Crystal Monastery's last sentence drives home the point—the full appreciation of life, just as it is. This is the direction of practice. Another teacher replied to a similar question about the effects of aging: Savor the deterioration and decline of your aging body.

Sometimes, I hear the answer 'same old, same old' to the question that asked 'What's happening?' Yet 'same old' can be very extraordinary. It is in the freedom of mind that the ordinary can be truly appreciated as extraordinary.

Freedom and The Blue Sky Bird

The natural behavior of a quail is to be free, to walk around in the underbrush, to eat, to drink, to fly, and to be quite sociable.

> Some quail were feeding at the edge of a clearing. A man crawled up behind them and captured four birds with his net. He put them in a cage. The quail were trapped, scared, and hungry. The man came and fed the birds. Three of them eagerly ate all that was given. The fourth bird just looked through the cage at the blue sky. Each day was like this—three birds eating and the other just looking at the sky. One day, the man saw that the birds were almost ready for market. But then he stared at the Blue Sky Bird, who was by this time quite emaciated. He reached into the cage to pull it out and inspect the skinny bird. However, the Blue Sky Bird, having waited for this moment, sprung into activity and flew immediately to a branch of a tree beyond the man's reach. The three caged birds looked up. 'How can we do this too?' The Blue Sky Bird replied: 'You ate the man's food and you will be captive until you die. I refused his food and now I am free.' And off she went into the expanse of the blue. (Adapted from Jataka Tale)

There are any number of reasons to forget what freedom is and to be content with what is presented. Conditioning takes a toll. Attachments, fear, and desires add to it. Three of the quail went in the direction away from freedom. Still there were glimpses of possibilities. The fourth bird saw them. The poet and hermit, Stonehouse, comments: "Nothing is better than being free, but getting free is not luck."[13]

Is working toward the direction of freedom worth the effort, even when there is no guarantee it will come to pass?

Freedom from Judging

Below is a workbook lesson from *A Course in Miracles* (#243). Consider the potential for freedom in terms of not making judgments and try the exercise out for a day to see if it's like taking a day off.

> I will be honest with myself today. I will not think that I already know what must remain beyond my present grasp. I will not think I understand the whole from bits of my perception, which are all that I can see. Today I recognize that this is so. And so I am relieved of all judgments that I cannot make. Thus, do I free myself and what I look upon, to be in peace as God created us (which is original nature).[14]

8

Illusions, Self, and Interconnectedness

> "Will not a tiny speck very close to our vision blot out the glory of the world, and leave only a margin by which we see only the blot. I know no speck so troublesome as the self." (George Eliot)[1]

In Eliots's classic novel *Middlemarch*, the first husband (Mr. Casaubon) of the central character (Dorothea) has a view of the world that is distorted by his ego: "To the facts he knew, he added imaginary facts, both present and future which became more real to him."

This quote is an example of the consequences of the idea of a separate self. The world is seen as separate from other, capable of distortions, and there is a strong attachment to one's own viewpoint.

The Buddha was directly asked the question: "Is there a self?" He did not directly answer it. However, the teachings that all beings are empty of independent existence and are impermanent negate the concept of a separate, permanent self.

Rahula succinctly connects the self to illusions and their consequences:

> According to the teaching of the Buddha, the idea of self is an imaginary, false belief which has no corresponding reality, and it produces harmful thoughts of 'me' and 'mine,' selfish desire, craving, attachment, hatred, ill-will, conceit, pride, egoism, and other defilements, impurities and problems. It is the source of all the troubles in the world from personal conflicts to wars between nations. In short, to this false view can be traced all the evil in the world.[2]

Illusions

Illusions are a beginning point for practice. Start with what you have access to. A first step is to recognize illusions:

> "Whatever the senses apprehend resembles an illusion, including everything ranging from mental concepts to living beings." (Huang Po)[3]

A demonstration is helpful. When a child waves around a Star Wars light saber in the dark (or failing that, a lighted stick of incense, a glow-stick, or a sparkler if they are still legal), all sorts of interesting shapes can be made to appear—a circle or a figure eight for example. When the motion stops, the shape is gone. More interestingly though, the shape was never there! It was just the way the motions were perceived.

Everything that is experienced by the senses is a similar illusion. That is, what is perceived in the dualistic everyday world is produced by the experience of the senses and is illusory. But illusions are useful as they allow experience and communication at a certain level. The difficulty arises when illusions are mistaken for the whole of reality, causing problems to originate. This mistaken perception is the cause of suffering. Illusions do exist, as the circle or the figure eight seems to appear when the child waves a light saber at night. We give them names and separate identities, but they are not us. Causes and conditions interact to give rise to these phenomena. However, the illusions that we experience as our world can be used as the entry ways into the full experience of life as it is.

Delusions are different from illusion. A delusion is mistaking an illusion for full reality, the root of which is clinging attachments. Everything in the dualistic world is a sense object and an illusion—past, present, and future.

The comments from earlier teachers complement this discussion:

> Illusions glitter like diamonds and people are drawn to them; illusions are what make human beings live, they are as necessary to us as air, because the end of illusion, the disappearance of phenomena, means the end of activity, the end of life, death. (Deshimaru)[4]

> The arising and the elimination of illusion are both illusory. Illusion is not something rooted in Reality; it exists because of your

> dualistic thinking. If you will only cease to indulge in opposed concepts such as 'ordinary' and 'Enlightened,' illusion will cease of itself. (Huang Po)[5]

> People set up views of delusion and enlightenment and hold to interpretations of turning towards and turning away, wanting to understand this mind and see this inherent nature; thus this mind and this nature immediately flow into wrong paths, following the person's inversions, errors, and confusion. (Ta Hui)[6]

Squashes: Exploring Self and Other

Here is a story from the Edo Period that shows that Zen can help squashes as well as people!

> Behind a temple, there was a field where a lot of squashes were ripening. One day an argument started. The squashes split up into two groups and they made a big racket shouting at each other. The head priest heard the uproar. He went to see what had happened, he found the squashes quarreling. The priest yelled to get their attention and scolded them: 'Hey, you squashes! The idea of fighting among yourselves! Everyone do zazen!' The priest taught them how to do zazen. 'Fold your legs like this, sit up, and straighten your back and neck.' While the squashes were sitting zazen, as the priest taught them, their anger subsided and they settled down. Then the priest quietly said, 'Everyone, put your hand on top of your head.' When the squashes felt the top of their own heads with their hand, they found some weird thing on their heads. It turned out that one vine connected them altogether. 'This is really strange. Actually we're all tied together and living just one life. In spite of that we've been arguing. What a mistake! It's just as the priest said.' After that the squashes got along with each other very well.[7]

The starting point of perception is self and other. Initially each squash views itself as a separate self apart from the others. There is inherently a relationship: in some cases, helpful, in other situations, perhaps antagonistic. Self and other, subject and object, always define a relationship. Generally, we think of relationships as being with other people. But there is a relationship with anything perceived as an object—a thought, the furniture, doing the dishes, riding a bike. Sometimes we can try to ignore it, figuratively burying our head in the sand. But inevitably, the relationship re-emerges as soon as attention is turned back to the world.

The next step is to investigate the relationship based on the idea that there is a separate self. The key word here is 'idea.' It is a thought that has taken on a life of its own. The idea appears to be reality. The practice of zazen is to investigate this illusion by releasing ideas, which leads to growing awareness. An important point is that this is not done by willpower, or by self-limited rational capacity, but by using the practice of zazen to transcend the intellect.

Then in the third stage, the squashes discover for themselves that they are one life. The differentiation between the individual squashes does not disappear—that differentiation is the manifestation of life. However, the entire experience of interaction with each other changes with the realization that there is just one life or one reality. It is one life working together. Instead of the term 'one life,' the expression 'one life force' is more descriptive.

Like the squashes, we also start with our own ideas of the individual self. The direction of Zen meditation is to let these ideas drop away and to experience this interconnectedness of life for ourselves. We are the manifestation of this life force.

In some sense, individual human beings may believe they are personally in control of something, perhaps even themselves. But a closer look, even at the rational level, calls this belief of control into question. What is the force that animates us? The force that allows us to move, to breathe, to be alive—it is not due to our thoughts! Life force goes well beyond that; it animates everything. Life force is beyond thought and is the reality of our life. Experiencing that reality is transformative and, as the squashes came to understand, changes the way we interact.

However even with this insight, differences do not disappear. The everyday world is still present—but the experience of it, in its always changing interconnectedness, is now different. There is the experience of unity within differentiation.

A passage attributed to Sengzhao (378- 414) gives a perspective on the differences and unity:

> Suppose there was a man who, in a treasure house of golden utensils, sees the golden utensils, but pays no attention to their shapes and features. Or even if he does pay attention to their shapes and features, he still realizes they are all gold. He is not confused by their varying appearances, and therefore is able to rid himself of their (superficial) distinctions. He always sees the

> underlying substance is gold, and does not suffer any illusion. This is an illustration of what a sage is.[8]

Buddha nature, represented as gold, is always present although the differentiated shapes may change as the gold is melted down and recast. The sage sees that there is only buddha nature. He is buddha nature. There is nothing outside of buddha nature. Everything that is experienced is the manifestation of life force.

Delusions to Explore: Self and Other

The world is typically perceived and experienced as Self and Other, subject and object, each being separate. The question explored in a Zen practice is whether subject and object is the ultimate reality. The exploration may begin in the intellectual realm and, with practice, be experienced. The ramifications of experiencing the reality as it is are enormous.

Maintaining the view that Self and Other are separate entities leads to opposition. There is a competition for resources. One takes from the other. The scenario manifests itself at every level—individuals, groups, and countries—all competing for their individual piece of the action. A further consequence of this perspective is that when circumstances do not work out as one desires or would like, there is some 'other reason' to attribute as the cause. Bankei gets at the root of the issue:

> Ideas of
> What's good, what's bad
> All due to
> This self of yours.[9]

Self and Other as one reality takes experience in an altogether different direction: sharing of life experience for mutual benefit, selfless individual behavior, respect, and compassion toward all phenomena.
Dogen sums this up:

> "It is the foolish man's idea that his own profit must decrease if he gives precedence to profiting others. But this is not so. The act of benefitting is one and it benefits both oneself and others."[10]

Self and No-Self

At the outset, it is almost a given that self and other are separate. The term 'self' generally refers to what Suzuki calls 'small mind'—our name, our body, sense perceptions, and all of the ideas and thoughts that contribute to the idea of self. This self constantly changes based on experiences, opinions of those experiences, time, and conditions. Each being seems to have a sense of independent existence which interacts with the surrounding world. There are egos, ideas, likes/dislikes, and attachments. All of this is the response to the conditioning elements in the culture, education, or upbringing. A consequence of this view of self is the strife that is manifested in the phenomenal world.

No-self is not the opposite. Rather, it is free of attachment to the idea of a self. There is functioning in the world without attachments to ideas or concepts. There is a natural, appropriate, spontaneous response to each situation as it arises. It is a nuanced state—acting from wisdom without the idea of wisdom. This is the functioning of mind. It should be noted that all of the above descriptions are not the actual reality. The experience of actual reality (neither self nor no-self) is what is termed as awakening. That experience ends the delusion.

One of the most quoted lines in the Zen literature comes from Dogen's *Shobogenzo*:

> To study the self is to forget the self.
> To forget the self is to be actualized by myriad things.
> When actualized by myriad things, your body and mind, as well as the bodies and minds of others drop away.[11]

This teaching is asking for an active inquiry into the nature of our perceived self. It can be helpful to consider this passage line by line:

To study the self is to forget the self.

The starting point can only be our current perspective, the dualistic view of self and other. One studies the self by growing awareness of self. This is done by practice and inquiry—to look inward and grow awareness. This is the practice of zazen. It is to become more aware of the attachments, ideas, and thoughts which are held. There are both obvious and subtle attachments which comprise the self. At the beginning, there is often a fondness for them. Over time, these attachments come into awareness and are allowed to dissipate on their own. The practice of thinking and letting go naturally leads to the falling away of self.

To forget the self is to be actualized by myriad things.

'Myriad things' is sometimes translated as the 10,000 things, the everyday phenomenal world. 'Actualized' is in the sense of making real. Actualization or realization is often the term used, but is frequently misunderstood in typical usage because of its association with mental activity. In this case actualization means to make it real and directly manifest the forgetting of self or 'no self' in the everyday world. What is manifested is life just as it is, the arising and falling of phenomena, all of which are interconnected. However, with the self forgotten, they appear as they are, unified and animated by the life force.

When actualized by myriad things, your body and mind, as well as the bodies and minds of others, drop away.

The expression 'drop away' is a reminder that the process is natural, that nothing has to be 'gotten rid of.' This can give way to pure awareness in which the self drops away. Having left behind the idea of self, our original nature emerges, just like that, with nothing 'special' to be done. To be enlightened by phenomena is to experience that there is one nature manifested in different appearances. The bodies and minds of others dropping away is well expressed in the teaching of the Diamond Sutra. There is no universal self, there is only impermanence. Life flows, everything in harmony, nothing lacking, and activity unfolds just as it is. There is an intimacy in the dropping away and a harmony when there is no self or other, when there is just one reality.

Ego and Individuality

Another way of looking at Zen practice is to move us in the direction of being fully who we are. Each of us is unique and has our own way of expressing ourselves. In a sense, we do not have to know who we are in order to be who we are. (Not knowing who we are will be discussed in Chapter 10.) However, on occasion the concern is raised that without an ego one would function in a passive way. The situation is the opposite. Without a blocking ego, one is free to function spontaneously and appropriately. In other words, you don't need an ego to express your individual personality. Deshimaru states this clearly:

> Individuality and a strong ego are different. Coming back to one's own originality is very important; you and I are not the same. You are you. You must find your own you. Through zazen you can end your own bad karma. Through zazen you can recognize your own individuality and make it strong .... You don't need to say to yourself, 'I must become like this or that.' Unconsciously, naturally, automatically, you become it .... Your personality becomes richer.[12]

Feynman and the Question "Why?"

I was educated in chemistry and then engineering. My inclination at that time was that phenomena could be explained or analyzed. That seemed to be true in the fields in which I was trained. Engineers fix problems and make things work. So, it was a sad day for me when I realized that there were more significant limits to understanding then I had hoped. These next few topics are presented to reinforce the limits of our understanding of the sensory world.

Richard Feynman, the Nobel laureate physicist, was deeply influenced by his father's encouragement to ask questions and notice things. As a boy, Feynman was playing with his pull train which had a ball in one of the cars. He noticed that when he suddenly stopped the train, the ball continued to move forward. He had made an observation about the law of inertia (a body in motion tends to stay in motion). He sought out his father and asked: "Why does the ball keep going after I stopped the train?"

The first reply from his father was "That, nobody knows ...." Then he explained inertia to his son, concluding with "but nobody knows why."

"That, nobody knows." It is a response that opens possibilities. Feynman's father was showing his son the difference between having a word or name that explains something and knowing what it really is or what causes it to be. It is easy to miss this distinction. While people may know a lot of names or labels, the labels become restrictive. They can trick us into acting from the belief that we actually know something. Most individuals have to make a real effort to understand that they do not know.[13]

A phrase from a koan, "Not knowing is the most intimate" (*Book of Serenity*, Case 20) is a reminder that not knowing is not the same as ignorance. Not knowing refers to the experience of our own nature which is beyond the intellectual realm. The term 'beyond knowing' may be helpful here. There is a world beyond knowing that can be experienced and expressed in our activities. A Zen practice can take you there.

The Fallible Senses

The empirical method has led to a heavy reliance on the interpretation of observations. Science tends to report its observation in objective terms—this is the way it is and there is data to substantiate the conclusion. The Feynman story presents an example of a scientific principle which is taken as an objective fact. Sensory perceptions can be challenged when opportunity arises in order to see how the conclusions hold up. Any event that weakens convictions in our beliefs and perceptions can begin to open the door to a wider and vast world that may not have been previously considered.

With that as an introduction, here is a sensory experiment that you can try at home:

> In the early evening when a full moon rises, you can see it large and luminous against the horizon. Later in the night, you can again observe the moon high in the sky and see for yourself that it has apparently shrunk to a small circle. Certainly, the size of the moon hasn't changed. For centuries, people, including Aristotle, have tried to explain this observation.
>
> It is easy enough to convince yourself that it is an illusion. For example, a photograph taken of a horizon moon will be smaller than that remembered by the observer. The size of the moon in the photograph will remain the same when taken at different heights in the sky. More simply, just compare the size of the moon to the tip of your little finger when held at arm's length. First, check the moon against your finger when it is first near the horizon, and then check again later in the evening when the moon is high in the sky and appears smaller. The relative size measured against the finger remains the same.
>
> There are many theories about the underlying cause of this illusion. An entire technical book, *The Mystery of the Moon Illusion*, examines these theories. The authors conclude that no single theory has emerged victorious. They further observe that "The moon illusion is one of the few perceptual phenomena that tap a broad spectrum of sciences: astronomy, optics, physics, physiology, psychology, and philosophy."[14]

Apparently, all human beings are wired to make the same perceptual error. The senses do not accurately register what is actually happening. The moon illusion is evaluated against our normal understanding. The assumption is that everyday perceptions and understanding are accurate, but evidently this is not the case. Having seen one inconsistency, it is easy to conclude that there very likely are other sensory illusions, even if we are normally unaware of them. These illusions throw further doubt on our understanding. We may not know what is 'out there' as reality, or even if there is an 'out there.' Bodhidharma is in agreement: "Using the mind to look for reality is delusion. Not using the mind to look for reality is awareness."[15]

Bodhidharma's comment points in this direction. A mind distorted by illusions from the senses cannot explore itself with accuracy. Such an exploration just adds error to error. But not using the mind to look for reality and instead practicing zazen and quieting the mind allow for the examination of reality through the development of refined awareness.

Moon Factoid: The moon waxes, becomes a full moon and then wanes in a 28 day cycle. People looking at the crescent moon very often are not clear which part of the cycle the moon is in. If you curve your right hand and it fits the crescent, it is a waxing moon. Conversely, if the curved left hand fits the crescent, the moon is in the waning stage. Many people report that this simple gesture increases their appreciation of the moon dramatically; it changes their lives.

Senses: Things Are Not as They Seem, Nor Are They Otherwise

The world which we appear to know is that which is processed through the senses. People trust those experiences as fact. In addition to the perceptual errors, such as the size of the moon, there are numerous omissions in our sense perception.

An occasional excursion into this area of omissions is helpful as a reminder of the limitations of our daily experience. At least on a rational level, it provides an opportunity to question and perhaps helps to undermine our attachments. This may make us more open to the vast possibilities that can be available to us by all the practices that can be used for the path of awakening. There is a lot going on that we don't know about. For those interested in perceptions of the physical world, this verse is a starting point:

"Fire is hot, wind moves, water is wet, earth hard.
Eyes see, ears hear, nose smells, tongue tastes the salt and sour."
(Sandokai)[16]

Earth seems to be hard, but it is mostly empty space. The smallest atom, hydrogen, has one proton and one electron. If the proton were increased to the size of a peanut, the entire hydrogen atom would occupy the volume of a baseball stadium. There really isn't much but open space.

Water seems to be wet to the touch. However, we really never actually touch water. That is a good thing because if we did, there would be a nuclear reaction setting off a large explosion. Objects never touch. The electrons in the atoms of all materials are negatively charged and repel each other creating a strong repulsive electromagnetic force. The brain perceives this repulsive force as touching. The hand is actually hovering at 10^{-8} m (0.00000001 meters) above the water. That force creates the sensation that is transmitted to the brain. The memories of these sensations (rough, smooth, etc.) are stored and referenced for future use. Touching is an illusion.

Space is not an empty vacuum. Particles are coming into and out of existence at time scales that cannot be registered by the senses. The material world (mass and energy) that is known to the senses is only about 1/20 (5%) of what is present in the universe. The majority of the known universe is either dark matter or dark energy. The existence of dark matter and dark energy has been inferred by many astronomical measurements over the last 50 years. No one has any idea of what is going on with that. It's possible though, that all of the theories are incorrect. Then we are even further in the dark!

The above examples reflect a rational understanding in the 21st century which allows us to function in the phenomenal world, but they are only provisional explanations. The truth of life lies beyond these explanations. Yet, there is a deeply conditioned belief in their validity and a strong desire to embrace them as anchors of security. These examples can be used both to undermine that security and to be encouragement to go beyond the explanations.

The physical definition of a sense is that it consists of a group of cells that responds to a specific physical phenomenon, and that response corresponds to a particular region of the brain where the signals are received and interpreted. Sense has two components—the physical response and the meaning associated with it. (Some languages distinguish both components.) It turns out that sensory experience is both

historically and culturally dependent. People of different times and places hear, see, taste, touch, and smell in distinctive ways. This might lead us to question the trust that we put in our own five bodily senses. Finally, although we refer to the five senses, there are at least three other recognized senses (and candidates for a number of others).
These are:

- Thermoception - the sense of heat.
- Equilibrioception - the perception of balance.
- Proprioception - the perception or awareness of the position and movement of the body. (Example: Close your eyes and touch your nose.)

All of the above examples reinforce the idea that it may not be so surprising how little is actually 'known' and even that which is called 'knowledge' cannot be relied upon. In a universe in which nothing can be relied upon, everything is possible. The universe is 'empty.'

Brushing Teeth

There are different ways of using the senses in doing everyday tasks. Brushing your teeth is an example. You can brush your teeth thinking about the day—who did what to you, how it went, what you are going to do differently tomorrow, and other commentary. At the end of the two minutes of activity, the teeth are clean. Alternately, you can brush the teeth following the attention to the bristles of the brush scraping the teeth, to the taste of the toothpaste, to the sound of the brushing as each sensation arises. At the end of two minutes, the teeth are clean. How is the mind? Is the condition different? Where has it been?

Absolute and Relative Are Empty and Identical

From the Buddhist perspective, the one reality is empty, that is it has no independent existence. This one reality is often described from two perspectives. While reflecting on these two perspectives, bear in mind that as with everything else, this explanation is just a description, a manner of communication, and is not the experience itself. The experience is what the practice is moving toward.

> The Relative refers to our everyday impermanent world experienced through the senses.

> The Absolute (Essential) is empty, it has no form, yet at the same time has limitless capabilities. Anything is possible. It is imagination and rational reasoning. There are experiences beyond the phenomenal world that cannot be grasped through the senses. From this the self cannot be 'known.'

Over time, many different terms have been used to describe these perspectives. This sometimes leads to confusion. For example different commentators have used these terms:

Absolute	**Relative**
Essential	Phenomenal
Emptiness	Form
Void	Cause and Effect
Essence	Phenomena
Mind	mind
Darkness	Light
True Self	Ego
Suchness	Discriminating

The essential (absolute) and the relative are not two things. Analogies have been made to one coin having two sides or one fraction having a denominator and numerator as described in the following section. These comments from Yamada may offer another way to look at absolute and relative:

> "Emptiness is the stage on which the myriad phenomena continually appear and disappear, without a moment's deviation, at the mercy of the law of causation."[17]
>
> "The standpoint of Mahayana Zen is that infinite, absolute reality wears the clothes of limitation and relativity."[18]

Awakening to True Self is to experience that emptiness and form are identical. It is seeing/experiencing both sides of the reality coin clearly and in balance. Each phenomenon that arises is a complete and perfect expression of the absolute. Everyday life is the scenery of the activity of essential nature unfolding right now:

> Cloudy days are cloudy; rainy days, rainy; clear days, clear; and it is only natural that the coming and going of thoughts and psychological and physiological conditions fluctuate accordingly. This very thing is the reality of life itself and its manifestations. Going beyond this, seeing it as the scenery of life, and not being carried away by it—this is settling down and this is the foundation of life.[19]

Uchiyama expresses the reality of life and its manifestations so succinctly. As it turns out, it is rainy as I write this. That is the scenery of life at the moment. A Zen practice helps to not be carried away by our reactions to the scenery, to just experience it and appreciate it.

Reality Expressed As a Fraction

Koun Yamada (1907-89) was a Dharma successor to Haku'un Yasutani. In addition to Zen teaching, he had a career in business and public health. As a leader of his lineage, Yamada differentiated his lineage from other Japanese Zen traditions by de-emphasizing the separation between lay people and the ordained. Yamada was also instrumental in bringing Christians to the practice of Zen, but he was clear that zazen was the focal point of the practice:

> The entrance into Zen is the grasping of one's essential nature. It is absolutely impossible, however, to come to a clear understanding of our essential nature by any intellectual or philosophical method. It is accomplished only by the experience of self-realization through zazen.[20]

However, he also maintained that some additional explanations of the concepts of the teachings were beneficial. Yamada has presented an analogy to reality in a symbolic way in several of his writings. This formulation may be helpful to point to the reality beyond the everyday world of the senses. It is useful, but provisional.

Yamada's approach to describe the one reality was to divide it into two perspectives: Phenomenal and Essential. The phenomenal is everything that is seen or experienced by the senses—seeing, hearing, tasting, smelling, touching, thinking. This is the world that is known. Everything we know resides in these experiences, including logic and rational analysis. The phenomenal may also be called the world of differences or things. The essential perspective is unknown to the senses.

It has no discernable characteristics.

One of the ways Yamada expresses the one reality is as a fraction. The numerator (the top half of a fraction) represents the phenomenal world that is subject to cause and effect, birth and death, impermanence, and change. This aspect is represented by the symbol alpha, α. The denominator (the bottom half of a fraction) represents emptiness, but full of endless potential, without beginning or end. The essential is represented by an infinity sign encircled by a zero (Θ). α and Θ are not two different things are but are one from the beginning. He says that α is the other side of Θ, and vice versa.

A fraction must have both a numerator and a denominator, α/Θ, which is to say that the changing world exists together with the essential. The complete fraction, α/Θ, the actual fact of reality, differs from the incomplete perception of the everyday world, α. However, without awareness of essential emptiness, the world of change and perception appears to us to be the full picture. He adds that although the full picture appears incomprehensible when viewed from the phenomenal world, once the world of α/Θ has been experienced, it is perfectly natural. It is a Zen meditation practice that takes us in the direction to have that experience.

In the Heart Sutra, a central line is:

> "Form is exactly emptiness. Emptiness is exactly form."

This verse expresses the same teaching. The use of the two aspects comprising one fraction can provide a different understanding of this teaching. Yamada has "set up the concept of a fraction and divided oneness into two, to try to help you understand that all phenomena have empty limitlessness behind them, so to speak."[21]

Perspectives on Interconnectedness

Interconnectedness and interpenetration occur in all of life, whether observable or not. However, there are different ways to see the phenomenal side of interconnectedness.

Shantideva views it from motion. There is one motion, all elements participating, but none on its own:

> A water-wheel turns, but
> The individual parts can't turn by themselves.
> In the same way, all the aspects of being

Exist in dependence on the combination of the others;
From the most distant past to the farthest future,
One of these existing by itself is not apprehended.[22]

Thich Nhat Hanh expresses interconnectedness using a chronological sequence. This excerpt from a longer essay brings to mind both these relationships, as well as the continuing interaction of causes and conditions, by looking deeply at a sheet of paper:

> If we look into this sheet of paper even more deeply, we can see the sunshine in it. If the sunshine is not there, the forest cannot grow. In fact, nothing can grow. Even we cannot grow without sunshine. And so, we know that sunshine is also in this sheet of paper. The paper and the sunshine inter-are. And if we continue to look, we can see the logger who cut the tree and brought it to the mill to be transformed into paper. And we can see the wheat. We know the logger cannot exist without his daily bread and therefore the work that became his bread is also in this sheet of paper. And the logger's father and mother are in it too. When we look at it this way, we can see without all of these things, this sheet of paper cannot exist. Looking more deeply, we can see we are in it too.[23]

It may be helpful to associate this passage with Yamada's expression of reality as a fraction.

The phenomenal world is interconnected. That corresponds to the relative. However, the interconnectedness extends not only to the phenomenal world but to all of life, including what can extend beyond our sensory experience.

Writer and teacher Nan Shepherd (1893-1981) loved the mountains and was able to express in her writings the relationships that are visible in the present. She lived near the Cairngorm mountains in Scotland and spent many days hiking thousands of miles observing them. She experienced the mountains as not just the earth; the 'non-mountain' elements were also an integral part of it. She keenly observed many of the elements of the mountains—geology, water, snow, light, plants, birds, and land animals, including man.

She expressed the effect of the mountains on her senses and awareness in *The Living Mountain*. She wrote this book at the end of World War II, but it was not published until 1977 and then reissued in 2011. In her writing, Shepherd takes these individual elements and sees them as one interconnected living being. Two excerpts show the relationship between the mountain and non-mountain elements:

> Individual: Water
>
> This is the river. Water, that strong white stuff, one of the four elemental mysteries, can here be seen at its origins. Like all profound mysteries, it is so simple that it frightens me. It wells from the rock, and flows away. For unnumbered years it has welled from the rock, and flowed away. It does nothing, absolutely nothing, but be itself.[24]
>
> Interconnected:
>
> But I have wanted to come to the living things through the forces that create them, for the mountain is one and indivisible, and rock, soil, water, and air are no more integral to it than what grows from the soil and breathes the air. All are aspects of one entity, the living mountain. The disintegrating rock, the nurturing rain, the quickening sun, the seed, the root, the bird—all are one.[25]

After reading this book, I immediately made plans to go the Cairngorms. Spending time in the mountains, without time pressure, or a destination, changes perspective.

The Center of the Universe and Indra's Net

Some people believe they are the center of the universe. They are correct. The center of the universe is right here where they are. Problems arise when this view is considered the whole story.

One can begin from the perspective of the earth. Looking into space with modern telescopes, it is observed that all planets and galaxies are moving away from the earth. A first conclusion is that the earth is the center of the universe. However, viewed from Mars, or any celestial body, the same observation would be made—that all the other planets are also speeding away. It could be concluded that Mars is the center of the universe. This conclusion is a consequence of the expanding universe. There is more than one center of the universe, in fact there is an infinite number of centers of the universe.

In addition, it has been now established that space is not an empty vacuum. There are many events—energy and particles popping into and out of existence in space. Space itself is not fixed, but may warp and bend. It is no longer accurate to maintain that each perceived object stands alone in space. All the phenomena are connected. In an expanding universe, the center does not have the usual meaning. An analogous teaching from ancient times is the Diamond Net of Indra.

The Diamond Net of Indra

The Diamond Net of Indra is a metaphor with a rich history that can be used to consider the interconnectedness, oneness, impermanence, and luminescence of the universe.

The universe is conceived as a multi-dimensional net with a jewel situated at each of its intersecting nodes, each jewel reflecting the light of all the other jewels.

> A net, going through space, with a jewel at each intersection.
>
> Each jewel represents a form or being.
>
> Since each jewel reflects the light of the others, a change in one is reflected in all the others. There is an interconnectedness of all forms or beings. None is independent. The radiant light is reflected everywhere and the reflection changes everywhere.
>
> The net does not have a beginning or end.

In the Indra's Net metaphor, there is just light reflecting. So the whole activity (however it began) is not known. Whatever is observed in the reflections is a temporary illusion. There is no particular individual source from which the light arises.

Just as a change in one jewel affects the others, each individual's behavior affects all beings. Each person or phenomenon reflects the radiance of the universe. The effects of these activities permeate throughout the entire universe. These effects may not be visible or conscious, but the interaction is occurring at some level. Some may argue that each interaction is too small to make a difference, but that view is based on a limited conscious perspective. The practice can extend the mind and its perceptions.

The metaphor is further extended so that all of the individual jewels of the net are tied together to form just one jewel. What this extension is pointing to is that all the phenomena are one reality. Dushun, introduced in the next section, emphasizes the consequences of the interconnectedness of all the elements in the net:

> Tying many jewels to form a net is itself just one jewel. Why?

> 'One' is the aspect of totality, containing the many in its formulation. Since all would not exist if there were not one, this net is therefore made by one jewel.[26]

Taking one sentence from the work "On the Zen Mirror," Yung-Ming states this even more explicitly: "The One Mind can take in all minds and return them to the One Mind, this is the meaning of Indra's Net."[27] The metaphor can be used as a story to reflect upon how each person's activity affects all else, a consequence of the interconnectedness and the one reality.

Indra's Net: Evolution of the Teaching

Teachings are often presented as fact. However, they have evolved over time to their current format. Elements of the local culture were incorporated with every geographical transition of Buddhism. Context can deepen appreciation for and the use of these teachings. It is also a reminder of their provisional nature. The origin of this particular teaching stirred my curiosity. Indra's Net metaphor has a long historical development. It is sourced from the traditions of the Hindus in India and then developed in China.

The namesake of the metaphor, Indra, is a high deity in Hinduism and is one of the most revered deities in the Rig Veda, often celebrated as the king of the gods. Over 250 hymns were composed in his honor well before 1100 BCE, perhaps as early as 1700 BCE. Centuries later, the Buddhists combined the mythology of Indra with themes from their primary text, The Flower Ornament Sutra.

This development was the work of a different school of Buddhism, the Hua-yen school. It was recognized as an independent school during the 6th century and its influence ended (in China) during purges in the 9th century. Dushun (557–640, C: Ta-Shun) was the First Patriarch of the school. The Hua-yen patriarchs engaged in an active tradition of thought and philosophy. Their contributions had a significant influence on the Chan (Zen) school, and the ideas that emerged from them are still incorporated in modern teachings. D. T. Suzuki has been paraphrased as calling 'Hua-yen the philosophy of Zen and Zen the practice of Hua-yen.'[28]

The Flower Ornament Sutra was composed in stages, in India, somewhere around the first to second centuries BCE and assembled as a complete work somewhat later. It is a large volume, 39 chapters in over 1,500 pages. It is breathtaking how deeply the sutras were studied by some during this period. The sutra does not mention Indra's net explicitly.

The Hua-yen patriarch's commentaries stressed the themes in the sutra of interconnectedness and interpenetration. They took the references in the *Flower Ornament Sutra* and developed them into the Indra's Net metaphor. An example of verses that contributed to this metaphor is in Chapter 30 of the *Flower Ornament Sutra*, "The Incalculable." After a series of complex calculations to illustrate the enormity of the universe and their interrelationship, there is a lengthy verse about magnitude and impermanence. Two excerpts:

> If untold buddha-lands are reduced to atoms,
> In one atom are untold lands,
> And as in one,
> So in each.
>
> In each of those pure lights
> Also appear various subtle lights;
> These lights also radiate various lights,
> Untold, unspeakably many.
> In each of these various lights
> Appear wondrous jewels like mountains;
> The jewels appearing in each light
> Are unspeakably many.[29]

This verse, occasionally modified with more descriptive language, is often cited in the description of Indra's Net.[30]

This concept was extended to the Indra's Net metaphor by the first patriarch, Dushun. He is generally credited with the work entitled *Calming and Contemplation in the Five Teachings of Huayan*. An excerpt:

> The manner in which all dharmas interpenetrate is like an imperial net of celestial jewels extending in all directions infinitely, without limit .... Because of the clarity of the jewels, they are all reflected in and enter into each other, ad infinitum. Within each jewel, simultaneously, is reflected the whole net. Ultimately, nothing comes or goes.[31]

Over the course of centuries, Indra's net has had contributions from the Hindus, the Flower Ornament Sutra, and the Hua-yuen school. The historical narrative adds to the depth of the metaphor and serves as a reminder of the debt of gratitude to the effort and dedication of the ancestors.

9

Co-Dependent Origination and Impermanence

This topic has come up before, but since it is central to the teaching, the entry point now will be from the words of the Buddha:

> When this is, that is
> This arising, that arises
> When this is not, that is not
> This ceasing, that ceases.
> (Ud 1.3 Bodhi Sutta)

Everything is interconnected with all else; no one thing is independent and there is only ceaseless change. This is called 'impermanence.'

All phenomena arise simultaneously in the moment. The appearances of this moment have arisen as a consequence of earlier causes and conditions, and the present will contribute to the next manifestation. The current appearances will fade when the causes and conditions change. This arising and fading is not predestination though since actions in the present will affect future appearances. Thus, the everyday world is impermanent and conditioned (influenced by environmental factors). Since appearances are impermanent and are not the experience of ultimate reality, these appearances are called 'illusions.' For many, experiencing what arises in life as 'illusion' presents a totally different perspective, which may be directly at odds with previously held ideas about life.

Uchiyama expresses the co-dependent origination in the context of the illusion of birth and death:

> We assume that there exists a world which you and I can experience, in common with all other human beings, that this world

> existed prior to our births, and that it will continue to exist even after our deaths. But again, this is nothing more than an idea. Not only that, we wind up thinking that we live and die within this world of fabrication. This is an utterly inverted way of looking at one's life. My true Self lives in reality, and the world I experience and is one I alone can experience, and not one anyone else can experience along with me. To express this as precisely as possible, as I am born, I simultaneously give birth to the world I experience; I live out my life along with that world, and at my death the world I experience also dies.[1]

He begins with the common perception individuals are born and die in a world which precedes them and that world continues after their death. This perception is an expression of the belief that there is an independent self which is not a fabrication of the rational mind. On the other hand, co-dependent origination, described by Uchiyama, means that the reality of life appears as an interdependent process where phenomena and activity are mutually dependent. There is always a flow of phenomenal events without permanent existence. In one moment, all life arises simultaneously, lives out, and fades away.

From this perspective, other teachings such as attachments, impermanence, and the cause of suffering, can be seen in a broader light. For example, since all phenomena arise at once and are fully interconnected, there can be no self and other, only the idea of self and other. Also, impermanence is inherent in the arising and fading of the moment. Suffering is a consequence of ignorance or misunderstanding the nature of life. The teachings are different aspects pointing in the same direction of helping people to experience their life as it is.

One Moment

In our everyday world, time appears to be linear—past, present, and future flowing in a line. Space also appears permanent or fixed and we are immersed in it. However, scientists currently have a different understanding of space and time. Einstein's Theory of Relativity shows that time slows as an object approaches the speed of light. Space is a field which can also be distorted. Further, physicists state that space is not an empty void, but that particles are always coming into existence and leaving existence. These scientific statements are additional indications that all phenomena are interconnected and impermanent even at the sensory level.

The Sanskrit word 'ksana' means instant or moment, the shortest possible time. When time is reduced to a singular point with no divisibility, this is 'absolute' present, here and now, and not a concept or mental idea of the present. The instant is alive with creative potential.

According to several early Buddhist sources and cited by Dogen, a day consists of 6,400,099,180 moments. (It's an interesting digression to investigate the source of this number. Some sources go back to references from the 2nd century—"In the time of a finger snap, there are 60 moments." There are a number of other ways to do this calculation. The actual number isn't an issue.) This consideration of the relativity of time was a significant conceptual and philosophical insight of the Buddhists, well ahead of its time.[2]

In each moment, all beings in the universe appear and disappear. They all arise together and do not exist independently (i.e. co-dependent). That is the basis of impermanence. Each moment arises independently. Everything is transient. Then the moment 'is' and all phenomena fade. It doesn't look that way though. Bushwell expands on the meaning of 'ksana':

> Physical objects or mental events that persist over time are posited in fact to be merely a collection of these moments. As a result of ignorance, these are falsely perceived as lasting more than one moment and having an independent existence. For example, sense experience is composed entirely of these moments of a given object, but this is not noticed by ordinary sense consciousness, and thought mistakenly projects continuity onto sense experience.[3]

A verse from *The Gateless Gate* (Case 21) gets at this using a physical example:

> Lightning flashing
> Sparks shooting from a flint
> A moment's blinking
> It's already missed.[4]

Not This Present Moment

The present moment is not what we think it is!

In Zen teaching, there is much emphasis on being present and mindful in the moment. But there is not always a clear meaning of what is meant by being present and mindful. As noted above, the right-now moment has no durability. When people speak of the present moment, it is just an idea of the present moment in the mind, not the right-now moment as it is experienced. In the everyday world, when cognitive activity begins to function, subject and object arise, and duality is experienced through the senses. Concepts such as past, present, and future are formulated and held as real.

One of those concepts is that this 'present moment' is the one being discussed. In considering an idea of the present moment other thoughts also arise, such as the past is gone, and the future is not yet here. These are all just expressions of thinking and speech and are not the experience of the present moment.

The 'present right-now' can be experienced as the moment of co-dependent origination before conscious thinking occurs. It cannot be grasped or discussed. As in the above verse, it is over in a flash. In this moment, comparisons and similar subject/object concepts have no meaning. That moment is our life. It is also the life and expression of the universe. When it is experienced, all beings are saved and suffering ends. The direction of Zen practice is to experience this right-now moment by moment.

Our entry point into this experience begins where we are, which is in the 'dualistic present moment.' It is by practicing fully in the 'dualistic present moment' that attachments and concepts can begin to drop away and the 'right-now' moment opens to us.

Moment by Moment Awakening

When people speak of awakening or satori, it is often implied that it is a one-time event of great magnitude. Another important point that can be misunderstood is that sudden awakening is just one step. But at each moment, there is the opportunity for a fresh awakening. Indeed, Zen is a life-long practice because each arising moment is fresh, with infinite possibility. Sawaki makes it clear that awakening is not a once and done event:

> Zazen means awakening from distraction and confusion and from dullness and fatigue, awakening to zazen billions of times. The zazen of living out this fresh and raw life means awakening the mind, certifying through practice billions of times. This is shikantaza.
>
> Some people begin with the practice of shikantaza (just sit-

ting) and then give it up quickly because it does not give them that feeling of fullness or because it bores them.

They do so because they only understand this awakening a billion times in their heads. That's why they think, 'Oh no! I have to awaken the mind a billion times? What I need is satori! If I hurry up and get one big satori, I can wrap up this billion-times business in a single stroke!'[5]

Another important point made here is that awakening is often described as if it were a state that can be attained. The idea of a single enlightenment stems from such a misunderstanding. However, in a world of impermanence, nothing can be attained. As each new moment arises, life arises and the opportunity to be awake to it and live it out is available. In any moment one can be awake or lost in distraction. That awakening to life is what Sawaki refers to as zazen or shikantaza. Awakening is an on-going moment-to-moment process. There are no laurels to rest on; even if there is a memory of an awakening, that too is an idea, not the experience itself. That moment is over and the attention has to be on what is now. In an impermanent world, how could it be otherwise?

The Individual Experience through the Five Skandhas

The Five Skandhas listed below are the elements that comprise the mental and physical self. (Other terms used are heaps, aggregates, collections, groupings.) Skandhas are not permanent elements, but transitory phenomena, analogous to energy.

The Buddha taught about the dispassionate view of the self and its aggregates:

> So seeing, bhikkhus (monks), the instructed noble disciple is dispassionate towards the body, dispassionate towards feeling, dispassionate towards perception, dispassionate towards mental activities, dispassionate towards consciousness. Being dispassionate he detaches himself, being detached, he is released and in release is the knowledge of being released and he knows: finished is birth, lived is the holy life, done is what had to be done, there is no more of this or that state. (SN 22.18)[6]

The following passage about the Five Skandhas is more often quoted, without primary source. It appears to be more technical, less personal and engaging then the one above: "When you understand that form, feeling, perception, formations, and consciousness are impermanent, then you understand right view."

The differentiated, individual personal self is a combination of these phenomena at a particular time. It is important to emphasize the impermanence of these phenomena. Since they are always changing, there can be no individual fixed self.

Examples of The Five Skandhas

Form:	Sights, smells, sounds
Feeling:	Sensations of the sense organs
Perception:	Identification and interpretation of sensations
Formation:	Conditioned response to object of experience, impulses (also called volition)
Consciousness:	Arising awareness of the process of the other skandhas. This is an awareness of the presence of a sense object and discrimination of its components and aspects. Consciousness depends on form, feelings, perceptions, and impulses for its arising and cannot exist independently of them. It is essentially an observing function. It is important to emphasize that it is also transient and not a permanent self.

Building a Self: An Exercise with Skandhas

There are six senses with which to experience the world (seeing, hearing, tasting, touching, smelling, thinking). Note that thinking is considered a sense in Buddhist thought. The sense of hearing is used in the example below, but the same steps could be applied to any of the other senses as well.[7]

The starting point is an arising sound.

1. Be aware of the presence of the ear and physical world. This is form.
2. Note the sensation of the sound on the ear. Does the sensation affect either your physical or mental state? This is sensation or feeling.
3. Observe the perception that instantly arises. Is the sound attributed to a car, footsteps, speech, etc.? This is perception.
4. Notice what you do with the perception. Does it turn into a story? Are there opinions? Some mental activity was en-

gaged to interact with the sound. This is formation.

5. Notice the condition of just being aware of the sound. Leave it alone, so to speak. Within that awareness, there is the entire process of raw sound and the fabrication of the story. This is consciousness.

This process is occurring each moment, with all the senses. Viewed from this perspective, forms seem to be constructed, and consequently there seems to be a fixed self. However, there are no fixed elements, including one's sense of self. We are the skandhas of the moment. The flowing activity of the skandhas is our experience of being alive in the everyday world. Since the activity is constantly changing, suffering results if they are viewed as fixed. The suffering follows from ignorance of the impermanent nature of life.

This point of no fixed elements is reinforced in the exchange below where Rahula questions the Buddha:

> "Is anything comprised within the feeling, perception, formations, and consciousness that arise with eye-contact as condition permanent or impermanent?"
>
> "Impermanent, venerable sir."
>
> "Is what is impermanent suffering or happiness?"
>
> "Suffering, venerable sir."
>
> "Is what is impermanent, suffering, and subject to change fit to be regarded thus: 'This is mine, this I am, this is my self'?"
>
> "No, venerable sir."
>
> Seeing thus, Rahula, a well-taught noble disciple becomes disenchanted … with anything comprised within the feeling, perception, formations, and consciousness that arise with mind-contact as condition.
>
> Now while this discourse was being spoken, through not clinging the venerable Rahula's mind was liberated from the taints. (MN 147)

If individuals attempt to define themselves, it misses the mark. As flowing energy, our life cannot be grasped, explained, or known. It can only be experienced.

The question arises: "What is a person?" Any attempt at an answer would become fixed and restrictive. That question was not addressed by the Buddha. This point is illustrated in a well-known exchange between Bodhidharma and the emperor from *The Blue Cliff Record* (Case # 1) that concludes:

> The emperor asked, 'Who is this facing me?'
>
> Bodhidharma said, 'I don't know.'
>
> The emperor did not understand. Bodhidharma then departed, and crossed the Yangtze River to the kingdom of Wei in northern China. (Blue Cliff Record Case #1)[8]

In a more contemporary exchange, a monk was asked essentially the same question posed by the emperor. The response: "It's a difficult question to answer."

In a flowing, changing universe, there is nothing that can be grasped, defined, or held onto as a unit. As the above example with hearing showed, a construct can be formed through a series of steps beginning with a sound and leading to consciousness; the idea of a person is one such construct. More generally, all phenomena are constructed in the same way. It is our conditioning that leads to the idea that these constructs have an independent identity rather than consisting of impermanent components. In the exchange with Rahula, it is asserted that these phenomena are impermanent and that holding on to them as fixed or permanent is the source of suffering. Finally, Bodhidharma and Rahula show the understanding that an individual 'person' cannot be defined. However, there is a direct experience of life, without the concept of fixed identities. The driving point here is that a correct view of life can put an end to suffering. This view is the direction of practice. Teachings can help, but there is no substitute for making the effort:

> Form is like a lump of foam;
> feeling is like a bubble;
> perception seems like a mirage;
> choices like a banana tree;
> and consciousness like a magic trick. (SN 22.95)

It's Too Late To Be Ready

Two temples each had a child protege. The children would pass each other on their way to the market each morning.

> "Where are you going?" asked the first child
>
> "I am going wherever my feet go," was the reply of the second

child.

This reply puzzled the first child and he went to his teacher for help. The teacher instructed him:

> "Tomorrow morning, ask him the same question. He will give you the same answer, and then you ask him: 'Suppose you have no feet, then where are you going?' That will fix him."

And so the next morning, the child again asked:

> "Where are you going?"
> "I am going wherever the wind blows," was the reply.

Defeated again, the first child returned to his teacher. The new instruction was similar:

> "Ask him where he is going if there is no wind."

On their third meeting, the first child asked with assurance:

> "Where are you going?"
> "I am going to the market to buy vegetables," was the final reply.[9]

The first child could not come up with an appropriate question to engage the second child, despite the coaching of his senior. A taut and flexible mind is needed to make an appropriate response to an arising situation. A taut and flexible mind is also the aim in zazen meditation. The first child's mind was blocked with ideas of what had happened earlier in the day and what he had projected to happen the next day. He was prepared for these imagined situations, but was not ready to spontaneously respond to the actual situation when it arose in the moment. Preparation has an important place and it is an important activity at many times. However, holding on to the preparation leads to blockage and sluggishness.

People spend much time preparing for events that never happen. It is a habit of almost everyone to rehearse scripts for situations such as difficult conversations with people. However, when the actual event occurs, somehow it never seems to follow the anticipated script. If the idea of the rehearsed script is not discarded, the mind is blocked and the opportunity to be present and to respond in the moment is lost.

A three step method for approaching a task might be useful. Prior to doing a task, some preparation is made. However, while the task is being performed, simply place full effort on it. Then, when the task is completed, a review and evaluation can be made in order to identify changes for the next time. Each of these three sequential activities is done with full attention, one at a time.

10

One Mind and Not Knowing

There are many facets to Buddhist teaching. Ultimately, they all interlock and point in the same direction. The teaching of One Mind dates from at least the first century and provides another perspective into other topics such as the equality (identity) of relative and absolute, and emptiness.

> The One Mind represents the absolute as it is expressed in the temporal order. The Mind necessarily contains within itself two orders or aspects—the transcendental and the phenomenal, the universal and the particular, the infinite and the finite, the static and the dynamic, the sacred and the profane, the absolute and the relative, and so forth. The absolute order, therefore, does not exist apart from the relative order; rather .... Human beings are presented as being located at the intersection of these opposing orders.[1]

The last sentence merits emphasis as it has been expressed differently earlier in the discussion of the Middle Way (Chapter 6). There the discussion was phrased: 'Everything exists' stands for the world of senses. 'Everything does not exist' refers to the absolute. The synthesis is the experience of the two in a realm beyond words. This is an example of approaching teachings from different perspectives.

As clarification, the word 'mind' is used in many contexts and the meanings are not always clear. For example, in 'One Mind,' 'One' indicates 'absolute' in the sense of 'one without any second,' not one among many. The word 'mind' is often used to designate the limited mind function in the relative world.

The term is even more problematic in English since mind is often associated with the psychological mind or brain. It is not only in English that there have been difficulties with 'mind.' Scholars note that individual Pali words originally used interchangeably for mind have taken on specialized meanings over time.

Huang Po very clearly presented a description that pointed at the One Mind:

> All the Buddhas and all sentient beings are nothing but the One Mind, beside which nothing exists. This Mind, which is without beginning, is unborn and indestructible. It is not green nor yellow, and has neither form nor appearance. It does not belong to the categories of things which exist or do not exist, nor can it be thought of in terms of new or old. It is neither long nor short, big nor small, for it transcends all limits, measures, names, traces, and comparisons. It is that which you see before you—begin to reason about it and you at once fall into error. It is like the boundless void which cannot be fathomed or measured. The One Mind alone is the Buddha, and there is no distinction between the Buddha and sentient things, but that sentient beings are attached to forms and so seek externally for Buddhahood.[2]

In just the few sentences above, Huang Po touches on a number of aspects of One Mind that will be considered in more detail:

> It encompasses all, there is no distinction between buddha nature and sentient things.
>
> It does not exist as a thing with dimensions or in a place.
>
> Thinking or reasoning about it leads to error.
>
> It is unborn and still, with nothing outside of it to search for.
>
> Thinking, reasoning, or attachments take one away from its experience.

Huang Po uses the example of mercury as a symbol illustrating the relationship of the one to all and all to the one. Mercury, when divided, becomes small pearl-like droplets, each separate and whole in and of itself. But when the mercury is allowed to run together, it forms one totality in which the separate parts are indistinguishable from the whole. In Huang Po's words, when things are separate, a mountain, for example, is a mountain, a monk a monk, an ordinary fellow an ordinary fellow, but the totality of the mind encompasses them all.[3] [4]

Analogies of One Mind

Centuries before Huang Po, a 1st century work long attributed to Asvaghosa, "The Awakening of Faith," used analogies to clarify the nature of mind with its relative and absolute aspects. The clarity shines through the complexity in this work.

Water, Wind, and Waves Analogy

This analogy has long been used to point at the relationship between phenomena and the absolute. It draws distinctions among the concepts of the nature of water, the wave motion of the water, and the activity of water caused by the wind. When the wind stops, the waves end, but the nature of the water remains. This relationship is then related to Mind and its stillness. Our true nature is represented by the unagitated still Mind. Asvaghosa makes this comparison:

> It is like the case of the wind which, following the surface of the water, leaves the marks of its movement. If the water should cease to be, then the marks of the wind would be nullified and the wind would have no support [on which to display its movement]. But since the water does not cease to be, the marks of the wind may continue. Because only the wind ceases, the marks of its movement cease accordingly. This is not the cessation of water.
>
> So it is with ignorance; on the ground of the essence of Mind there is movement. If the essence of Mind were to cease, then people would be nullified and they would have no support. But since the essence does not cease to be, the mind may continue. Because only stupidity ceases to be, the marks of the [stupidity of the] mind cease accordingly. It is not that the wisdom (i.e., the essence) of Mind ceases.[5]

Pottery Analogy

Asvaghosa further states that enlightenment and non-enlightenment may be viewed together in two ways, namely, where they are the same and where they are different, and uses pottery as an analogy:

> Same: Take, for example, the various kinds of pottery: they are all made of one clay. In the same way non-enlightenment [phenomena] are manifestations of the One Mind .... Perfect enlightenment can-

not be cultivated or made, can never be added to, and has no form which can be seen. That which has form to be seen accompanies useful transformations. It is not the nature of real Wisdom for this Wisdom is invisible.

Different: It is like speaking of the different kinds of pots made. Infinite enlightenment and finite enlightenment differ according to their useful transformations, and the infinite nature appears different in the transformations.[6]

The last sentence connects back in a different context with a teaching from Yamada (Chapter 8) "The standpoint of Mahayana Zen is that infinite, absolute reality wears the clothes of limitation and relativity."

Aspects of One Mind

In addition to the two analogies above, Asvaghosa also described the two aspects of the One Mind in "The Awakening of Faith":

> The principle of One Mind has two aspects. One is the aspect of Mind in terms of the absolute (suchness) and the other is the aspect of Mind in terms of phenomena (relative). Each of these two aspects embraces all states of existence. Why? Because these two aspects are mutually inclusive.
>
> The Mind is eternal, permanent, immutable, pure, and self-sufficient. All explanations by words are provisional and without validity, for they are merely used in accordance with illusions and are incapable (of denoting suchness).
>
> Human beings are originally enlightened or saved, but suffer because they do not realize that they are enlightened or saved and continue on as blind or faithless persons, groping for enlightenment or salvation elsewhere .... Since all unenlightened people discriminate with their deluded minds from moment to moment, they are alienated (from suchness) ... but once they are free from their deluded minds, they will find that there is nothing to be negated .... The degrees of ignorance are infinite, therefore the natures of people differ in character accordingly.[7]

Asvaghosa lived about 800 years before Huang Po, whose passage was presented earlier in this section. Both passages point at similar descriptions the Mind. Some people compare them point by point, but others select one that speaks more directly to them.

Thoughts as Opportunities

Thoughts get a lot of bad press in Zen. There are always complaints about how distracting they are and talk of getting rid of them. A different view is to use them as an aid to grow awareness. They are the tools of the present that are available to work with during meditation.

A few observations:

Thoughts are fully appropriate in the conduct of daily life. Examples are problem solving, doing taxes, etc. These types of thoughts are characterized by a full effort to the activity at hand.

But the thoughts referenced here are those that compare, make value judgments, ruminate about the past or future, or are similarly non-directed. They include ideas of what we are and what we think we have been. This type of mental activity is comparable to the winds over the water in the analogy above. These thoughts may be considered as 'agitation of mind.' Below are some characteristics of thought:

> Thoughts are a natural product of the mind. Sometimes they are referred to as secretions of the mind.
>
> Thoughts have the same empty nature as all phenomena and are not an inherently special category.
>
> Thoughts exist only in mind. They persist only when held onto.
>
> Thoughts arise haphazardly, a product of time and conditions.
>
> Thoughts have nothing to do with what is actually happening.
>
> Thoughts are thoughts. They are a closed system and thus do not provide insight into life as it arises.

These characteristics of thoughts come to play in meditation. An awareness of thoughts as they arise in meditation can reduce the agitation in the mind so that the true essence of mind can be experienced. In meditation, when we become aware of our thoughts, they can be acknowledged and released, as if letting go of a feather, and attention can be returned to the moment (i.e. the breath or open awareness). The empty (no independent existence) nature of the thoughts is experienced and reflects our own empty nature.

Blocking thoughts or attempting to do so is a negative proposition. It is like adding fuel to the fire. Similarly, to continue with the water analogy, thoughts are like wind increasing the turbulence of the water. Once the thought appears, it can be used from the more positive perspective of just looking at it, which reduces the tendency to fight with it or to become frustrated by its appearance. Each thought that appears has to be acknowledged, since unacknowledged thoughts are the ones that are most debilitating. Instead of becoming entangled with the content of the thought, which is the habitual approach, one works with its empty nature. When the attention is directed back to the moment and away from the thought, it fades and is gone. It had no independent existence.

Thought content can be viewed like candy. It's enjoyable now and then, but it does not make for long term health. Thoughts and memories from the past can have the intensity of a present experience, yet cannot be changed. Looking forward in time, the scenarios and stories that are pondered in mind rarely occur. We are shackled by them. The tendency to repeat such thoughts can condition us to become entangled in them. So, it is not an easy matter to look at them and dismiss them as impermanent phenomena. Such thoughts are not released at once, but gradually, as a repetitive process of having them arise, acknowledging them, letting them go, and returning to the moment. Returning to the moment and growing awareness is really the heart of the practice.

Zazen is working with thoughts. Sometimes it works like this:

An awareness of a thought arises.

Decide not to pursue the thought.

Drop the thought.

An awareness of another thought or the same one returns.

Frustration with the thought "Is this the best that can be done!"

Sit with that frustration.

Release the story or thought about frustration and return to attention and just be with whatever is there (even if it is the energy of frustration).

The cycle may repeat. It does not matter if the same thought or distraction recurs almost immediately.

The real engine of meditation is being aware and returning attention to the moment. That is why it was earlier stated that thoughts are viewed as opportunities for work. They are not judged. This is zazen. Period. It may strike some as not what they signed up for; it's too ordinary. But this is exactly what being present in the moment is.

In summary, thoughts are to be used rather than allowing them to use us. Nothing is to be discarded out of frustration, but rather allow the process to occur in a natural fashion as captured by this verse:

> Faults and delusions
> Are not to be got rid of
> Just blindly.
> Look at the astringent persimmons!
> They turn into the sweet dry ones.[8]

Dissatisfaction and Peace of Mind

Many people come to a meditation practice with the goal of calming their everyday mind. Sometimes that happens. However, the idea of meditating toward a goal represents a searching outside of oneself for something to be different. It is an idea of peace of mind. A different way to look at peace of mind is to begin with the everyday agitated mind and work with that to experience our own peaceful nature.

Earlier, Sawaki expressed some very direct comments about zazen (Chapter 2). He has the same direct style when commenting on the quest for peace of mind. The narrative below is crafted directly from Sawaki's oral teachings. He begins with the everyday mind, then shows the role of zazen in this process of experiencing peace of mind, and concludes with his understanding of what peace of mind is. He has little patience for complaining.[9]

Dissatisfaction is first viewed from the everyday perspective. The annoyances are seen to be illusions that are mistaken for the actual fact of reality:

> "You say you're seeking the way, but what does it mean if you're seeking the way just to satisfy yourself?"
>
> "Zazen is unsatisfying. Unsatisfying for whom? For the ordinary person. People are never satisfied."
>
> "Isn't it self-evident? How could that which is eternal and infinite ever satisfy human desires?"

The last line in the above section is especially provocative—the satisfaction of human desires is not met by zazen. Then in the following section, Sawaki issues a reminder that the practice is not about improving or purifying the senses, particularly thoughts. Practice is to go beyond the senses and deeply realize that emptiness is our nature. At each moment, phenomena arise and fade, without external plan or progression. It is only thoughts that hold together the illusion of something happening. Zazen is the practice which goes beyond the illusion that something more is happening beside being present to yourself in the moment. Sawaki further states:

> "You say you want to become a better person by doing zazen. Zazen isn't about learning how to be a person. Zazen is to stop being a person."
>
> "Nothing is ever happening, no matter what seems to be going on—that's the natural condition. Illusion means losing this natural condition. Illusion means being unstable. Illusion means being controlled by the situation."
>
> "Zazen means putting into practice that which cannot be thought."
>
> "When you practice Zen, it has to be here and now."

Finally, Sawaki makes a distinction between the idea of peace of mind and the actual experience of peace. A common idea of peace is tranquility in the face of arising events. He explains that peace of mind is not an idea of unbroken tranquility, but the acceptance of things and situations just as they are, even when they do not match one's concept of what is peaceful:

> You lack peace of mind because you're running after an idea of total peace of mind. That's backwards. Be attentive to your mind in each moment, no matter how unpeaceful it might seem to be. Great peace of mind is realized only in the practice within this unpeaceful mind. It arises out of the interplay between peaceful and unpeaceful mind.

As an example, illness afflicts human beings. But if the illness is not troubling, then there is peace of mind in an unpeaceful situation:

> "A peace of mind that is totally at peace would be nothing more than something readymade. Real peace of mind only exists within unpeaceful mind."
>
> "When dissatisfaction is finally accepted as dissatisfaction, peace of mind reigns."
>
> "When peace of mind only means your personal satisfaction, then it's got nothing to do with the buddha-dharma."

Don't Know Mind

'Don't Know Mind' is leaving behind questions, explanations, opinions about right and wrong and exploring or experiencing what lies beyond rational. There is always an element of uncertainty in leaving rational knowing behind, and so moving in this direction requires trust. However, there is also spaciousness in not knowing since restraints are relaxed

As the earlier Feynman story (Chapter 8) suggests, there is a premium on knowing and providing explanations. Holding onto the explanations, as if they were 'right and complete,' limits the experience to the rational, and cuts off the experience or raw life force. Moving beyond the scientific story brings up fundamental questions. "Who am I?" "Where did I come from?" "What is the world about?" The explanations that can follow are opinions really, limited in context by the rational system that produced them. But if the questions are pursued, there is no rational answer.

Don't Know Mind is the dropping of thinking to experience this vastness. Cutting off or interrupting the thinking process brings one directly to the present moment, the heart of nature. This expression references the absolute nature, and is not at all related to knowledge, ignorance, or rational insight. Being present in the moment is what Zen practice is all about. It is being present to whatever the activity is—writing, walking, eating, even appropriate thinking. What is going on now! At each moment!

Zen meditation practices train one to grow awareness and to allow thinking to drop off. It is not always pleasant because it takes us to the abyss of emptiness. Yet in a seeming paradox, it is the way of freedom. The practice is being aware of all the thoughts and opinions and letting go of ideas about how things should be.

Seung Sahn emphasized Only Don't Know in his teaching:

> "The name we give to clear mind is don't-know mind. So you must understand don't-know. Don't-know is don't-know. This is very important."
>
> "If you are not attached to don't-know, there is only don't know."
>
> "When you are thinking, your mind and my mind are different. When you are not thinking, your mind and my mind are the same."[10]

Katagiri:

> Even though I say I am Katagiri, this is just kind of a fixed idea—a very narrow understanding.[11]

> If you try to examine your life analytically, asking yourself who you are, finally you will realize that there is something you cannot reach. You don't know what it is, but you feel the presence of something you want to connect with.[12]

Provisional Truth and Opinion

The comment is sometimes heard: "People speak to me as if they know with certainty what the truth is. Do they?"

There is only provisional knowledge. Constraining yourself to the world of rationality, it certainly appears that some statements are presented more forcefully and have apparent validity. But beyond the world of rational knowledge, there is nothing to rely on except life itself.

Still, we are in the everyday world and have to hear and deal with everything that is around us. Roshi Bernie Glassman offered some good advice about responding to these situations. He suggested imagining that the opinionated speaker is wearing a red clown nose. Then, listen to them with this image and see what a difference it makes to your reception of their opinions. As advice to ourselves, he also reminded us to remember that what we say is also just our opinion, and to conclude our own comments with a reminding remark (even if it is said only to ourselves) that they also are just opinions.

Thinking about 'Nonthinking'

> Once, when the Great Master Hongdao of Yaoshan was sitting [in meditation], a monk asked him, 'What are you thinking, [sitting there] so fixedly?' The master answered, 'I'm thinking of not thinking.' The monk asked, 'How do you think of not thinking?' The Master answered, 'Nonthinking.' [13 or 14]

Nonthinking is a term used frequently and the exhortation to "Go beyond thinking!" is often heard during retreats. How can that be explored? The term is easily misunderstood. Nonthinking is not the same as not thinking. Typically, when one begins a meditation practice, the mind moves from awareness of thinking to the suppression of thinking which is not thinking. However, this is still in the realm of conceptual activity.

The Japanese word 'hishiryo' has been variously translated as 'nonthinking,' 'beyond thinking,' or 'without thinking.' One explanation is that nonthinking is a happening, a dynamic activity that escapes any dualistic definition. It is the ongoing activity of a mind without entanglements.[15]

In fact, nonthinking can only be experienced; the explanations fall short of this event. Nevertheless, it can be useful to have at least some flavor of the state that is being referenced. Since attempts at explanations of nonthinking resonate differently, a few are listed below.

Dogen:

> Do not think of good or evil; do not deal with right or wrong. Halt the revolutions of mind, intellect, and consciousness; stop the calculations of thoughts, ideas, and perceptions. Do not intend to make a Buddha, much less be attached to sitting still.[16 or 17]

Deshimaru:

> You do not think, but your unconscious mind becomes active and you think unconsciously. What comes out is true thought, unthought thought, beyond thought.
>
> How do you think without thinking? That is the whole art of zazen. Concentrate on your posture and let your thoughts pass, without dwelling at any point of consciousness .... We can get to this ultimate consciousness, but we cannot do it through our personal consciousness.[18]

The common elements of nonthinking:

Dynamic activity of mind
Not willful activity
An expression of zazen

Nonthinking activity arises naturally from the practice: When a thought arises, be aware of it. Then let it drop like a feather, it will fade on its own. This leads to nonthinking. Nonthinking manifests as appropriate activity. It is an active, not a passive state.

Belief and Don't Know

Although we are often asked to believe in one thing or another on a conscious matter, it ultimately does not matter what we believe. Conscious belief has its utility in the present, but ultimately, it has to be left behind. For a time, belief can be a useful tool, but it can become fixed as a desire and thus limiting to one's potential.

From the perspective of emptiness, our being has infinite possibilities. To believe that something cannot possibly occur is to limit oneself to the known sensory perspective of one's being. Reality functions as it is. The functioning is not dependent upon our rational or irrational beliefs.

So, how does someone investigate the nature and function of a belief story? Some suggestions for starting points:

> Is the belief system due to something that we have learned from conditioning or based on our own experience?
>
> Has this belief system led to self-imposed limitations?
>
> Has this belief system led to direct experience of the end of suffering?

The questioning is more important than any answers. The activity of questioning can erode the surety that is often attached to belief systems. That surety is a rigidity of mind that obstructs its natural fluidity and restricts responses to situations as they arise. The intent is not to discard beliefs since they do have an important role in daily life. Rather, it is to place them in a relative perspective so that they serve as guides or aids, rather than restrictions to our responses.

Another's Perspective of Not Knowing

Not knowing sometimes refers to not seeing what our assumptions are. It may refer to assumptions about everyday activities or even what we think our life is. As noted in a previous section, "Only Don't Know" was emphasized by Seung Sahn. This story is a reminder of those teachings in an everyday situation:

> A child of two or so noticed that the leaves of a plant were dried out. Asking a parent about watering them, the reply was to go ahead, but use care not to spill the water. The child went off and soon returned with disappointment stating that the water spilled because whenever it was put on the leaves, it ran off and onto the floor.

This is straightforward example that makes a significant point. One acts from one's own perspective, with the assumption or belief that others can also see from that same perspective and share it. The assumption of shared perspectives may also be made in many more complex situations. How can one have certainty about what another knows or needs? This is difficult enough in the everyday realm. But it goes beyond that because life and suffering go beyond thinking and our sensory experience. Suffering in the realm beyond senses cannot be ended by thought and words. However, addressing the needs of both realms is the work in the spiritual world by bodhisattvas (Bodhisattvas Chapter 11).

11
Bodhisattvas

The origin of the word 'bodhisattva' is from *bodhi* (enlightenment) and *sattva* (a being). In practice the term is used in a number of different ways. A bodhisattva may refer to one who has generated a spontaneous wish and compassionate mind to become enlightened, and is dedicated to help other beings to end suffering and to become enlightened themselves. Bodhisattvas are not fixed beings, but may manifest when the situation is appropriate. In some usages, bodhisattvas postpone their final stage of enlightenment to remain in the world to do this work.

Some traditions divide bodhisattvas into two groups. The first group consists of special students of the Buddha who appear in the Sutras. Kannon, Manjushri, and Maitreya are the names of three in this group. In art, these bodhisattvas are often depicted in peaceful god-like poses and are venerated as deities by some Buddhists. The second group are those who participate in the path of enlightenment and are considered to be ordinary bodhisattvas.

Colloquially, a bodhisattva can refer to anyone who lives in the spirit of the bodhisattva vow with the commitment to put others' well-being in front of one's own. The Bodhisattva Vow can be taken by anyone with the intent to liberate all sentient beings from suffering. In this sense, a bodhisattva is anyone on the path to becoming a buddha. Thus, the Buddha is known as having been a bodhisattva in past life times.

Interactions with All Beings

In the everyday world of phenomena, it is usual for people to experience interacting with others to generate new ideas, insights, directions, and methods of actions. As described previously in terms of Yamada's fraction (Chapter 8), there is a part of the life of all sentient beings which is beyond knowing. This is the essential perspective, our original nature with infinite potential. We are the essential and the sensory, whether we are aware of it or not. Our being is not just what we know, but also what we do not know, and this whole being is always functioning. Our whole being is interacting with all other beings. We may not be able to 'know' this, but that reality can be experienced and lived out.

Just as our being extends beyond our sensory experiences, interactions also occur at the level beyond sensory experience. The interactions are always occurring, not only between sentient beings but also with awakened beings, buddhas, and bodhisattvas. In fact, sentient and enlightened beings can and do interact at both the sensory and essential levels. Awakened beings radiate the energy of compassion and wisdom, which is available to us in the sensory world to assist us and reduce suffering. A key point here is that their compassionate energy can influence us, whether we are conscious of it or not. At the everyday level, the energy may show itself in the sensory world, perhaps manifested by the desire to move in the direction of our own awakening. The process of interaction is always going on between buddhas, bodhisattvas, and sentient beings.

This may sound preposterous and certainly makes no sense to the rational mind. It does not have to be rejected or accepted on faith. To do either is to go in the wrong direction and is a mistake. The words of Tung-Shan in the "Song of Focusing the Precious Mirror" can be borrowed in a different context for use here:

> Rejection and attachment are both wrong;
> It is like a ball of fire.[1]

There is another option beyond rejection and attachment. It can be explored, through the process of sitting and quieting the mind. A story illustrates this process:

> Nan-in, a Japanese master during the Meiji era (1868-1912) received a university professor who came to inquire about Zen.
>
> Nan-in served tea. He poured the visitor's cup full, and then kept on pouring.
>
> The professor watched the overflow until he could no longer restrain himself. 'It is overfull. No more will go in!'
>
> 'Like this cup,' Nan-in said, 'you are full of your own opinions and speculations. How can I show you Zen unless you first empty your cup.'[2]

Just as the continuing of pouring tea into the overflowing cup must be stopped, we need to make space by reducing the activity of the mind in order to experience the messages of the buddhas and bodhisattvas. Our minds can be emptied of attachments and opinions through a meditation process. The buddhas and bodhisattvas are always interacting with us, and it is possible to experience this directly.

Bodhisattva Activity

The entry point is an episode where the Buddha is confronted by the bandit, Angulimala. The Buddha arranged for conditions so that the bandit could not catch up with him even though the Buddha was walking at normal walking pace. Angulimala called out for the Buddha to stop. The Buddha replied:

> "I *have* stopped, Angulimala. *You* stop."
> Angulimala: "How have you stopped? How haven't I?"
> "I have stopped, Angulimala, once and for all, having cast off violence toward all living beings.
> You, though, are unrestrained toward beings. That's how I've stopped and you haven't." (MN 86 Angulimala Sutta)

What has stopped? It is the mind that has stopped the arising thoughts of violence. It has stopped the arising of all thoughts. An enlightened being acts in the world with the capability of reasoning and thinking. However, there is no attachment to a separate self. The enlightened are beings whose spiritual insight has gone to the foundation of knowledge and whose life and thought are in harmony with the universe. They are motivated by love to end suffering, and their actions are guided by wisdom. The spiritual love of the bodhisattvas perspective is "most comprehensive and universal as to embrace the entire universe … there is not a trace of partiality or discrimination."[3] It is available to all.

More than that though, it is the bodhisattvas' vow to save all sentient beings with no exceptions. This vow is not viewed as an obligation since it arises from the spiritual love of all that comprises the entire universe. The possibility of excluding something or acting from ego simply does not arise, and desires or petty emotions simply are not there. It is not a matter of having willed them away, rather it is due to a change in the functioning of mind. There are no obstructions in the mind of the bodhisattva so that it functions in its natural state.

To recap, bodhisattvas are beings (sattva), either seemingly ordinary people or transcendent beings, who are on the path to awakening (bodhi), but who remain here with the aspiration to work for the end of suffering and the awakening of all sentient beings. Their motivation is based on selflessness and the understanding of the interconnectedness of all beings. Compassion for all beings is the hallmark of the bodhisattvas and this work is as natural to them as breathing is to us.

An equivalent, but more expansive view is stated in the Vimalakirti Sutra:

> "Though he attains Buddhahood, turns the wheel of the Law, and enters into Nirvana, in fact he never forsakes the bodhisattva way—such is the practice of the bodhisattva."[4]

In this description, the bodhisattvas move freely in the world of life and death and are not bound to either. They turn towards it and not away from it. As Pye points out, this is a different understanding than postponing entry into nirvana.[5] Bodhisattvas do not exactly forego nirvana. But they do not aim for it prematurely. Entering nirvana as a bodhisattva while there is still suffering is not satisfactory. Bodhisattvas must deliver all beings from suffering. This image brings to mind a train conductor, who is always the last to board the departing train.

It is important to emphasize again that bodhisattvas are real, just as buddhas are real. Still, they are not fixed beings and may spontaneously manifest according to need. Bodhisattvas actually exist and interact with human beings. Some humans have direct experience with this interaction; many do not. In their work in the world, bodhisattvas respond to the time and conditions immediately, though the response may not be one that can be understood or expected, or even noticed by the senses. Bodhisattvas harmonize with the situations of the world, rather than direct them.

Kannon

As a practice, any person can follow the path of the bodhisattvas but it may often appear as a hopeless task. Still, inspiration can be found in the Buddhist traditions, such as Kannon who is revered as the Bodhisattva of Compassion, and is known by many names: Avalokitesvara (Sanskrit), Kanon, Kwanon, Kanzeon (Japanese), Kuan Yin, Guanyin (Chinese). Depending upon the culture, Kannon may be represented as male or female.

In Buddhist art and literature, many bodhisattvas have demonstrated such a high level of active virtue that they are also regarded as deities, but because they are active in our world, they are more than just symbols. The bodhisattva Kannon, the embodiment of great compassion who vowed to free all sentient beings from suffering, is such a deity. Kannon is both a powerful force in the world and an inspiration to practitioners on the path.

The name Kannon has been translated as "one who perceives the world sound." For some, this is interpreted as hearing the physical cries of the world and responding to all those who call for help from the deity of mercy. Shaku, among others, comprehends the phrase "perceives the world sound" as inward or spiritual rather than physical. He maintains that the sound is perceived from insight into true nature and that the suffering being attended to by Kannon is due to separation of self and other.[6]

There are many art representations and stories about Kannon. One story relates that Kannon saw the vastness of suffering of the world and became so despairing of the vow to end suffering that the body shattered. With help from other Buddhas, Kannon then attained a new form and renewed the vow to save all sentient beings. The new form is reflected in the often referenced image that has 11 heads and 1,000 arms. The many heads are in order to know the needs of the world. They represent 11 principal virtues, which are used to conquer the 11 desires that obstruct the path to enlightenment. Some images show the hands with eyes in order to emphasize the ability to see suffering in all directions.

Takuan Soho commented on the difference between Kannon's clear mind and one that is obstructed by attachments. In this passage 'stopping the mind' is used to mean stopping the mind from attaching to an object:

> Kannon has a clear and tranquil mind which cannot be obstructed. When Kannon looks, it is just being aware so that they see everything. If Kannon were to concentrate on one hand, the other 999 would be of no use.
>
> As for Kannon, to what purpose would it have a thousand arms attached to one body? This form is made with the intent of pointing out to men that if their fixed ideas are let go (immutable wisdom), even if a body has a thousand arms, every one would be of use. While hands, feet and body may move, the mind

> doesn't stop anyplace at all.[7]

Factoid: The Bodhisattva and Canon Cameras

In 1934, the first focal plane shutter camera in Japan was produced by devout Buddhists. They named it after the Bodhisattva Kwannon. According to the 2014 press release commemorating its invention:

> The engineers who created the camera decided to name it after Kwannon, the Buddhist goddess of mercy, hoping the deity would share her benevolence as they pursued their dream to produce the world's finest camera. The camera's lens, called Kasyapa, was named after Mahakasyapa, a disciple of Buddha. Additionally, the top portion of the camera body featured an engraving depicting the thousand-armed Kwannon.

In 1947, the name of the company was changed to well known 'Canon,' which is still a leader in imaging technology.

The Centipede's Dilemma

The mind can be free, or it can be stopped, that is attached, to an object. Kannon's mind was free. The centipede had a different problem:

> Once a centipede was asked how he could operate all of his numerous feet in such an orderly manner without getting them confused. The centipede shook his head, shrugged, and said that he had never given it a thought. From that time on, the centipede became unable to move, the legs all got in the way of one another. Only when there was a loud noise that frightened him could he move as before. The rest of the time he stumbled. (Adapted: Katherine Craster [1841–1874])

The activity of the centipede had been interrupted by stopping the mind at a point of thought. Takuan Soho comments on the paralysis of the centipede:

> The mind that is stopped on (an object) is sent into confusion—this is the affliction of the common man.
>
> No matter where you concentrate your mind, the rest of the body will lack its functioning.

If one thinks, he will be taken by his thought.[8]

Soho's example is viewing a tree. If the focus is on a single one of its leaves, you will not see all the others. When the eye is not set on any one leaf, and you face the tree with nothing at all in mind, any number of leaves are visible to the eye without limit. But if a single leaf holds the eye, it will be as if the remaining leaves were not there: "One who has understood this is not different from Kannon with a thousand arms and a thousand eyes."[9]

As noted earlier in the example when the Buddha said "Stopped" (Bodhisattva Activity), for the enlightened being, nothing moves in the mind, but the functions of the mind are still present. Enlightened beings function in the world with the normal senses of reasoning and thinking, however they are not attached to the idea of a self; consequently they are aware of the world and its needs and are able to act spontaneously and appropriately. The vow that guides their actions is the intent to end suffering and aid people on the path to enlightenment.

The Four Bodhisattva Vows

The foundational vows which express the aim and direction for the practitioner are called the Four Bodhisattva Vows. In many zendos, they are chanted at the end of the final sitting period of the day. More formal ceremonies which include many additional vows are also occasionally conducted.

There are numerous interpretations of these vows. Different groups have devoted much effort trying to capture the meaning and spirit from a variety of available sources. Some have attributions with discussions about context, others appear without sources. There are many translations, but they all have the same spirit of compassion. The first is widely chanted at many zendos. The second is from Hui-Neng and has a different flavor:

Sentient beings are numberless: I vow to liberate them all.
Desires are inexhaustible: I vow to end them all.
The Dharma gates are infinite: I vow to master them all.
The Buddha way is unsurpassable: I vow to attain it.
(J. Kornfield)

The beings in my own mind are infinite, I vow to liberate them.
The afflictions in my own mind are infinite, I vow to end them.
The teachings in my own nature are inexhaustible, I vow to study

> them.
> The buddhahood in my own nature is supreme, I vow to attain it.
> (Sutra of Hui-Neng) [10]

The words of the first line 'to liberate all beings' often leads to either confusion or a sense of hopelessness at the magnitude of the task. How is it possible to save all sentient beings? Many have offered commentaries on this line. Some emphasize the perspective of the phenomenal world while others stress the essential perspective. The two excerpts below provide some directions for perspective. Katagiri responds from the position of the everyday world:

> If you believe that saving all sentient beings is a ridiculous idea, your life is already rigid. Then no matter how long you practice, there is no space to be flexible, no space to manifest the unknown world through the form of your zazen or the form of your standing posture. So try not to think why manifesting the whole world is not an abstract idea, because it's something we have to do right now. We have to manifest the unknown world simultaneously with the known world.[11]

Katagiri is reminding people that our phenomenal world is limited and if we are attached to those ideas, saving all sentient beings does not seem possible. However, the practice of zazen allows one to release attachments and experience or, in his words, manifest the unknown, with its infinite possibilities. It brings to mind an earlier quote from Nagarjuna: "All is possible when emptiness is possible." (Chapter 2) Hui-Neng answers from the absolute perspective in which these beings are delusions springing from our mind:

> Learned Audience, all of us have now declared that we vow to deliver an infinite number of sentient beings; but what does that mean? It does not mean that I, Hui-neng, am going to deliver them. And who are these sentient beings within our mind? They are the delusive mind, the deceitful mind, the evil mind, and such like minds—all these are sentient beings. Each of them has to deliver himself by means of his own essence of mind. Then the deliverance is genuine.[12]

This last passage is from the Sutra of Hui-Neng. He adapted it from the Diamond Sutra (Chapter 25) where he further emphasizes that there is no individual soul or self and the practice is to be released from such ideas.[13]

The apparent differences between these two responses to the vow to free all sentient beings reflect the positions of the speakers at the time. This is a reminder that apparent contradictions arise from a fixed viewpoint. It is useful to keep in mind that the response to them by a reader also changes with the reader's individual time and conditions.

Limited by Experience: The Cicada and the Wren

Here, life for the cicada and the wren is as it seems:

> There are birds that fly many hundreds of miles without stopping. Someone mentioned this to the cicada and wren. The two animals decided that such a thing was impossible. "You and I know very well that the furthest one can get, even by the greatest effort is that elm tree over there; and even then, one cannot be sure of getting there every time. Sometimes, one finds themselves dragged back to earth long before reaching that elm tree. All of these stories about birds flying hundreds of miles at one stretch must be sheer nonsense."[14]

The cicada and the wren have valid experiences; their thoughts and imagination are shaped and confined by the view that their experiences are the complete story. This story echoes the comments of both Katagiri and Hui-Neng. There can be a limited response to the activity of ending all suffering if we believe that something is not possible based on our experience to date. Further, our idea of what it means to deliver beings from suffering is just an idea. The suffering originates in the delusive mind and ending that delusion is the direction of Zen practice.

Shantideva and *The Way of the Bodhisattva*

There is little reliable information about the life of Shantideva. He was no ordinary eighth-century monk. He did not participate much in the daily activities and to the chagrin of the other monks, seemed to only eat and sleep. However, unbeknownst to them, he had developed deep insight. The monks waited for an opportunity to embarrass him. On a particularly important occasion, the monks forced him to give a talk on the Dharma from the high seat. Shantideva asked if they would like to hear an old teaching or a new work that he had composed. The monks asked for something new, believing that this would lead to embarrassment. He then offered a recitation of a new work *The Way of the Bodhisattva* that was a clear, precise verse describing the range of practices needed to become a Bodhisattva. Legend has it that he levitated toward the end of the talk and left the monastery. He disappeared for a while and was eventually located and taught at other places. A number of miraculous events involving settling disputes and dealing with famines are attributed to him in the literature.

Shantideva's book of verse, *The Way of the Bodhisattva*, is the classic expression of the practice of becoming a Bodhisattva. It is a discourse on moral commitments, the awakened mind, practices such as patience, meditation, wisdom, and the exchange of self and other. It has been very influential and is a major text in Tibet. These verses capture the direction, work, and joy of the bodhisattvas:

> Thus the suffering of everyone
> Should be dispelled, and here there is no debate.
> To free myself from pain means freeing all;
> Contrariwise, I suffer with the pain of beings.
>
> May all bodhisattvas now fulfill
> Their high intentions for the sake of beings,
> And sentient beings likewise now receive
> The good the Buddhas have in store for them.
>
> Like those who take great pleasure in their games,
> The Bodhisattvas in their every deed
> Will feel the greatest joy, exhilaration,
> Pleasure that will never fade or pass."[15]

The Work of a Bodhisattva in the World

It has been emphasized that bodhisattvas are not fixed beings, but manifest in our everyday world according to time and need. In the Lotus Sutra, Kannon is described as manifesting in over 30 different ways—anything required for the occasion, with the objective of delivering beings from suffering. As noted earlier, there is always a response, but the response may not be at the sensory level. In fact, one may not be aware of or recognize the response of the bodhisattva.

In the 1960's an older woman's brother was involved in a con-

> struction accident, suffered severe brain damage and was hospitalized in a city two hours away from his sister. He did not know his old life or recognize his family. Still, twice every week, the woman would go into her town to the bus station, board a bus for the two hour trip to the hospital to visit her brother, and then make the return trip home. For 11 years this woman visited her brother though he did not recognize her as his sister, only as a nice lady. He appreciated her visits.

The woman in this story simply responded to the suffering in front of her. Her act of relieving suffering, with no expectation, reward, or recognition, is the work of a bodhisattva. Was she an ordinary person or a bodhisattva, or neither, or both? There is no answer to that question. But we have to keep in mind that bodhisattvas are not fixed beings, they manifest as needed. Also, they are always among us whether we are aware of them or not. Finally, it is a reminder than anyone can aspire to take the path of the bodhisattva.

12

Karma: Causes and Conditions

No Small Thing To Be a . . .

This moment is a result of causes and conditions of all that has come before. It is easy to forget how these causes and conditions create a unique moment that we take as just 'usual.' More specifically, it is easy to forget that all beings, sentient and insentient, are also singular events. When one looks at the sensory world, one can appreciate the complexity of the interactions of causes and conditions that come together in this moment.

As a volunteer at Yosemite National Park, I became fascinated with the giant sequoia trees. Each tree in the Mariposa Grove is a consequence of what happened before. What are the chances that a seed actually grows to a tree? By spending some time considering the likelihood of one sequoia tree actually growing into a mature tree, we can become more aware of how fortunate we are to have the opportunity to experience life.

No Small Thing To Become a Sequoia Tree

Sequoia trees illustrate causes and conditions in the physical world. These trees grow far inland along the western slope of the Sierra Nevada mountain range at altitudes between 5,000 and 7,000 feet above sea level. This elevation range provides the trees with dry mountain air necessary for their cones to open and to release seeds. The elevation also has a deep snowpack which supplies the large volumes of water required for growth.

It is interesting to note that in the last 500 years there has been no evidence of change in the boundaries of the Mariposa Grove in Yosemite National Park. In order to sustain the boundaries of the grove, a tree must generate one successor which grows to reproductive maturity during its life span. In this case, the seed is the cause, which then interacts with the environmental conditions that allow for the seed to germinate and grow.

A mature Sequoia can have 50,000 cones that may be on the tree for 20 years before they open. Another perspective is that one tree produces approximately 1,500 new cones per year. The number of seeds per cone vary widely and the typical range is from 200-400 seeds per cone. A sequoia tree has an estimated life span of 1,800-2,700 years, although some have lived for much longer. Thus, during the span of a single tree, it may produce one billion seeds.

Then, there are the conditions of the environment to be considered. When a cone opens and the seeds fall to the ground an opportunity to germinate is present. Those seeds that fall on forest debris have no chance to germinate because they will dry out without moisture. The optimal conditions for germination are for the seed to be slightly buried in moist soil and to have restricted light. Still, even under these conditions, the initial germination rate is small. In 1938, it was reported that a 15% germination rate was a fair average under the best of conditions, but the study estimated that only one of every million seeds germinates under natural conditions.

Even after germination has been successful, the microenvironment of the forest ground surface conditions (i.e. moisture, minerals, competitors) determines the development and survival of the seedlings. The early seedling stage is probably one of the most critical as far as the survival of the species is concerned. Under the best controlled laboratory test conditions, 98.6% of seedlings did not survive after two years.

Beyond the initial germination, a number of other factors are needed to be favorable for growth to maturity. Fire is among the physical factors that are beneficial to sequoia seedling survival through both direct and indirect means. The heat and smoke from the fire can cause the cones to open and release the seeds. Fire also kills off competitor trees, allowing additional light through the canopy, light that is needed by the seedlings. In addition, fire disrupts and opens up packed soil allowing the roots to penetrate. Perhaps if all the conditions are favorable, a seed will have a chance to become a mature reproductive tree.[1]

Causes and Conditions for a seed to mature: One in a billion. Just for one sequoia tree. And what would they be for humans!

Perspectives on Karma

A concept of karma (kamma) has found its way into common expression with different connotations than the original sense of the meaning. Perhaps the most common use of it is in the lament expressed when things don't go as planned: "I have bad karma!" This wail conveys a sense of inevitability. It expresses the belief that some circumstances have conspired against an individual. It takes away any sense of responsibility and leaves one a victim of the circumstances.

In the Buddhist sense, karma is the force generated by a person's actions which has ethical consequences contributing to the manifestation of a future event. Karma may be positive or negative depending upon the action. A person's actions can be in thought, word, or deed, which are sometimes expressed as mind, speech, and body. Not all actions generate karma. The major action or cause of karma is ignorance, which is not knowing reality as it truly is. On the other hand egoless actions, such as those performed by enlightened beings, without desire or attachment, do not produce karma.

The entry point is the Buddha's response to a question from a student about the differences in the conditions of human beings:

> Beings are owners of kammas, heirs of kammas, they have kammas as their progenitor, kammas as their kin, kammas as their homing-place. It is kammas that differentiate beings according to inferiority and superiority. (MN 135 The Shorter Exposition of Kamma)

A more concise, colloquial rendering of the same passage is:

> All living beings have actions (Karma) as their own, their inheritance, their congenital cause, their kinsman, their refuge. It is Karma that differentiates beings into low and high states.

The Law of Causation can be simply expressed:

> Causes + Conditions ▸ Effect 1 + changing conditions ▸ Effect 2 and so on.

Good causes lead to a good result, bad causes lead to a bad result. In colloquial usage, karma is often expressed as a negative force.

Key Points for Considering Karma

The Law of Causation operates in the relative world without the intervention of any external force or being.

Karma is not fate, since one's action in the present will contribute to their state in a future moment. One way to think about karma is as 'energy' created by a past action which then later manifests in a present situation. But it would be a simplification to believe that there is an identifiable cause and effect relationship which can connect one single event directly to a specific result. Many conditions combine to contribute to the manifestation of the moment. Consequently, a single individual action does not fully determine one's future. There are many variables. Everything is interrelated—the karma of family, country, culture, and gender. All the variables contribute to the present conditions. There is also the variable of time, since karma from a past action may not be immediately manifested, but may be held and come to fruition at a later time.

Karma does not just refer to past actions. It can be generated by both past and present activities. Hence in one sense, we are the result of what has happened in the past; we will be the result of what we are choosing to do now, or in other words, the activity of all beings creates the future.[2] A primary teaching of the Law of Causation is that all beings are fully responsible for their own actions. A motivation of the teaching of karma is to take responsibility for the past and to direct positive energy in the present.

Karma: The Best Laid Plans for College Applications

These are the summary elements of karma:

- Responsibility for actions
- Interrelationship of karma
- Not fate
- Manifested and unmanifested karma
- No ability to control

These elements all are evident in the process of the college application. The entire application process now spans years, and has taken on a life of its own in complexity and induced anxiety. As the deadline nears, the pressure on students becomes oppressive because all of the components must be completed by the deadline—SAT exams, the life essay, transcripts, and supplementary essays.

When students asked for perspective on how to get through it, my response was:

> Put your best and full effort into the process. One is only responsible for bringing their full effort into each task that is in front of them.
>
> Once the application is submitted, there is nothing more to be done.
>
> The students are not responsible for the next outcome.

The law of cause and effect functions without any external direction and does not respond to entreaties. Admission decisions can be affected by any number of factors which range from the objective evaluation of an application to how well the admission officer slept the night before! (Later addition: Bribes and payoffs.)

The good news: No matter what the outcome of the application process, events will not unfold according to the plan.

The students did not initially accept this as good news. Yet, life is so much more vast than rational imagination. The possibilities that can arise are endless and the one that does manifest in the present may be totally unexpected. No one event can be explained as the result of one individual act.

In general, rational planning and full effort are needed in the everyday world. However, our lives are greater than the rational mind can know. As in the college application example, planning for the future is an appropriate activity. Having done the preparation, the next step is to not be attached to the plans, accept what comes, and live in the moment of the situation.

How Can There Be Merit if Everything Is Impermanent?

> There are these three grounds for meritorious activity. Which three? The ground for meritorious activity made of generosity, the ground for meritorious activity made of virtue, and the ground for meritorious activity made of development [meditation]. These are the three grounds for meritorious activity. (ID 3.11: The Group of Threes)

Merit here has a slightly different emphasis than its Western use because it refers to an inner sense of well-being, rather than being particularly good or worthy of deserving praise. An inner sense of well-being can arise from beneficial actions. When action is taken in the everyday world, karma is created and at a later time an effect can manifest.

The understanding of merit and transfer of merit depends upon perspective. In the world of self and other, actions are influenced by self-attachment or ego, and karma will be created. This understanding of merit can be seen as another provisional teaching and has been termed the causal position. So from this perspective, it is misleading to say there is not merit.

From the causal position, practitioners were told that the accumulation of merit could lead to rebirth into a higher state of being. This transfer of merit has developed into an integral practice in the liturgical chanting services of most schools of Buddhism. The practitioners' merit may be transferred to the deceased, to deities, or sentient beings. Shantideva has offered this dedication:

> May beings everywhere who suffer
> Torment in their minds and bodies
> Have by virtue of my merit,
> Joy and happiness in boundless measure.[3]

However, there is also the different perspective of enlightened beings. Since they have realized the nature of emptiness and no-self, their actions transcend the everyday world and therefore do not produce karma. Enlightened beings understand that merit only exists in relation to a self, therefore for them, there is no such thing as merit. As in the case of Dana, there is no giver or receiver, but a formless field of benefaction moving through the universe. Sheng-Yen has called this the 'consequential' position.[4]

Cause and Conditions for an Accident

> There was a man in a small canoe out in the bay. The man was quite proud of his boat, which he had just refinished. The day began as clear and bright, but rather unexpectedly, clouds quickly gathered and a dense fog rolled in. The man brought the canoe about and headed for shore. As he headed home, he could just make out the profile of another boat in the fog-obscured distance. He kept that outline of a boat within his view and noticed that the boat was moving in his direction. This observation caused him

> some concern and when the boat was within earshot, he called out "Keep your distance so that we have plenty of room to pass." However, the other boat continued to move closer and was now on a direct collision course. He called out again louder, "Keep your distance!"
>
> He was quite skilled with the oar, knew a number of strokes, and could maneuver the canoe quite adroitly. He changed course and paddled away from the other boat. However, as he changed direction, he was upset to see the other boat also change direction and again move directly toward him. The man could also see that it was significantly larger than his canoe. He called out again "Watch out. Don't hit my boat, it has just been repainted!" None of this shouting had any effect. The larger boat continued to bear down on him. "Stay out of my way!" But it was of no use. Whenever he tried to change direction, the maneuver was matched by the on-coming boat. The boat went straight at him until there was a loud crack from the crash. The man saw his new boat damaged by this senseless accident.
>
> His rage knew no bounds. "You idiot, look what you did to my boat!" He continued his rampage, screaming and getting quite worked up. Suddenly, the fog lifted. The man could see the larger boat clearly now. There was no one in it. The boat was a long-abandoned shell of a boat and its movements were random.

One of the Bodhidharma's *Four Practices was Repaying Wrongs* (Chapter 2):

> When encountering suffering or injustice, accept it without complaint. This suffering is a manifestation of past actions which have now ripened and manifested. Just endure it without anger or complaint."

This admonition can now be appreciated more fully in the perspective of karma. For the man in the canoe, it seems like 'bad luck,' often stated as 'bad karma.' However, no one event of the past defines the manifestation of the present. In this case, in addition to the man's past actions, there were other events; someone abandoning the shell of a boat, the man's decision to go out on the lake at that time, the sudden storm, and the currents that brought them together with a crash, all as contributing causes and conditions. All of these conditions were working together in harmony. The result was the crash of the moment. There was no one to blame. Consequently, Bodhidharma advises that the practice is to endure it without anger. Perhaps it is easier to see in this case where no other person was involved. But it seems different when other people are doing foolish or unjust actions that affect us. Acceptance in those situations is where the difficult practice is done.

Shantidiva combines the interdependence of karma with the resulting anger of the man in the canoe:

> All things, then depend on something else;
> On this depends the fact that none are independent.
> Knowing this, we will not be annoyed at objects
> That resemble magical appearance.[5]

Situations such as the unexpected storm on the lake arise every day and there are many different ways to respond to them. The most common reaction is a conditioned, reflexive response, characterized by 'our' way of responding. Alternatively, an awareness of the responsibilities of actions due to karma, coupled with an understanding of interconnectedness, can lead to more freedom and options in responding to these situations.

13
Awakening and the Way

What Is the Way?: Different Perspectives

The term 'Way' is often used, without explanation. It seems as if it is assumed everyone else knows what it is. Actually, it is the opposite. No one can really say what the Way is. Without trying to say what it is, teachers use pointers to direct people to have their own experience of the Way. While each teacher has an individual way of showing a pointer, all of their responses are in the same direction. Still, one response may speak more directly to an individual than another.

Nansen's exchange with Joshu introduces the first of these apparent contradictions—there is not something that can be sought or known, yet Nansen speaks of the Way as if it were something:

> Joshu: "What is the Way?"
> Nansen said: "Ordinary Mind is the Way. "
>
> Joshu: "Then may I direct myself towards it or not?"
> Nansen: "To seek (it) is to deviate (from it)."
> Joshu: "If I do not seek, how can I know about the Way?"
>
> Nansen: "The way does not belong to knowing or not knowing. To know is to have a concept; to not know is to be ignorant. If you truly realize the Way of no doubt, it is just like the sky: wide open vast emptiness. How can you say yes or no to it?"
>
> At these words, Joshu had sudden enlightenment. His mind became like the clear moon.[1]

Bodhidharma reinforces the idea that there is nothing to seek outside of oneself and the way is already perfect, our own nature is perfect. To describe it is useless, yet everyone tries. Ultimately, there is nothing to seek or find, yet it is the effort of a meditation practice that takes us in the direction of realizing the truth of the Way:

> The Way is basically perfect. It doesn't require perfecting. The Way has no form or sound. It's subtle and hard to perceive. It's like when you drink water: you know how hot or cold it is, but you can't tell others .... The ultimate truth is beyond words. Doctrines are words. They're not the Way. The Way is wordless. Words are illusions. They're no different from things that appear in your dreams or at night.[2]
>
> Someone who seeks the Way doesn't look beyond himself. He knows that the mind is the Way. But when he finds the mind, he finds nothing. And when he finds the Way, he finds nothing. If you think you can use the mind to find the Way, you're deluded.[3]

Huang Po talks about the provisional nature of the teachings. He recognizes that words are needed to get started, but after that, he warns about the use of concepts and words. Like Nansen, he states there is no thing to be sought. This admonition is repeated continually in all of his passages because the most comfortable way we have to investigate a question is through words and ideas. In his last comment in the excerpt below, Huang Po emphasizes that wisdom is prevented by such words and ideas:

> The Way is not something which can be studied. Study leads to the retention of concepts and so the Way is entirely misunderstood. Moreover, the Way is not something specially existing; it is called the Mahayana Mind: Mind which is not to be found inside, outside, or in the middle. Truly it is not located anywhere. The first step is to refrain from knowledge-based concepts.
> The Way is spiritual Truth and was originally without name or title. It was only because people ignorantly sought for it empirically that the Buddhas appeared and taught them to eradicate this method of approach. Fearing that nobody would understand, they selected the name Way.[4]

In his responses to questions, Huang Po does not mince words:

> Q: "What is the Way and how must it be followed?"
> A: "What sort of THING do you suppose the Way to be, that you should wish to FOLLOW it?"

Q: "What instructions have the Masters everywhere given for practice and the study of Dharma (teachings of the Buddha)?"
A: "Words used to attract the dull of wit are not to be relied on."

Q: "Since there is no need to seek, why do you also say, not everything is eliminated?"
A: "Not to seek is to rest tranquil."[5]

Huang Po adds:

> Mind is fundamentally without error, whenever thoughts arise, you will be fully convinced that they are responsible for errors. If you could prevent all conceptual movements of thought and still your thinking processes, naturally there would be no error left in you. Therefore it is said:
>
> 'When thoughts arise, then do all things arise.
> When thoughts vanish, then do all things vanish.'[6]

In the interchange below, Joshu is at his elegant best here. He simply demonstrates the Way.

> A monk asked, "What is the Way?"
> Joshu said, "You're too kind."[7]

Joshu is using his response, essentially 'thank you,' as an example of ordinary words. The Way is right here in the exchange.

Key phrases about the Way that recur in the teachings: no seeking, no form or sounds, not a thing with a location, perfect without error, no concepts.

One of the above responses may be more helpful than the others. It's worth sitting with the Way to see for oneself the direction to which these teachers are pointing. Whatever the experience of the Way is, the entry point is from the full awareness in the moment. The entry point takes the comments about the Way back to practice. The call is to stop seeking an entry point with the senses and use the gift of meditation to go beyond them.

Picking and Choosing

The most well-known verse about the Way is by the Third Patriarch *Seng-Ts'an (J:* Sosan d 606). The verse appears near the beginning of

"Trust in Mind":

> The Great Way is not difficult,
> Just don't pick and choose.
> Cut off all likes or dislikes,
> Everything is clear like space.[8]

"The Great Way is not difficult,"

There is no simple statement to define the Way. If it could be written in a sentence, it would not be the Way! The teachers have provided a number of pointers to direct students in the direction of experiencing the Way. The reminder here is that it seems difficult because the effort is not always in the appropriate direction.

"Just don't pick and choose."

The use of the word 'just' is an underappreciated modifier. 'Just' means simply or not complicated to do, but it may not be easy. The activity of not picking and choosing is a matter of avoiding discrimination and attachments as a matter of course of everyday comings and goings. When the activity is zazen, the practice is to gently let go of concepts and ideas. There is no need to add drama by making the arising of thoughts and ideas into a big deal.

Picking and choosing can occur on many levels of awareness. The obvious examples are with material possessions and people, but the phrase can also refer to choosing states such as anger or greed. Analysis by any of the senses leads to discrimination. Picking and choosing can only happen, and indeed must happen when there is a boundary between two things that gives rise to subject and object. Subject and object is an artificial boundary that is created by our conditioned mental activity. Since we are creating them, we can also stop making them.

"If you cut off likes and dislikes,
Everything is clear like space."

The expression 'cut off' is often used to describe the process of allowing increased awareness to bring discrimination and illusory boundaries to an end. This method is the opposite of trying to 'get rid' of the discrimination and boundaries forcibly by rational analysis.

There is a tendency to focus on the discriminating perspective, avoiding the original self as expressed in the first line. The point emphasized by Yasutani below is that nothing is excluded in buddha nature:

> Where is there room for picking and choosing? .... If you think that the discriminating function of picking and choosing is outside buddha-nature, then Buddha isn't telling us anything either—the whole existence of all sentient beings is buddha nature.[9]

In the absence of any boundary, life simply arises each moment and flows. All creations are in harmony. We are free to fully experience the moment without adding anything extra to it.

Text Perspective: There is a bias to take the translation one is most familiar with as the 'correct' translation. At different practice centers, different translations are used. As noted earlier, there is no 'definitive' translation of these works.

The following verses are presented as a reminder that teaching in words is provisional and that it is our own responsibility to experience the spirit or ultimate meaning of the teaching (Chapter 3). The first verse could be interpreted to be in conflict with Yasutani's comments about discriminating functions. How can anything be excluded?

> The best way is not difficult
> It only excludes picking and choosing
> Once you stop loving and hating
> It will enlighten itself.
> Translated by Dusan Pajin

> The Great Way is not difficult
> For those who have no preferences,
> When love and hate are both absent
> Everything becomes clear and undisguised.
> Translated by Clarke/Osho

In closing, it is noted that the term 'no preferences' extends in all directions. This instruction includes having no preference for not having preferences!

Ripening of Awakening

'Sudden Awakening' usually refers to the view that the mind is innately pure and that enlightenment entails an instantaneous recognition of this purity. Experiencing one's nature is to realize one is exactly buddha nature. This experience is often presented as a two-tiered path, sudden awakening followed by gradual cultivation. Zongmi (780-841) describes it as a ripening:

> In terms of the elimination of hindrances, it is like when the sun immediately comes out, yet the frost melts gradually. With respect to the perfection of virtue, it is like a child which, when born, immediately possesses four limbs and six senses. As it grows, it gradually develops control over its actions.[10]

There can also be multiple awakenings at different levels. So although there may be significant differences in clarity and depth, depending on the individual's experience, since the experience is of one's inherent nature, the 'content' is the same. The initial experience may not be sufficient to generate the complete, perfect enlightenment of a buddha because at that profound level, one not only knows they are a buddha, but also how to act like one; it is a full integration of experience, wisdom, and activity.

In the Mahaparinirvana Sutra, the elusive nature of the awakened consciousness is described in a series of metaphors, two of which are quoted here:

> Good people, it is like looking into the distant sky at a bird flying; at one moment it seems there is nothing there, at another moment there is a bird flying. One is not sure, but it seems as if one has seen something.
>
> Good people, it is like a man walking home at night. Suddenly there is a flash of lightning that causes him to think he has seen a group of cows, but he is not sure if they were really cows or just shadows in the midst. After peering into the dark for a long time, he determines it must be a group of cows he has seen and yet he is not completely sure.
>
> Bodhisattvas perceive the buddha nature that lies within them in much this same way; they are not completely sure about what they are seeing.[11] [12]

Yasutani comments that enlightenment and the person do not obstruct each other. The person still has the range of emotions and adventures, and enlightenment is undefiled.[13] This observation is made to express the fact that the personality does not change; for example, an abrasive personality may not be transformed.

Sudden and Gradual Awakening in Chinese History and Legend

The terms 'sudden' and 'gradual' awakening are often cited in an interesting historical context. In the 8th and 9th centuries, there were serious arguments in the Chan (Zen) schools in China about teaching practices. In brief, teachers in the 'Southern' school believed that the 'sudden' approach was superior and attacked the 'Northern' school as inferior and accused them of teaching a 'gradual' method.

Over time, the position of the Southern school won out. The winner writes the history. The Platform Sutra,[14] attributed to Hui-Neng, the revered 6th Patriarch of China, is the most important document from this period. It contains the major teachings of 8th century Chan. The story of the dispute between the two schools became legend and was taught as history for 1,000 years. This dominance of the Southern School set the direction for Zen in China, Japan, and the West.

Then in 1900, a huge trove of documents dating from the 4th to 11th century was discovered in the Tun-huang caves in China. There were 1,100 bundles of scrolls, and over 15,000 paper books and shorter texts. Some of these were dispersed around the world, but it was almost another 50 years until they became generally available and widespread scholarly study began. The documents chronicled the historical situation over the centuries. In some respects, the historical record differed from the legendary accounts.

The documents outlined the conflicts between Buddhism, Taoism, Confucianism, and the Tang dynasty in the 7th and 8th centuries. Further, different schools of Buddhism were in conflict with each other for dominance. Within the Chan school itself, teachers had their own disputes. Although the full story of this internal dispute cannot be known, the information challenged many accepted facts. The following are three examples of the dispute: (i) The initiator of the attack on the Northern school, Shen-hui (670-762) was a man willing to stretch the truth for his own purposes. He had personal ambitions such as control of the teaching lineage. (ii) The Northern school was quite prominent at the time and the differences in the teachings of the two schools were not as pronounced as had been claimed. (iii) The Platform Sutra was written in sections and completed about 100 years after these events. The facts, legends, and fabrications about the life of Hui-Neng are contradictory. However, it is not likely that Hui-Neng is the author of the Platform Sutra. This sutra is one of most influential teachings and addresses both spiritual and political agendas. [15] [16]

The religious traditions and teaching legends are rich and are not diminished by such scholarship because the effectiveness of teachings is more important than its history. The significance of the legends is that they have been instrumental in the awakening of countless people over the centuries. Thus, these legends are true in the sense that they reflect teachings of the Buddha, even if some historical facts are not accurate. Legend and history have different functions. McRae clarifies the difference:

> Legend reflects the school's total creative output and is an important guide to its self-image, whereas history is the modern understanding of the dynamic cultural and intellectual realities of the school's development.[17]

For practitioners however, an awareness of the historical context is helpful to avoid distortions and idealization.

There is a reference to this dispute in the Sandokai (Harmony of Relative and Absolute) composed by Sekito Kisen (C. Shitou Xiqian) in the eighth century. It is one of the most chanted verses. The opening lines are:

> The mind of the great sage of India
> is intimately transmitted from west to east.
> *While human faculties are sharp or dull,*
> *the Way has no northern or southern ancestors.*
> The spiritual source shines clear in the light;
> the branching streams flow on in the dark.
> Grasping at things is surely delusion;
> according with sameness is still not enlightenment.

Suzuki comments:

> Sekito's understanding is that the true teaching of the great sage, Shakyamuni Buddha, includes both the Southern school and Northern school without any contradiction .... If you have the eyes to see or the mind to understand the teaching, you will see it is not necessary to be involved in such a dispute. Because some of the descendants … didn't completely understand the teaching of the Buddha they got into a dispute. From Sekito's point of view, there is no need for contention.[18]

Legend, History, and Significance

Sometimes, it is useful to look at legend and history from a different setting. Events are what they are. The public reports of the events are another matter. The significance of the events is yet another consideration. In the 'sudden awakening' dispute above, the significance is not always emphasized. The significance is that the teachings of the Buddha to end suffering continued in an effective way. The dominant side in a dispute invariably chooses to portray the outcome as the only right one. However, teachings are provisional so that a dogmatic statement about a right way of teaching is flawed. No one can know where different alternatives may have led.

The difference between history, legend, and significance is illustrated in the story of the Great Race of Mercy. In the winter of 1925, there was an outbreak of diphtheria in the frontier town of Nome, Alaska. The nearest antitoxin was located in Anchorage. In order to get the antitoxin to Nome, the last 674 miles had to be covered by a succession of dog sled relay teams. Despite great dangers and -80°F wind chill temperatures, the 20 teams of men and 150 dogs made the entire trip in 5.5 days. The medicine arrived intact and the outbreak was contained. There was great excitement and the grateful people and the press focused attention on the lead dog, Balto. The news of the heroic rescue was broadcast everywhere almost immediately by the new technology of radio. Balto became famous and a statue of Balto was erected in Central Park in New York City.

The facts were a little different. Balto did lead the 55 mile last leg into Nome. As the first face of the successful expedition, the press had their hero. However, a different dog, Togo, led the teams for 255 miles through far more treacherous conditions. Although people involved tried to correct the record, public enthusiasm for the story could not be changed.

The difference between the facts and the legend are clear. The legend continues to inspire. The significance was that the rescue was successful and the people in Nome were saved. In a bit of irony, compared to the awakening dispute above, the dogs performed selflessly to help people.

14
People of Zen

Dogen: *Shobogenzo* + 800 years

Today, Eihei Dogen (1200-1253) stands out as the founder of the Soto sect and as the author of the collection of works known as the *Shobogenzo* (*Treasury of the True Dharma Eye*). He is now one of the most revered teachers in the Soto sect of the Zen school. However at the time of his passing he was not prominent. The change in his standing over the 800 year period is dramatic. There are both idealized accounts of his life as well as ongoing scholarly research of his life and times. The following is a brief summary of the latter.[1,2]

Dogen trained in Japan and then went to China for more depth in his training experience. After his return to Japan in 1227 or 1228, he had several residences in established monasteries. In 1242, he and a small group of students moved to a rural location. There he ultimately established the monastery Eihei-ji, incorporated Chinese monastic practices, and founded the Soto sect. He emphasized single-minded practice and was a forceful teacher and writer.

Buddhism had been in Japan since the 8th century or, by some accounts, as early as the 6th century. Zen was introduced in the 12th century. Dogen was the first to establish the formal Chinese monastic practices and structures at Eihei-ji. The clear intention of establishing Chinese Buddhism in Japan was evident in both the meditation discipline and the monastic regulations (i.e. schedule, meal procedures, evening lectures). However, he also incorporated features of Japanese Buddhism including lay activities such as precept recitation ceremonies. There are contemporaneous reports of mystical events surrounding Dogen at several of these events which further increased his teaching authority.

At that time, the Soto community at Eihei-ji was geographically isolated by its rural location and relatively small size. Its continued operation relied upon the warrior class for financial support and was dependent upon Dogen's formidable teaching authority. In the eyes of the established, patron-funded Buddhist prelates, Eihei-ji was not prominent. Dogen's passing in 1253 attracted little attention at the larger monasteries in more populated areas. However, at the time of his death, the Eihei-ji monastery was the location of one of the earliest viable independent Zen sects in Japan.

Both Dogen's prominence and the status of Eihei-ji changed dramatically over the next 800 years. Today, the Soto school is the largest Zen school in Japan; the *Shobogenzo* the most used Soto text; and Eihei-ji is one of the two head temples.

Rise to Prominence

Dogen's successors spearheaded a number of activities to enhance his standing. Perhaps the large Memorial Services which grew over the centuries were the most influential. It is not clear when the services began, but by the 350th anniversary, the memorial ceremonies at the monastery were major events which took place every 50 years on the nominal anniversary of his death. These memorials grew in importance for both enhancing Dogen's reputation and supporting the well-being of Eihei-ji. Monks traveled great distances to make pilgrimages and funds were collected for the expansion of the monastery. In addition, regulations were enforced on the participants to ensure that Eihei-ji was recognized as the custodian of the authentic monastic practices. These events grew to such proportions that it was reported that 27,000 monks attended the memorial in 1752, the 500th anniversary.

Biography

Dogen's life was chronicled in 1452 by Kenzei near the 200th anniversary of his death The work included a chronological account, quotes, letters, and similar historical documents. However about 300 years later, in 1754, another monk, Menzan Zuiho, produced an annotated edition and included new idealized details of his own creation. These details soon became regarded as established facts. Zuiho's work was later illustrated and became both a teaching vehicle about Dogen and the reference work used for more than 20 subsequent biographies and similar articles. However, in 1975, a scholar (Kodo) located and analyzed six versions of the original work by Kenzei. This work showed the extent of the additions fabricated by Menzan.

As a consequence, the historical accuracy of biographical information depends fully on the source.

Dogen's Shobogenzo

The *Shobogenzo*, which is comprised of 95 fascicles (chapters, the number of which depends upon the edition,) also had an uneven history in its rise to be recognized as a renowned and well-studied text. Originally, access to the manuscripts was limited to senior monks who had a relationship with a monastery or temple possessing a text. In many locations, the complete work was not available and by the 15th century, many of the fascicles were hidden from view. Over the years, the works were recopied independently at different monasteries and errors were introduced.

At some point in the 17th century, comparisons of different versions were made. Major issues arose as there were significant discrepancies among the texts. Since they are difficult to interpret, differing conclusions were drawn. In short, no one understood with confidence the original intent of Dogen. The situation was ultimately resolved because two of Dogen's direct students had composed voluminous commentaries immediately after his passing. These commentaries were crucial for the authentication of his work and aided in assembling the *Shobogenzo* for the first time.

Later, Tenkei Denson (1648-1735), a Soto scholar, conducted the first full-length, line by line study of the *Shobogenzo* since Kyogo, one of the two students mentioned above. In addition to editing out passages that failed to agree with Tenkei's own understanding, he also 'corrected' Dogen's readings of Chinese passages by adding additional words or changing the punctuation.[3]

For a period of time in the 18th century (1722-1796), publication and dissemination of the *Shobogenzo* was against the law in Japan. After the ban was lifted in 1796, a major effort was made to analyze the existing versions and publish the entire work. It was a very arduous process because there were many contradictions, and the entire project was not completed until 1820. There have been reanalyses and revisions since that time in order to publish editions that more closely conform to the original.

Even after the entire work was published, there were few reports of public lectures on the *Shobogenzo* until the conference at Eihei-ji in 1905. The conference was a great success and became an annual event. These conferences continued to bring attention to the depth of this work, and subsequently it became the primary reference work that it is today. It was never a foregone conclusion that either Dogen or his masterpiece would rise to the central positions they hold in the Zen community today. It is the consequence of the beliefs, energy, and savvy of his followers.

Yasutani's Commentary on the Title of Dogen's Treasury of the True Dharma Eye

Yasutani wrote a commentary on the "Treasury of the True Dharma Eye" (*Shobogenzo*). His comments below are limited just to the title and begin to reveal the different levels at which the *Shobogenzo* can be experienced.

Yasutani points out that the meaning of "true dharma" is usually misunderstood:

> 'True' is not used as the opposite of false. True is the world of *absolute* equality.
>
> 'Dharma,' in this usage, is the world of absolute differences (the world of phenomena).
>
> 'Absolute' is not used for emphasis. It is used for both True and Dharma .... 'Absolute' means that the whole universe is nothing but equality, the whole universe is nothing but differentiation ... they are the same thing.[4]

His interpretation of the title is "The Entire Phenomenal World is the Living Buddha-Way." Nothing is excluded. There is nowhere outside to look. So, there is no choice but to 'turn the light inward' in meditation, rather than searching outside for a teacher, book, or experience to rely on unconditionally. Yasutani continues:

> It's as if the whole universe is nothing but the continuous development of the complete, perfect performance of one great living drama, with all the best actors. Further, this great drama is always limited to one time only. There are never any retakes .... To say it truly, it's all the actors plus the stage, the scenery and the small props, the theater, and the audience; all are parts of the self, or better, each is the whole of the self.[5]

He emphasizes that "True Dharma" is just the conceptual representation of the title and it is up to the individual to realize the spirit. Yasutani is especially critical of the numerous commentaries that miss this point since they are conceptually based, and in some cases disregard awakening. His analogy is that analytical thought and reality are as different as clouds and mud.

This above commentary refers to just the title of Dogen's work. There have been countless commentaries published on the entire work.

Dogen's Instructions to the Tenzo

Dogen described the administration of the monastery. There were six senior positions in the monastery, one of which was the tenzo, the head cook. Dogen gave three guidelines for the seniors: Work to benefit others, contribute to the growth of the monastery, and learn from the masters of old. The tenzo was expected to demonstrate these guidelines in the role of preparing the meals for the monks. The tenzo was far more than a cook and the position required a deep practice and mindfulness. Dogen's short essay "Instructions to the Tenzo" includes specific kitchen instructions which apply to all areas of practice. The following excerpts are from that essay.

Experience is Individual

Dogen had gone to China to study. It was summer and very hot. There was an old monk spreading mushrooms out in the sun to dry. Dogen said to him:

> Why are you working? You are an old monk and a superior of the temple. You should get younger people to do this work. It is not necessary for you to work. Besides, it is extremely hot today Do this another day.

The monk replied:

> You are intelligent and you understand Buddhism, but you do not understand the essence of Zen. If I do not do this, if I do not work here and now, who could understand? I am not you, I am not others. Others are not me. So others cannot have the experience. If I don't work, if I do not have this experience here and now, I cannot understand. If a young monk helped me to do the work, if I were to stand by and watch him, then I could not have the experience of drying these mushrooms. If I said, 'do this and do

> that,' I could not have the experience. I could not understand the act that is here and now.[6]

Dogen commented:

> There was nothing else for me to say. As I walked along the passageway, I began to sense inwardly the true significance of the role of the tenzo.

The old monk had a different attitude than most people. He understood that there is only this moment and it has to be lived to the fullest. When judgments and opinions intervene, they become filters and the experience is clouded. In this view, there are no favorable or unfavorable tasks, there is just the meal to be prepared. It is the attitude of the tenzo and the respect for all of the activities in preparing the meal and serving the community that make it a task of joyfulness and gratefulness.

The old tenzo gave Dogen a glimpse of his understanding of the significance of individual experience. It is a challenge to allow the filters and opinions to weaken so that the direct activity of the moment is experienced. This is the direction of a meditation practice.

Reminders from "Instructions to the Tenzo"

In this set of instructions, Dogen emphasizes using kitchen work as a metaphor for how every single activity is about life in the moment:

> Handle even a single leaf in such a way that it manifests the body of the Buddha. This in turn allows the Buddha to manifest through the leaf. This is a power which you cannot grasp with your rational mind.
>
> If the head cook throws all his energy into whatever the situation truly calls for, then both the activity and the method by which he carries it out will naturally work to nurture the seeds of the buddha-dharma.
>
> Your attitude toward things should not be contingent upon their quality. A person who is influenced by the quality of a thing or changes his speech or manner according to the position of someone they meet is not a person working in the Way.

This last statement is a particularly challenging statement to practice. For example, throughout a day, people in all positions are encountered.

Attitudes and behavior may very well differ depending on with whom we are engaged. That is the situation of the moment. The practice is to grow awareness of those changes in attitude and behavior. With practice, there may be a shift in how these situations are perceived and the response might not be governed by conditioned opinions. It can be observed that there is a change in reaction to people and arising conditions.

> When working in any position of responsibility, not only as tenzo, but as any officer or assistant, strive to maintain a spirit of joy and magnanimity, along with the caring attitude of a parent. A joyful spirit is one of gratefulness and buoyancy.[7]

The attitudes and perspectives highlighted in this essay can be used by anyone preparing a snack or meal which is then taken to the table. Here Dogen is extending the attitude beyond the kitchen to each situation as it arises throughout the day.

No Work, No Food

On the subject of food, there is an illustrative story from an earlier time:

> Hyakujo (720-814), the Chinese Zen master, used to labor with his pupils even at the age of eighty, trimming the gardens, cleaning the grounds, and pruning the trees. The pupils felt sorry to see the old teacher working so hard, but they knew he would not listen to their advice to stop, so they hid away his tools.
> That day the master did not eat. The next day he did not eat, nor the next. 'He may be angry because we have hidden his tools,' the pupils surmised. 'We had better put them back.' The day they did, the teacher worked and ate the same as before. In the evening he instructed them:
> 'No work, no food.'[8]

Hyakujo had an understanding of the depth of work responsibility. He put his full effort and attention into each task required to keep the monastery in good order. The students viewed the responsibility as a burden and moved to relieve Hyakujo of that burden. It cannot be taken away however, since one is always responsible for the activity in the present. As shown by Hyakujo's response, in order to experience the moment, one must place full effort on that activity. It cannot be taken away by others. Further, an attempt to take away the responsibility, even with good intentions, is an intrusion into someone else's life.

Vimalakirti: A Towering Layperson

Vimalakirti was a contemporary of the Buddha. He was a very realized lay person and was considered to be a bodhisattva. Beginning in the early days of Buddhism, ordained monks held and also enforced the monastics special position. Vimalakirti was not constrained by the trappings of religion in order to have the experience of reality. Consequently, the monks at the time had a special respect for this lay practitioner. His style of living merits special attention independent of the sutra which bears his name. Vimalakirti lived immersed in the world and did not fit the mold of piousness often preached by the hierarchy. He had a wife and children, apparently great wealth, and interacted with respect toward people he met.

However, there was an extraordinary dimension in his interactions. He made a skillful effort to give the people what they needed to support them in their life and practice, whether they were aware of it or not. His response was flexibly appropriate to the time and conditions. This skillful means was the connection between his own attainment and his service to others. He demonstrated that the affairs of the world have their own provisional value, but his actions showed that he was not attached to them.

More concisely, he was immersed in the world, but not entangled in it. As a lay person, he demonstrated that the one reality can be manifested to people in their interactions and does not depend on hierarchical status or approval.

Vimalakirti Sutra: Aspects of Renunciation and Sickness

Near the beginning of the Sutra which bears his name, the Buddha recognizes that Vimalakirti is ill and suggests that someone be selected to visit him. Sequentially, the Buddha asks ten of his followers to go to Vimalakirti's home and inquire about his condition. Each person in turn states their reluctance and declines. (Declines the request of the Buddha!) They each relate an incident in which they were involved in an activity and Vimalakirti appeared and directly corrected or contradicted their position on meditation or teaching. In these encounters Vimalakirti pointed out how they were still attached and had not realized or expressed the emptiness of all illusions. These interactions made the monks uncomfortable to visit him at his home. Finally, Manjushri agreed to visit and they had a far-reaching teaching conversation on renunciation, the nature of sickness, emptiness, duality, enlightenment, and the responsibilities of bodhisattvas. The excerpts below, concerning renunciation and the nature of sickness, illustrate the style of the sutra.

The Real Meaning of Renunciation

The perceived advantage of the monastic path compared to the lay path was brought up in the Vimalakirti Sutra during a discussion with Rahula, the son of the Buddha. Rahula had renounced both his family's throne, his household, and the world. He was explaining the benefits and blessings of this renunciation to some young men when Vimalakirti butted in and said Rahula was off-track:

> Renunciation is itself the very absence of virtues and benefits. Reverend Rahula, one may speak of benefits and virtues in regard to compounded things (phenomena), but renunciation is uncompounded, and there can be no question of benefits and virtues in regard to the uncompounded. Reverend Rahula, renunciation is not material but is free of matter. It is free of the extreme views of beginning and end.[9]
>
> In all of the things that are conditioned in nature (everyday phenomena) one may speak of having benefits and blessings. But one who leaves the household life enters the realm of the unconditioned, and in the realm of the unconditioned there are no benefits, no blessings.

Vimalakirti emphasized that often the focus is on the appearance of renunciation. Outward renunciation is a metaphor for ultimate renunciation. Renunciation is the absence of benefits and blessings. It is a spiritual, not material activity. Leaving home is not an end in itself. It is not a matter of gaining benefits or virtue, but one of growing. Renunciation is not an outward action, but an internal one. Vimalakirti then added:

> It is without ties and attachments, without personal possessions, without thought of possessions, without fluster or confusion. It means harboring joy within, guarding the minds of others, pursuing the practice of meditation, freeing oneself from all fault. If one can do all this, then one has truly left the household.[10]

There is no a priori exclusive position for the monastic tradition compared to the householder. Being immersed in life and free of entanglements is a moment-to-moment activity that needs no fixed setting. It requires genuine effort though. For some, the monastic tradition is an attractive location. For others, working through the affairs of the world is a path to renunciation. Rather than extend the discussion about the two paths, Suzuki frequently remarked "Not always so."

Nature of Sickness

Each culture has its own view of sickness and methods of healing. In Western medicine, a diagnosis is made of a physical ailment and an approach to alleviate that condition is prescribed. In many cases, this approach works for the specific condition. Since our organism is interactive, all medicines have side effects, so that there is a risk/benefit for all treatments. In Traditional Chinese Medicine, such as acupuncture and herbal treatments, the diagnosis is made by discerning patterns of energy (qi) flows and blockages rather than specific ailments, and treatments are based on this analysis.

In Buddhism, there is a different understanding of sickness. Sickness is separation from self and other, a separation from the experience of reality as it is. That separation is the cause of suffering. Excerpts from the Vimalakirti Sutra make this clear:

Manjusri: Layman, what is the cause of this illness?

Vimalakirti: This illness of mine is born of ignorance and feelings of attachment. Because all beings are sick, therefore I am sick. If all living beings are relieved of sickness, then my sickness will be mended. Why? Because the Bodhisattva for the sake of all living beings enters the realm of birth and death, and because he is in the realm of birth and death, he suffers.[11]

Sickness arises from total involvement in the process of misunderstanding from beginningless time. It arises from passions that result from unreal mental constructions, and hence ultimately nothing is perceived which can be said to be sick.

What is the elimination of this sickness? It is the elimination of egoism and possessiveness. What is

> the elimination of egoism and possessiveness? It is the freedom from dualism. What is freedom from dualism? It is the absence of involvement with either the external or the internal[12]

The first sentence is a reminder of how seriously the bodhisattvas take their vow to end suffering. Vimalakirti states that all beings must be relieved of suffering. He also stresses again that illness/suffering is the consequence of believing and holding on to either the idea of a separate self or the idea of sickness and health. Both are errors of attaching to conditioned responses. All conditioned responses by the senses contribute to this suffering. The exchange also emphasizes that the remedy to end illness or suffering is non-attachment. The medicine to release attachments is a meditation practice.

Layman P'ang and Playful Samadhi

P'ang Yun (704-808) is revered in China as an example of a layman with a family, who was also a serious student of Buddhism. P'ang studied with two prominent masters of the time. Layman P'ang had a wife, daughter, Ling Zhao, and a son. His wife and Ling Zhao were also adepts. Ling Zhao showed she could be a match for her father in wit and responses. In later years, it is speculated that P'ang and his daughter traveled together in pilgrimages and ended up living in a cave. The son is mentioned once, with a hoe, and is presumed to be a farmer.

At some point, P'ang gave up his material lifestyle. He gave his house to be used as a temple and viewed possessions as a hindrance to practice. He put the possessions on a boat and sank them in the river. Asked why he did not donate them to the needy, he replied that he did not want others to be so entangled in materialism. He then lived as an itinerant. There are no accounts of whether Layman P'ang's family was involved in the decision to get rid of their possessions or if they had an opinion in the matter!

The published collection, *The Sayings of Layman P'ang*, is generally regarded as the only Chinese classic about a Zen layperson. The book only exists because P'ang had an influential friend. Shortly after P'ang's death, Duke Yu Ti (soon to become the Imperial Commissioner) made the effort to send out requests for anecdotes about P'ang's life. P'ang was well known to have engaged in quick and sharp exchanges with teachers, monks, and other laymen. However, these exchanges were collected and compiled after the fact so there was some variation in the anecdotes. Some of these stories were compiled into an edition that was later preserved as a woodcut. The different English translations that are available are from that woodcut.

Playful Samadhi

Samadhi is a centering of mind which leads to a concentrated mind of attentiveness and an internal tranquility. Playful samadhi is the condition in which everything is all right and beautiful just as it is. In this exchange, P'ang was essentially asked by a Master: "What have you been doing recently?" Two versions of his reply are shown:

> What I do every day is nothing special:
> I simply stumble around.
> What I do is not thought out,
> Where I go is unplanned.
> No matter who tries to leave their mark,
> The hills and dales are not impressed.
> Collecting firewood and carrying water
> Are prayers that reach the gods.
>
> (Green)[13]

> My daily activities are not unusual,
> I'm just naturally in harmony with them.
> Grasping nothing, discarding nothing,
> In every place there's no hindrance, no conflict.
> Who assigns the ranks of vermilion and purple?—
> The hills' and mountains' last speck of dust is extinguished.
> [My] supernatural power and marvelous activity—
> Drawing water and carrying firewood.
>
> (Sasaki)[14]

The flavor of playful samadhi is shown here. In playful samadhi, everything is in harmony and appreciated just as it is: Life flows in ordinary activities, direct interaction, nothing lasts, everything in harmony, the whole event is a miracle. It is this experience that P'ang is communicating.

The last two lines, particularly of the Sasaki version, are very well known and often quoted. This type of experience is showing our own nature. Interpenetration, connectedness, harmony are all experienced simultaneously. This is within the potential of everyone's experience through practice.

These translations are from the same Ming woodcut. In the transcription of this verse, the best that one can hope for in words is a flavor of the experience that the enlightened P'ang was attempting to communicate. First there is the experience, then the capturing of it in Chinese, and then the differing English translations.

However, for an individual, a specific sentence or phrase in one of the translations may spark resonance. This energy can be incorporated into meditation practice. Like many other teaching examples, the verse both provides an example of playful samadhi and also can be used directly to bring energy into one's practice.

An Enlightened Family at Home

In addition to the above translations from the wood-cut, there are earlier versions in which the stories and details differ, but these are not so readily available. As noted earlier, the concern is not with the historical facts, both are right teachings; the concern is what can be done to skillfully use the teachings. The two passages below, describing the same episode, are an exchange among the family members about the practice. The first is well known:

> The Layman, sitting quietly in his temple, made this remark: 'How difficult it is! How difficult it is! My studies are like drying the fibers of a thousand pounds of flax in the sun by hanging them on trees.' His wife responded: 'My way is easy indeed! I found the teachings of the Patriarchs right on the tops of the flowering plants!' When the daughter overheard this exchange, she sang. 'My study is neither difficult nor easy. When I am hungry I eat. When I am tired I rest.'[15]

In this version, one member of the family takes the positive position, another, the negation of the position, and the third takes the Middle Way. The approaches are different, but they all reflect their experience of original nature.

The second version is obscure and is from a story told and published by Seung Sahn and takes a different tack. The original source was not cited; Seung Sahn could have adapted it himself for his own teaching! It shows the same three approaches and adds one more:

> One day, someone asked Layman P'ang, 'Is Zen difficult or

easy?' 'It's like trying to hit the moon with a stick. Very difficult!' Then this man thought, 'Oh, Zen is very difficult.' So, he asked Layman P'ang's wife, 'Your husband said Zen is difficult. I ask you, then, is Zen difficult or easy?' She said, 'Oh, Zen is very easy! It's like touching your nose when you wash your face in the morning!' The man could not understand. He thought to himself, 'Layman P'ang says Zen is difficult; his wife says it is very easy. Which one is correct?' So he went to their son and said, 'Your father said Zen is very difficult; your mother said it is very easy. Which one is correct?' The son replied, 'If you think it's difficult, then it's difficult. If you think it's easy, then it's easy. Don't make difficult and easy!' But the man was still not satisfied, so he went to the daughter. 'Everyone in your whole family has a different answer to my question. Your mother said Zen is easy. Your father said Zen is difficult. And your brother said don't make difficult and easy. So, I ask you, is Zen difficult or easy?'
'Go drink tea.'[16]

As in the first example, the family members take the positive, negation, and middle way positions. However, the ending has been modified and is quite direct—stop the discussion and be present to the moment! Enough talk! Just do what is in front of you. You can ask all the questions you want. Some questions are not worth pursuing. On one level, all of the answers that come back are provisional. On another level, they are directing our energy to the present. The second version has an even more direct instruction to the reader: "Cut the discussion and be present to the taste of life!"

P'ang's Invitations to Ordination

P'ang lived during the Tang (618-907) dynasty, the golden age of Buddhism in China. The monastic community enjoyed state support at that time. Monasticism was considered both more prestigious than lay life and the path for serious practice.

P'ang was recognized as having great insight. He was invited to join the monastery on more than one occasion. Once he replied, "I want to do what I like." So he did not take the formal vows. Another time, the teacher Tan-hsia said P'ang looked like a Master. P'ang's response was that the Master looked like an unskilled laborer. Just think of the consequences of saying that to most teachers! Many would have banished the student for disrespect. But Tan-hsia recognized the situation and agreed with him! P'ang lived in playful samadhi.

The exchanges show that P'ang was free from attachments to either the monastic or lay life. There was no self-analysis of what he should or should not do. Nowadays, there continue to be many discussions about the merits and restrictions of the two paths. It is a debate that remains at the rational level. P'ang, as Vimalakirti did earlier, shows that these discussions are provisional and the direction is to experience one's own life just as it is.

Bankei: A Shooting Star

Bankei (1622-1693) was like a shooting star in his time. During the 15th and 16th centuries, the major schools of Zen were in decline. Bankei emerged with his teaching of the Unborn Mind, a real departure from traditional teaching. Although his own practice had been strenuous, he rarely spoke of zazen or the precepts. Unconventional in several ways, he talked directly to the lay people—often thousands at a time. He ordered that his writings be destroyed and left no successors. Consequently, his teachings were largely neglected. In the 20th century, scholars and translators brought them back to view.

His sermons, documented surreptitiously by a follower, were not mainstream, but they may resonate with some today as they did in earlier times. He composed the 50 stanza "Song of the Original Mind." One well known follows:

> Unborn and imperishable
> Is the original mind
> Earth, water, fire and wind—
> A temporary lodging for the night.[17]

Each person always has this Mind and the differentiated elements of phenomena are the temporary manifestations of it in the moment.

Here's the frustrating thing: Bankei was never really explicit about the meaning of 'Unborn Mind.' Other terms that he used were 'having no origin, 'not coming into existence,' 'not taking effect,' 'Buddha mind.' Another phrase, 'beyond measurable time,' is also used for unborn. Similar to the use of the term 'Way,' Unborn Mind is a pointer to reality rather than a concept (Chapter 13).

He said that Unborn Mind is the Buddha-mind, with the 'marvelous working of illuminative wisdom': "It deals perfectly with every situation and all things fall into place and remain in perfect harmony."

Bankei elaborated on the Unborn Mind in his sermons about thoughts, ideas, and the illusions that are created:

> "What we call a thought is something that has fallen one or more removes from the living reality of the Unborn."
>
> "Let them arise when they arise. Don't have any thought to stop them. If they stop, let them stop."
>
> "If you fix onto images as they reflect, you are unwittingly creating illusions."

Ideas and thoughts have no substance. They exist, but they are a product of our own building of a self through conditioning. It is easy to forget that the designations 'good' and 'bad' are opinions.

Thoughts are naturally arising phenomena. Bankei is emphasizing that giving them special treatment leads to an error. In Zen meditation, there is a tendency to 'get rid' of thoughts. This is an attachment no different than holding onto them. It is our attachments that are at the root of illusions. We create illusions ourselves:

> So whatever else you may do or say, whatever happens leave things as they are. Don't worry yourself over them and don't side with yourself. Just stay as you are right in the Buddha-mind, and don't change it into anything else. If you do that, delusions don't occur. (4 quotes above)[18]

In another direction, Bankei reminds us that there is no way to predict or control situations that arise. It is the Unborn Mind, one that is clear without hindrance, that can respond to the situation appropriately:

> When someone tosses you a tea bowl
> —Catch it!
> Catch it nimbly with soft cotton
> With the cotton of your skillful mind![19]

It may be a tea bowl coming your way or an unexpected outcome. The skillful mind, our Unborn Mind, allows us to respond to such outcomes appropriately with 'the marvelous working of illuminative wisdom.' Bankei's approach and style may be different from other teachers, but the overall aim of his teaching is to end suffering. He brought fresh energy to the people of his time. Today, his teaching still brings a fresh perspective for some practitioners. There is not one fixed way to point to the reality.

Therigatha: Verses of the Elder Nuns

The Therigatha (Verses of the Elder Nuns) is a collection of the enlightenment poetry of nuns at the time of the Buddha. It is remarkable that these women's verses were preserved and included in the Pali Canon. The Therigatha is the earliest known collection of women's literature composed in India. There are always historical issues of dating, timing, original language, and multiple translations, but to be entangled in these issues is to obscure the significance of the work.

Susan Murcott (1992) pieced together historical information and legends that she could find, but lamented the possibilities of incompleteness. More recently, Anagarika Mahendra (2017) has published new ('for free distribution only') translations with extensive references. It is the tone of these backstories that sets the verses in more human relief. The women came from many different and difficult circumstances to meet the Buddha. Some fled their homes, others were wives, widows, mothers, prostitutes, or were held in harems. Each made their way to the teaching of the Buddha. Some of the women formed different communities to teach and to support each other. Others lived in the forest. It was difficult to gain recognition and ordination from the Buddha. This eventually happened for the women, not fully equal to the monks, but far in excess of other religious traditions at the time.

Many of the women wrote poems and 73 of them were later inscribed on palm leaves and included in the Therigatha. Many others were not included and lost. Some women never escaped their condition or found community with others. Their stories and hopes can be found on the palm leaves also. These stories are incredibly inspiring to read. The themes of the verses include seeking freedom from previous constraints and the struggles to awaken. There are many translations from the Pali and they vary over a broad range of interpretation. The poems below were composed by these women.

Mutta was the daughter of a poor brahmin and given in marriage to a hunch-backed brahmin. Unwilling to live with him, she persuaded him to allow her to join the order where she became an arhat. Her name means 'free woman' in the enlightened sense:

> Freed, good to be freed,
> freed from three crooked things;

From mortar, from pestle, from crooked husband too;
Freed from birth-death, lead to becoming fully destroyed.[20]

Sangha may have been a farmer's wife. However, in some accounts she was a member of Siddhartha's court. She left everything behind and followed the Buddha and experienced enlightenment:

I gave up my house
And set out into homelessness.
I gave up my child, my cattle,
And all that I loved.
I gave up desire and hate.
My ignorance was thrown out.
I pulled out craving
Along with its root.
Now I am quenched and still.[21]

Dhammadina set an example well ahead of her time. She was the wife of a prominent man. Her husband announced that he had heard the Buddha speak and was going to renounce everything, including her, to become a monk. She decided to renounce the world as well and became a nun. Dhammadina developed great insight and skill as a teacher, had a great gift for preaching, and was approved by the Buddha. However, her husband decided not to become a monk and returned to his former lay life. He was still interested in the teaching and came to her for explanations:

Eager for the end of suffering,
full of awareness,
that's the way.

When one's heart is not
Attached to pleasure, we say,
'That woman has entered the stream.'[22]

Citta was a long-time practitioner and an old woman when she was awakened. She expressed determination very simply:

Although indeed I am thin, sick and very weak;
Leaning on the walking stick I go, climbing the mountain.
Having put down the double robe, and having turned bowl upside down;

Sitting in meditating posture on rock, I shattered the aggregate of darkness.[23]

15

Zen Perspectives in Art

Basho: Haiku

Basho (1644-94) was a great poet and Zen practitioner. He stated his principle in writing poetry very clearly:

> Go to the pine tree if you want to learn about pine, or to the bamboo if you want to learn about the bamboo. And in doing so, you must leave your subjective preoccupation with yourself.
>
> Otherwise you impose yourself on the subject and do not learn. Your poetry issues of its own accord when you and the object have become one—when you have plunged deep enough into the object to see something like a hidden glimmering there. However, well phrased your poetry may be, if your feeling is not natural—if the subject and object are separate—then your poetry is not true poetry but merely your subjective counterfeit.[1]

The elements of Zen shine through: dropping opinions, interconnectedness, no separation from self and other, energy, spontaneity, and freedom.

Basho was not the first to write in the 17 (5-7-5) syllable structure, but he emphasized techniques which continue to be stressed in haiku. The overall mode or emotion is evoked with a simple description, which suggests a picture. Natural phenomena, such as referring to the seasons to indicate the time of year, also help to set the mood. Two different parts of that picture are often compared to each other, for example stillness and motion. In Basho's haiku there is a spirit of solitude and mystery in which the readers discern the meaning for themselves.

Basho's most famous haiku

Rendering a haiku in another language is a difficult art since the aim is to transmit both the meaning and spirit. This task is often a daunting proposition since some words and their associative emotions have no real English equivalent. Also, there is no punctuation or reference to verb tense to use as a guide. Nonetheless, many people have been attracted to the challenge. Actually, there is a book with 100 translations of this poem edited by Sato, the most respected translator in Japan today:

> The old pond,
> A frog jumps in—
> Plop!
> (R.H. Blyth)

> An old pond:
> a frog jumps in—
> the sound of water
> (Sato Hiroaki Sato)

There is an internal comparison between the old pond and the sudden sound. Yuasa, translator and editor of Basho's work, comments further:

> On the surface, the poem describes an action of the frog and its aftereffects—a perfect example of objectivity. But if you meditate long enough upon the poem, you will discover that the action thus described is not merely an external one, that it also exists internally, that the pond is, indeed, a mirror held up to reflect the author's mind.[2]

Some translations go in different directions and constructions to try to capture the spirit:

> Breaking the silence
> Of an Ancient pond,
> A frog jumped into the water—
> A deep resonance
> (Nobuyuki Yuasa)

This haiku is the work of a master poet and incorporates the principles that he stated earlier. Basho's work, either consciously or spontaneously, has many levels that can be experienced.

There have been countless translations; a meaning cannot be captured or defined. One can select a translation that has some attraction for them. It is generally suggested that haikus be read a number of times with reflection and meditation. Different meanings arise at different times for the individual. The experience that comes from this interaction with the poet's mind is uniquely one's own.

Sumi-e

Sumi-e is the ancient Chinese and Japanese art of black ink painting. The intent is to capture the essence of an object. The same principles described by Basho above are applied here as well. There is an emphasis on simplicity and intuitiveness. Subjects are painted in black ink with gradations from black to light shade; the tonal variation may give the appearance of depth and color. The spirit must be free from a voluntary desire for success.

Many masters have practiced both sumi-e and Zen meditation. The intentions of dropping body and mind and being present are emphasized in both disciplines. When the mind is empty, life flows. In sumi-e, the work develops freely and the artist flows with spontaneous energy and activity to create the art. The artist paints what they feel, rather than what they see, but only after they have first seen it distinctly. One's individuality has to be expressed. There must be living movement so that the nature is transferred to the paper.

The basic instructions of body, mind, and breath are right in line with the Zen teachings of learning to forget oneself and experience the emptiness of all things. Chiura Obata (1885-1975) was the foremost sumi-e artist in America in his time and is particularly well-known for his nature paintings of Yosemite National Park. He describes the three disciplines essential to the practice of sumi-e:

Composing the Mind

> "The mind must be as peaceful and tranquil as the surface of a calm, undisturbed lake. Let not a shadow be cast on it, nor the slightest thought of self-conceit or egotism."

Correcting the Posture

> "The mind cannot be composed until one has learned to assume

a position in which the body is held straight and erect without being rigid or stiff."

Attending to the Breath

"Respiration is adjusted according to the physical quality exhibited by the object to be drawn. One should take a deep breath when the brush is about to be laid on paper."[3]

The beginning instructions, as taught by the Sensei Koho Yamamoto, founder of the oldest Sumi-e school in New York City, also are succinct and require the student to understand them by practice and experience. The practice instructions are generally oral and without detail. They can't be internalized without working with and being confused by them. For example:

"Fingers, arm, and body work together."

"The stroke should be fast, but not too fast."

"Press with your fingers, but not too hard."

"Make mistakes, have no expectations for success."

"Do 1,000 bamboo leaves, then 10,000 more."

"Each stroke is important. It reflects your mind."

It is for the student to experience the internal meaning of these instructions. Every now and then, fully unexpected, a truly special bamboo leaf appears on the paper. The student knows it is special even before the brush stroke is completed. There is no formula, it cannot be reproduced by direct will:

And what is the mind
and how is it recognized?
It is clearly drawn
in sumi ink, the sound
of breezes drifting through pine.
(Ikku Sojun[4])

When the inexpressible has been made visible, there is nothing else to do but to put it aside and place attention on the next stroke. The same intention as in Zen practice.

Do 1,000 bamboo leaves, then 10,000 more.

Fully unexpected, a truly special bamboo leaf appears on the paper.

Koho Yamamoto

Hesse and Siddhartha's Resume

Hermann Hesse (1877-1962), awarded the Nobel Prize for Literature in 1946, was one of the first Western fiction authors to focus his work on Eastern thought and practices. In 1922, he published *Siddhartha,* the story of a young Indian man's quest to experience the truth. It was translated into English and was very influential in the 60's as awareness of Eastern thought grew in the United States. Hesse has gone in and out of favor several times since then. There are now many works in this genre and his early contributions do not stand out as they once did. In this passage, from Hesse's *Siddhartha*, the title character, having lived as an ascetic for three years in the forest has returned to a city. He is being interviewed by a merchant and has been asked what he can contribute. His response was nine words which have resonated with many readers:

> "I can think, I can wait, I can fast."

The merchant's reply: "Of what use are they? For example, fasting, what good is that?"

> "It is of great value, sir. If a man has nothing to eat, fasting is the most intelligent thing he can do. If, for instance, Siddhartha had not learned to fast, he would have to seek some kind of work today, either with you or elsewhere, for hunger would have driven him. But as it is, Siddhartha can wait calmly. He is not impatient, he is not in need, he can ward off hunger for a long time and laugh at it. Therefore, fasting is useful, sir"
>
> The reply: "You are right."[5]

In Siddhartha's experience as an ascetic he has learned lessons that seemingly have no value to others. This is a question that often arises from others: "What good is it?" Siddhartha had the opportunity to explain. In the passage above, Siddhartha knew what he had learned and if his answer had not been accepted, he would very likely just have moved on to the next situation, with his calmness undisturbed.

Many long time Zen practitioners are asked this same question: "What good is it? Why do you do it?" As with Siddhartha, they know what they have experienced or learned and value it. They may not be able to explain it to another or give a good rational explanation that satisfies them.

Later in the novel, after experiencing his truth, Siddhartha distinguishes between seeking a goal and having a direction in a statement to a follower of the Buddha:

> When someone is seeking, it happens quite easily that he only sees the thing that he is seeking; … because he has a goal, because he is obsessed with that goal. Seeking means: to have a goal; but finding means: to be free, to be receptive, to have no goal. You, O worthy one, are perhaps indeed a seeker, for in striving toward your goal, you do not see many things that are under your nose.[6]

This comment echoes those by Zen teachers everywhere: when one stops seeking peace in other places, the mind will naturally come to rest and one will be present to life just as it is.

Bird in the Cage Story Revisited

This story was presented at the beginning of the Introduction. It is included here with additional commentary made to the Bard High School Early College Graduating Students.

There are a couple of points to keep in mind when listening to a Zen story. First, the story is always about you. This one appears to be about a bird, but see how it resonates in your own life as you hear it. Even if you have heard it before, the reaction today may be different, because the time and conditions are changed. Second, the story does not have a traditional ending; rather it is your individual response to it that gives it power.

> A bird found himself in a cage. He did not know how he got there. The cage life was really all he remembered and, as such, it seemed like a normal life for him.
>
> The cage was decent sized and there was enough room to move around comfortably, although not to fly. He regularly toured the cage, often finding twigs, straw, and cloth, as well as food and water. Well, the bird thought, since he was here, he may as well make himself comfortable. So, he began making a crude nest. As time went on, he found other things around to make himself a first class home, with plenty of diversions and sufficient food. Not too bad, he thought. It might be nice to try out the wings, but then again, he was comfortable.
>
> One day, during his regular inspection tour, he was surprised to see that the cage had a door! The cage had not been changed, the door had always been there; the bird had simply not noticed it before. The bird was intrigued and inspected it further. To his

astonishment, the latch of the door was not locked. With one peck on his part, the latch disengaged and the door swung open. He was free to go if he chose.

There were never any constraints, just the lack of recognition of the actual situation. It only appeared to be a new condition. The bird perched at the threshold of flying into freedom. The bird could go through the gate into the unknown. Perhaps he would experience the true freedom of the flight of the bird, or be eaten by a predator. Another option was to stay inside and maintain his comfortable style.

Life is always bringing new situations that require us to act; it is the nature of life itself. But how do you choose? What abilities or insights have to be developed or grown in order to proceed well with our life? It is true for all of us and it is especially relevant as you leave the school and push off in new directions.

The first is to have eyes that see the truth. Not physical eyes, but the ability to experience life just as it is. Not how we want it to be, not how it should be, not how our parents or others told us how it is. Life just as it is in the moment. Some people may call it understanding one's own nature, but that is a different conversation.

Second, feet that can function (metaphorically), that can move or stand still as appropriate for the situation. Storms often arise in life. Think about the summer storms—they come on suddenly and with disrupting power, wreak havoc, and then just as quickly are gone. Sometimes they may be emotional or physical, but they come through us with power and perhaps leave a mess to be cleaned up. Our storms may be emotional or physical, we cannot run from them, but stand firm and upright, weather them out. Other situations are different. They require initiative action, a stepping out, if you will, into a new situation, a new set of experiences. Our feet must have the capability to do both.

Third is the heart of intuitive courage. The strength to be able to choose to do what is appropriate once the situation has been recognized. This is not easy. Internally, it is often a struggle between the intellect and the heart. On occasion, it requires a decision directly in conflict with the mind or emotions.

Eyes that see the truth, feet that can function, a heart of intuitive courage. Where do these come from? The good news is that we already have them. It is our responsibility to develop them, allow them to grow and to express themselves in our own life. The other news is that no one but ourselves can do this. There are no teachers or books that can make this happen. It takes work and effort. Each individual has their own path for this growth, but there are some guides.

APPENDICES

APPENDIX A

Clarifying Terms for Context

Most terms are defined in the text. Some require additional clarification.

Arhat (Arahant) One who has attained liberation.

Bodhisattva An enlightened being who vows to remain in the world until all other beings are also liberated. Sakyamuni, World Honored One, Tathagata, Thus Come One.

Buddha nature The inherent nature that exists in all beings. All beings have the potential to realize it.
The following terms have been used more or less interchangeably by different teachers or translators over the ages. Perhaps they are not quite the same, but they can provide a context for this introduction.

Buddha nature	Dharma nature	Dharmakaya
Tathagata	Mind	One Mind
Original Mind	Universal self	No-self
Suchness	Non-duality	Middle Way

Chan See Zen

Co-dependent Origination. See Chapter 9. Other translations: dependent origination, conditioned origination, causal interdependence

Dharma and dharma The word 'dharma' (also used as 'dhamma") has many meanings and has been difficult to translate. The commonly accepted usages are:

Dharma refers to the teachings of the Buddha. This would include meditation practice (zazen), precepts, sutras, and rituals.

dharma are the phenomena of the world. As such, they have causes and conditions and do not exist independently. dharma are always arising and disappearing based on the previous conditions.

Dharma Body means the essence of Buddhahood, the ultimate truth of all things, and the true nature of the Buddha's life. The term body refers to a group or collection. With this meaning of body, the dharma body is composed of qualities and teachings which represent the truth that the Buddha embodied. In Buddhist teaching, there are three bodies or aspects of the Buddha: an ordinary person (manifest body), Buddha as seen by enlightened beings (reward body), and the dharma body.

Emptiness is the absence of an independent nature of all phenomena. Emptiness is not nothingness. It is not the absence of existence but the absence of a falsely perceived independent existence.

The perceptions of phenomena that are experienced through the senses give rise to the erroneous concept that the phenomena have an independent existence. This false impression leads to the concept that beings have an independent 'self.'

Koan Originated as a saying or anecdote from a Zen teacher used to investigate the nature of the mind. The purpose is to help go beyond rational analysis to have a direct perception of emptiness.

Mind is used in different contexts. See Chapter 10.

Nirvana Extinction of desire and suffering, the state of liberation through full enlightenment.

Precepts Basic guidelines for moral behavior.

Samadhi States of meditative absorption in which mind and environment are innately one.

Sangha Buddhist community.

Satori The experience of one's true nature, translated also as enlightenment.

Three Treasures Buddha, Dharma, and Sangha.

Zazen Zen Meditation.

Zen (C. Chan) School of Buddhism characterized by its teachings of enlightenment through direct experience of the nature of mind. The word 'zen' has its story. It is derived from the Chinese word 'chan' which is a Chinese transliteration of the Sanskrit word 'dhyana,' which means meditation.

APPENDIX B

Outlines of Meditation Practice

The Zen meditation methods outlined in this Appendix can serve either as a broad introduction to meditation practices or as a review of the methods. It is suggested that the reader have personal instruction in these methods either by an experienced practitioner or an online video.

Following the Breath

Meditation develops the capacity to live and experience the present moment without being pulled into a story of what is happening. The meditation process allows us to observe our conditioned patterns of using our mind (e.g., planning, recalling arguments, fantasizing, worrying) and work to sustain our awareness without these habits of mind. Our own experience shows us how these conditioned responses cause suffering and pain in our daily life. It is not necessary to judge them, or try to get rid of them. Meditation is about observing our state of mind (often out of control) and working with it.

Posture

In order to observe and work with the mind, it is necessary first to hold the body still so that it is not a distraction. This is the basis for the posture instructions. The important point is to position the base of the body so that it is stable and can be held still. The principle is that three points of contact make a stable position.

Chair: Sit on the forward third of the chair with the feet flat on the floor. The back is held erect as described below and is not supported by the back of the chair. The feet should be at shoulder width to provide the three points of contact.

Cushion: Sit on the forward third of the cushion. The cushion elevates the buttocks so that your knees can meet the ground firmly.

The Burmese position is more accessible for beginners since

it puts the least stress on the joints. In this position, the right foot is pulled close to the thigh, allowing the foot and calf to rest on the floor. The left foot is placed in front of the right calf so that both knees touch the mat.

The important point is to make sure that the knees are solid on the ground in order to form a stable 3 point position. If the knees do not touch the ground, try a higher cushion or an additional support pillow under one knee. If this position cannot be held with both knees down, it is advisable to try a chair.

Spine is centered by rocking side to side in gentle arcs of decreasing size to come to an upright position. Straighten the spine from the small of the back. (There will be a slight curve in the lower back.)

Head is aligned by pushing up toward the ceiling and relaxing. The base of the neck is in a line with the spine. Head is straight, with the tip of the nose centered over the navel and the ears parallel with the shoulders. Chin is tucked in slightly.

Eyes are neither fully opened nor fully closed, but lowered to a 45 degree angle and unfocused, directed toward the floor approximately three feet in front.

Mouth is closed.

Hands can be in the more comfortable of two positions. The favored hand, palm up, holds the other hand. The middle knuckles overlapping slightly and the thumb tips lightly touching, forming an oval. The oval is perpendicular to the floor. This is frequently referred to as a mudra. The arms and wrists can rest on the legs in a comfortable position. If the hands are held in space, without support, the shoulders will quickly become tired or sore. Alternatively, if this position does not feel comfortable, the hands, palms down, may be placed on the thighs, at a comfortable distance. This position may be more comfortable when sitting in a chair.

This posture will allow you to hold the body still, without undue tension. It is essential to remain still during zazen.

Breath

The breath is used as a reference point. It is always present and has a cyclical quality.

Breathing is from the abdomen. Breathe through the nose unless congested. To check breathing, you can place your hands just below your rib cage on each side. During diaphragmatic breathing, you will feel the rib cage gently rise and fall with each breath. After this pattern has been established, return your hands to the mudra position.

Breathing is slow and rhythmic. A natural rhythm will be established. Typically, this may be ~4-6 inhalation/exhalation cycles/minute.

Mind

Put your full attention on the breath. Count inhalation (1), exhalation (2), inhalation (3) and continue through ten and repeat the cycle. The counting is an aid to help you to be aware of the activity of the mind. There is no goal or reward for getting to ten.

As thoughts appear, acknowledge them, let them go, and bring your attention back to the breath. Random thoughts are natural. If the thoughts develop into a train or story, your attention will go with it. As soon as you become aware of it, simply acknowledge the thought, let it go, and return your attention to the breath starting at 1. Continue this practice.

At some point, some practitioners drop the counting and simply put the attention on the breath.

As you let go of the thought, do not judge it, your sitting, or anything else. Let the thought go as if dropping a feather. Simply resume your attention on the breath. Just practice. The crux of meditation is to be aware and when the mind drifts, just return the attention to the present moment of the breath each time.

Just Sitting: Shikantaza/Silent Illumination

Just Sitting is another method of zazen meditation. It is sitting in an alert condition; one just sits in expanding awareness, aware of the sensations of being alive. The breath is not followed. When one becomes aware of a distraction (disturbance in the mind), one returns to open awareness. In this section, the background of this method is discussed and the instructions outlined. Silent Illumination/Shikantaza is not typically the beginning practice and can be carefully introduced after the mind has settled somewhat.

In Zen, the practice is called Shikantaza. In Chinese Chan, it is the 'Silent Illumination Method.' The practices are similar. Silent Illumination has been referred to as 'Shikantaza with more instructions.' In this outline, both will be in the same discussion.

Shikantaza

> Shikan is translated as wholeheartedness .... Shikan is exactly becoming one with the process itself. Literally, Za of taza is zazen and ta means to hit; so, from moment to moment, we have to hit the bull's eye of zazen itself. This is not a technique ... (because) Shikan is exactly taza—full devotion (effort) to the process of zazen itself, that is, to the process itself and not to a concept.[1]

Silent Illumination

> Silent: No reactivity in the mind; nothing to be added to the experience.
> Illumination: The mind is engaged and bright.

An important point is suggested in the title: A quiet mind does not mean stopping the activities of mind. It means your mind pervades your whole body. In the Silent Illumination method, there is no object to limit the awareness. 'Ordinary' mind is aware, or in other words, it is the natural state of just being with what is. This practice is about expanding awareness and can lead to the unification of mind and environment.

Hongzhi Zhengjui (1091-1157) first formally described the practice of Shikantaza, which was later expanded by Dogen. Hongzhi states:

> "Respond unencumbered to each speck of dust without becoming its partner. The subtlety of seeing and hearing transcends mere colors and sounds."
>
> "The practice of true reality is simply to sit serenely in silent introspection. When you have fathomed this you cannot be turned around by external causes and conditions." [2]

'Ordinary' mind is aware, the natural state of mind; often we do impede the natural flow. The practice is just to get out of the way and fully inhabit the moment.

As noted above, Shikantaza is generally not the initial practice. Usually, a practice such as following the breath is first introduced so that the mind can be settled. Personal instruction or guidance in the method is usually recommended.

Method

The body posture is the same as described earlier.

Scan the body to identify tension and relax it. One may begin with the forehead, soften the face, and work downward through the body. Wherever tension is identified, place the attention there in order to release it.

Stabilize the mind. A relaxed mind is not a striving mind. Full effort is often associated with the tendency to become tense to reach a goal. On the other hand, a relaxed mind is often associated with less than full effort. Full effort can be made with a relaxed mind. A useful analogy is with performance athletics, where the athlete must have a relaxed mind in order to respond spontaneously with full effort. In meditation, a full effort can be made when the attention is complete, yet without tension.

Move Toward Open Awareness. Allow the attention to be on the sensations of just sitting in the room and being alive in the present moment. Just experience each sensation as it comes and goes with no disturbance. As a reminder, there is no special attention placed on any phenomena, including the breath. Some examples of open awareness:

> Thoughts/Emotions/Sensations that appear to arise from the outside environment.
>
> Hear/Don't Listen: Hearing is attention to what is present. Listening is placing attention somewhere, with intention.
>
> Labeling a thought or sensation is not helpful since it limits the awareness. A sensation labeled "wind" or "breath" leads to a brief attachment and puts a constraint on the openness.

When a sensation (thought, emotion, feeling) stays in the mind. The sensations that disturb the mind are the manifestation of the moment, neither good, nor bad. The process is to work with them, not try to eliminate them.

When a sensation moves through the mind without a disturbance, the mind is silent. However, the mind is bright and alert to being aware of any sensation that lingers or disturbs the mind. That's illumination.

Let it in— No exception—the thought is already in the mind, let it in. It is not to be gotten rid of.

Not to be afraid of thoughts. The only thoughts to be afraid of are those which are not in awareness.

No thought is dismissed.

Let it be— Be with it—observe the contents of the mind to clearly see them and their effect. Examine, but do not add to it or become entangled with it. Feel it. Experience it.

Let it go—The thought will disappear if the origin comes into awareness. Let it pass and return attention to the sensations in the environment.

Return to Open Awareness

Some teachers, but not all, suggest that if the thought sticks in the mind or continues to return, it can be gently investigated for sub-stories to see their effect. Then, let them fade. Some different categories of sub-stories that occasionally arise:

Attachments
Self-interest such as self-promotion
Something is lacking in the present moment
Shame: Confession and repentance

As a closing note, open awareness is not a 'goal.' Rather this is a process in which awareness grows and the mind naturally moves to its natural, quiet state. The only thing to do is to sit here in the present and be aware of being alive. Hongzhi summarizes:

> "Silent and serene, forgetting words, bright clarity appears before you.
> When you reflect it, you become vast, where you embody it, you are spiritually uplifted."[3]

Koan Study

The intent here is to begin to address the initial question "What is a koan?" Originally a koan was a saying, question, or anecdote from a Zen teacher used to investigate the nature of the mind. Koan study developed as questions and answers between Master and students. The method was initially a response to quietism (passive meditation). During the 10th and 11th centuries, the questions and expressions were gathered into collections. The most well-known is the Mumokan (*Gateless Barrier*) by Wu-men compiled in 1228. Since that time, many teachers have published their commentaries on this collection. Each commentary offers a different perspective and is not at all an answer.

There are popular misconceptions about koans. They are not puzzles to be solved. Also, there are no fixed or correct intellectual responses to a koan. In the past, there has been a corruption of this practice. There was a book published (and still available) with 'answers' to koans; these are not answers of course, but they lead to a misunderstanding that there are short-cuts.

The purpose of koan study is to go beyond rational analysis in order to have a direct perception of emptiness. It is a method of meditation in which the meditator wholeheartedly sits with an enigmatic statement or question assigned by the teacher. The process is sometimes referred to as developing a 'mass of doubt.' The response can only be made by going beyond rational thinking to have the same experience as that expressed by the Master when the original statement was made.

As noted, the direction of koan study is to experience the same state of consciousness as the master's state of consciousness when the statement or question was made. This awareness developed in koan study enlivens the person to experience reality as it is. The experience of a koan must be demonstrated in order to 'pass' it. The response is not to provide an explanation or an imitation. Since words are only a vehicle for the truth, a gesture or some type of spontaneous demonstration of experience is usually required to demonstrate insight.

Some examples of koans that have found their way into popular discourse:

> What is the sound of one hand clapping?
> Does a dog have Buddha nature?
> What was your original face before your parents were born?

Requisites for Koan Study

Teacher: A teacher is essential for guidance in formal koan study. There are many ways to go astray working with koans. The teacher's responsibility is to keep the direction clear and comment as appropriate. It is not to provide clues or hints. The teacher's responses are generally spontaneous to the situation and may differ completely from one interview to another.

Spirit of inquiry, without a fixed goal: Practice is about investigation into one's life. Koan study is an intensification of that investigation and is likely to lead to unexpected places. It is a method to go beyond the reliance on the rational. Since there is a component of 'passing' a koan, there can be a real urgency to have a goal in mind. However, one can work with a koan in a joyful or playful state of mind to ameliorate this tendency. This state of mind can help one make the full effort to let the process unfold, even to the point of frustrating the rational mind, rather than forcing it. One can both have a playful attitude and make an intense effort at the same time.

Taut but flexible mind: Koans are not usually the first practice. Generally, a different practice (such as following the breath) is employed initially to settle the mind to some degree. Stable, or not slack, is the working meaning of taut. Flexible means being responsive to the time and conditions. Nothing is forced. For example, some days one can be fully immersed in the koan, other times perhaps not. On those latter days, the activity is to bring attention back to the koan, without recrimination or frustration; that is the way it is.

Full effort with intent and courage to be prepared to move beyond the intellect: There may very well be confusion, uncertainty, and a range of emotions during work with koans. At some point, the powers of the intellect may be exhausted and there will appear to be nowhere to go. The advice is usually to keep going.

Persistence and remaining with the koan at every moment: One stays with the question and allows it to burn inside constantly. The approach here is to be with it in spirit and energy even when engaging in other activities. Just to live with it.

An Example: "Who is calling?"

"Master Zuigan Calls to Himself"

> Every day, Master Zuigan used to call to himself, 'Master!' and would answer, 'Yes!'
> Again, he would call, 'Thoroughly awake! Thoroughly awake!'
> And he would answer, 'Yes! Yes!'
> 'Don't be deceived by others, any day or any time.' 'No! No!'
> (Case 12 Gateless Gate) [4]

What is this calling about? Possibilities:

> Is it Master Zuigan calling to himself?
> Is it Master Zuigan calling to the absolute nature?
> Is there only calling?
> None of the above?

From a personal perspective of the koan, the 'I' who is calling is the small self of sensory perception that appears to inhabit a conceptual world of changing time and conditions. From this discriminating perspective of the everyday world, 'I' am calling to another. This calling to another is an illusion, which can be mistaken for reality.

From the perspective of forgetting the self, there is no one to call and no object to receive the call. There is only the universe talking, manifesting as the appearance of Master Zuigan calling out in the moment.

None of the above: All views are conceptual descriptions. The questions may be starting points, but no rational answer gets at what was going on with Zuigan's experience. The state of mind is still different. This is the focal point of practice, to clear attachments and thinking in order to experience the original mind.

Reject them all. So what's left? To experience the original state of mind as Zuigan.

The verse at the end of the case reinforces the consequences of mistaking the small self as the essential self:

> The reason those who learn the way don't realize the truth,
> It's simply that they perceive the discriminating consciousness they've had all along.
> It is the origin of endless life and death,
> But fools take it for the essential self.

This introduction is a brief response to the initial question of what a koan is. If there is interest, there are countless books and articles which delve into the subject. In the book *Meditating with Koans*, assembled by Zhuhong around 1600 (translated by Cleary), there are many examples of practical instruction and first person accounts of experiences of Masters. These accounts can be used for elaboration and encouragement. This collection of articles is a highly focused work and not a word is wasted.

APPENDIX C

Chronology of Quoted Teachers

Century	**Name**, Dates, Birthplace; Perspective
BCE	**Buddha** (563/480:483-400 BCE, other dates used), Nepal; b. Siddhartha Gautama
	Zhuangzi (4th century BCE), China; Credited with a foundational text of Taoism
1st CE	**Asvaghosa** (80-150), India; Buddhist philosopher
	Nagarjuna (~150-250), India; Buddhist philosopher, including wisdom sutras
	Sengzhao (384-414), China; Blended Buddhist doctrines with Taoism
5th	**Bodhidharma** (5th century), India; Credited with bringing Zen to China
	Hui-Neng (638-713), China; Sixth Patriarch of China, Sudden Enlightenment School
	P'ang, Yun (740-808), China; Esteemed layman
	Joshu (778-897), China; Chan master of Tang dynasty, many koans attributed to his activities
	Zongmi (780-841), China; Patriarch of Hua-Yuan School, harmonized teaching of schools
	Shantidiva (late 7th to mid-8th century), India; Credited with Way of the Bodhisattva
	Huang Po (d 850), China; Master during Tang dynasty founded Rinzai School
	Yang-shan (813-819), China; Abbot of the Kuei-Yang House
	Yung Ming (904-975), China; Hua Yan and Zen writing
	Ta Hui (1089-1163), China; Rinzai teacher, advocate of koan practice
	Hongzhi Zhengjui (1091-1157), China; Described method of Shikantaza

12th	**Dogen E.** (1200-1253), Japan; Founded Soto School, see Chapter 14
	Muju, I. (1227-1312), Japan; Compiled *Sand and Pebbles*
	Stonehouse (Shiwu) (1272-1352), China; Chan poet and hermit
	Bassui, T. (1327-1387), Japan; Revitalized Rinzai school
	Zhu Hong (1535-1615), China; koan guidance
16th	**Soho, T.** (1573-1645), Japan; Rinzai teacher, affected direction of swordsmanship training
	Bankei Y. (1622-1693), Japan; Taught "Unborn Mind"
	Basho, M. (1644-1694), Japan; Haiku
19th	**Shaku, Soyen** (1860-1919), Japan; Represented Zen in Parliament of Religions 1893
	Suzuki, D.T. (1870-1965), Japan; Writings contributed to spread interest in Zen in the West
	Sasaki, Sokei-an (1882-1945), Japan; Founded Buddhist Society of America
	Sawaki, Kodo (1880-1965), Japan; See Chapter 3
	Yasutani, H. (1885-1973), Japan; Soto School, founder of Sanbo Kyodan
20th	**Dumoulin, H.** (1903-1995), Germany; Jesuit theologian, published Zen articles
	Suzuki, Shunryu (1904-1971), Japan; Soto teacher, founded the Zen monastery in San Francisco
	Yamada, Koun (1907-1989), Japan; Prominent in business and Zen, Zen heir to Yasutani
	Uchiyama, K. (1912-1998), Japan; Soto Abbot and encouraged Westerners
	Deshimaru, Taisen (1914-1982), Japan; Founder of Association Zen Internationale
	Beck, Joko (1917-2011), United States; Ordinary Mind Zen School co-founder
	Thich Thien-An (1926-1980), Viet Nam; Founded Buddhist Meditation Center in Los Angeles
	Thich Nhat Hanh (1926), Viet Nam; Founded Plum Village Monastery for Engaged Buddhism
	Sahn, Seung (1927-2004), Korea; Founder of Kwan Um School

	Hsing Yun (1927), China; Taiwanese teacher and proponent of Humanistic Buddhism
	Mazeumi, H. (1931-1995), Japan; Founder of Zen Center of Los Angeles and White Plum Asanga
	Katagiri, D. (1928-1990), Japan; Founder of Minnesota Zen Center
	Sheng-Yen (1931-2009), China; Scholar and Chan teacher
	Dalai Lama (1935), Tibet; b. Tenzin Gyatso, Leader Gelug School of Tibetan Buddhism

APPENDIX D

Bard HSEC Zen Entry Course Summary

I have supported many Zen groups for over 10 years. Most of the people that I have worked with had their first exposure to Zen an older age. When I was teaching Engineering at Bard High School Early College, I took the opportunity to see if college level students would be interested in exposure to a Zen Meditation Practice. To the best of my knowledge, such an experience is not generally available at public schools. In response to their interest, a Zen Practice/Seminar was offered to students. The Seminar was fully subscribed for 20 semesters. This project has been shaped by these experiences.

The initial course was offered at Bard High School Early College in Manhattan. This public school was formed as a partnership between Bard College and the NYC Department of Education in 2001. The premise of the partnership is that motivated students are quite capable of doing advanced and challenging work. The curriculum allows the students to take two years of high school courses and then two years of college courses. They can graduate with an Associate's degree from Bard College at the end of four years and then transfer these credits to their next school.

Each term, about a dozen students expressed interest in the college level Zen Seminar. Each had their own motivations—most were curious, some had exposure to meditation, and others simply needed a credit that fit into their schedule. Over the years, about 300 students elected to have this experience. The diversity of the school was reflected in the class roster. In the last class, there were students from Buddhist, Hindu, Christian, Jewish, and unknown traditions as well as a representation of various ethnic groups.

What was particularly fun was their approach to the course. Their comments, questions, and responses reflected their interests. Their initial questions were often different from those elicited in the traditional introductions to zazen to adults. Over the course of the term, many topics were covered and a not-quite-random framework invariably emerged, covering both mainstream teachings and their own interests.

My intention was to use a combination of meditation, literature responses, stories, and open questions.

Meditation

In the practice component, Zen meditation instructions were presented several times at the beginning of the term, followed by a sitting period. The first week of sitting was five minutes, then ten minutes, and increased each week to extend to 25 minutes, which was one-half of the class period. Then there was discussion time for students to ask questions or make comments about the experience.

It was generally observed that the first two weeks were the most difficult for the group. The ten minutes of sitting seemed like an eternity for some. Since the students voluntarily signed on for the entire semester, they essentially committed to sit through their initial resistance. By the 3rd meeting, sitting still seemed to get easier and the extension of the sitting periods progressed to 25 minutes. Some of the students were quite surprised and pleased that they could make the effort to meditate for 25 minutes. There was no request for them to meditate on their own, some did though. (Asking someone to sit outside of class as a requirement is often a lost cause for all.)

Literature

The literature component consisted of a weekly reading. The selections listed below generally followed the geographical progression of Buddhism from India, China, Japan, and then to the West. Each week, the participants submitted a one-page response to the reading. The instruction was to choose a sentence or paragraph that resonated with them and explore and respond to that selection. It was emphasized that the work was a personal response and not a summary.

A short paper (3-5 pages) was assigned at the end of the term. Typically, a few lines from a sutra (for example from the Heart Sutra: "Form is Exactly Emptiness, Emptiness Exactly Form") were provided, together with two different commentaries. After digesting and responding to the commentaries, the students wrote their own original commentary on the passage. This work allowed them to see for themselves how they internalized their experience of sitting and reading into the larger framework of Zen practice.

Questions

In addition to the weekly response paper, two original questions were also required. The only stipulation was that the questions had some connection to the experience of Zen or Buddhism. Individuals took advantage of that freedom and the submitted questions were wide ranging, including some that are rarely heard in a formal setting. I responded to each person with a short reply. Later, some were discussed with the group.

The response topics and questions are the basis for some of the sections in this book. In class, my immediate response was my synthesis of my own experiences. The intent here is to take a step back and allow the distinctive voices of Zen teachers throughout the ages to contribute to the conversation. Sources are included so that a deeper interest can be satisfied if desired.

One of the joys for all concerned was that there was no curriculum of topics that had to be covered. Individual topics such as impermanence, interconnectedness, emptiness, and original nature naturally appeared. From this exploration over a range of topics, a framework of the group's making developed, and with it an opportunity to see the teachings from different perspectives. The topics discussed here have been developed and written about more carefully than the immediate answers given in the classroom setting.

At the end of each period, a Zen story was presented and left without further elaboration or comment. The very nature of these stories tended to take the students aback and gave them something to think about on the way out. Some of these stories have been included in this work.

Readings

Many, if not all, of these readings have been available online.

Topic	Author	Article	Source
Zazen Instructions		Outlined in Appendix	Zen Entry Points
American Contemporary	Beck	What Practice Is/ Is Not	Everyday Zen
Meditation Practice (Zazen)	Yasutani	Theory and Practice of Zazen	Three Pillars of Zen (Kapleau)
Primary Canon	Buddha	Setting in Motion the Wheel of Truth (First Sermon); Fire Sermon Getting Rid of Cares and Troubles	What the Buddha Taught (Rahula)
Zen from India to China	Bodhi-dharma	Outline of Practice Bloodstream Sermon	Bodhidharma (Red Pine) (3-7, 9-19)
Zen from China to Japan	Dogen	Instructions to the Tenzo Genjo Koan	Moon in a Dew Drop Tanahashi (53-66)
Zen in Japan	Bankei	Sermons	Bankei Zen
Zen Stories	Muju	Stories	Zen Flesh/Zen Bones 1-18, Senzaki and Reps
Introductory Visual Art (12th Century)	Kuoan	10 Oxherding Pictures/Verse	Riding the Ox Home (Loori)
Zen to America	D. T. Suzuki	The Reason of Unreason: The Koan Exercise	Suzuki: Selected Writings
Koan	Wumen	Koan 1: Mu with Commentary	Gateless Gate (Yasutani)
Poetry	Basho	Poetry/Haiku	The Narrow Road to the Deep North (Basho)
Verse	Sozan	Trust in Mind	Zen Source Book (Addiss)

Acknowledgments

Special gratitude to Roshi Robert Kennedy, SJ for taking me on as a student after an extended search for a teacher. When I began, just the two of us sat together in a three seat Zendo in Jersey City. At the time, my children were small. Years later, I became his Dharma Heir and the children had grown to young adults. I express appreciation and admiration to both Finn and Kelsey for living out who they are.

On the academic side, Dr. Michael Lerner, Principal of Bard High School Early College, encouraged the proposal to have a Zen Seminar at the college level when he was Dean of Studies. My colleagues in the Science Department supported me teaching both an engineering course and the seminar. I offer a special recognition to the 287 students who fully subscribed to the course over its 20 semester run. Their wide ranging interests in both the formal teachings of Zen Buddhism, as well as background issues, widened the scope of the discussion and my own understanding. On the technical side, I remember the late Dr. David Pall, founder of the Pall Corporation, for showing me how to move beyond perceived limits. My Sumi-e teacher, Koho Yamamoto, held my hand to the brush and brought out previously unknown artistic potential.

Dr. Michael Russo, Professor of Philosophy at Malloy College, was the motivating force for this work. He encouraged me to undertake the project over a number of years. He graciously took no for an answer and then repeated the proposal several times before it stuck.

My major teaching activity has been the support of independent Zen meditation groups in the New York metropolitan region. These groups meet at their home locations each week and are open to all. The sanghas sponsor retreats which are attended by the others. I have been a primary or a monthly visitor to these groups for between five and ten years. Remarkably, they continue to invite me, and it is a privilege to support them. The current groups with the leaders include: City Tiger @ Xavier (NYC, Marie Bannister), Inisfada (Manhasset, JoAnn Miller), White Plains (Russ Michael), Empty Cup (Brooklyn, Christopher Smith), Malloy College (Rockville Center, Michael Russo), Immaculate Conception (NYC, Genoa Sosa) and previously Fordham (NYC,

Sheila Ross). Their diversity and dedication have challenged and extended my practice.

Parrish Turner provided the initial editing and general guidelines. His suggestions to restructure the work were invaluable and the comment "unpack" still echoes in my mind. James Safarti designed the thoughtful and beautiful cover. There was a major learning curve in making a transition from technical writing for engineers. The three people below worked generously and tirelessly to patiently teach me the art of unpacking. Peggy Schubert dismantled the first draft with a Sawzall and reassembled the debris in the direction of clarity. Marianne Schubert did yeomanlike service in editing the document. She enthusiastically offered organizational suggestions and repaired a semi-infinite number of grammatical errors. Kay Corkett has a fine sense of flow and spared no effort to impart it to me in her extensive revisions. Having a pacer was very motivating to help me to stay on-track. Thanks to M.C. Halfpenny for providing GPS updates of her steady progress on her 2,200 mile Appalachian Trail thru-hike.

Bibliography

Addiss, Stephen, Stanley Lombardo, and Judith Roitman, eds. 2008. *Zen Source Book.* Indianapolis: Hackett.

Anderson, Reb. 2001. *Being Upright.* Boulder: Shambala.

Armstrong, Karen. 2019. *The Lost Art of Scripture: Rescuing the Sacred Texts.* New York: Knopf.

Asvaghosa. 1907. *The Awakening of Faith.* Translated by Timothy Richard. Chennai: Christian Literature Society; (Internet Sacred Text Archive).

—. 2005. *The Awakening of Faith.* Translated by Yoshito Hakeda. New York: Columbia University Press; reprinted dBET Beta PDF: 2017.

Bankei, Yotaku. 1984. *Bankei Zen.* Translated by Peter Haskel. New York: Grove Press.

—. 1984. *The Unborn.* Translated by Norman Waddell. New York: Northpoint.

Basho, Matsuo. 1966. *The Narrow Road to the Deep North.* Translated by Nobuyuki Yuasa. New York: Penguin Classics.

Bassui, Tokusho. 1989. *Mud and Water.* Translated by Arthur Braverman. New York: North Point.

Beck, Charlotte Joko. 1989. *Everyday Zen.* New York: Harper Collins.

Bhikkhu, Thanissaro. 2010. *Skill in Questions: How the Buddha Taught.* Valley Center: Metta Forest Monastery.

Bhikkhu, Ṭhānissaro. n.d. *To Kaccāna Gotta Kaccānagotta Sutta (SN 12:15).* Accessed 2020. https://www.dhammatalks.org/suttas/SN/SN12_15.html. Accessed 2020.

Blum, Mark. 2014. *The Nirvana Sutra: Volume 1 Bdk English Tripitaka: Taisho, 374.* Moraga: BDK America. Accessed 2020. https://www.bdkamerica.org/system/files/pdf/dBET_T0374_NirvanaSutra1_2013_0.pdf.

Bodhidharma. 1987. *Zen Teaching of Bodhidharma.* Translated by Red Pine. New York: North Point.

Bodiford, William. 2008. "Dharma Transmission in Theory and Practice." *Zen Ritual: Studies of Zen Theory in Practice.* Steven Wright and Dale Heine, eds. Oxford: Oxford University Press.

—. 2006. "Remembering Dogen: Eiheiji and Dogen Hagiography." *Journal of Japanese Studies* 32 (1): 1-21.

—. 1993. *Studies in East Asian Buddhism and Soto Zen in Medieval Japan.* Honolulu: Kuroda Institute Book, University of Hawaii Press.

Bolokan, Eitan. 2016. "An Embracing Thought: Contemporary Soto Interpretations of Hishiryo." *Journal of Contemporary Buddhism* (Taylor and Francis Routledge) 17 (1): 17-29.

Buddhist Text Translation Society. n.d. *Sutra in 42 Sections.* Accessed 2020. http://www.cttbusa.org/42s/42sections.asp.

Bushwell, Robert and Donald Lopez, eds. 2017. *Dictionary of Buddhism.* Princeton: Princeton University Press.

Chang, Garma C. C. 2001. *The Buddhist Teaching of Totality: The Philosophy of Hwa Yen Buddhism.* University Park: Pennsylvania State University Press.

Chuan-Yuan, Chang. 1969. *Original Teaching of Ch'an Buddhism: Selected from The Transmission of the Lamp.* New York: Pantheon.

Cleary, J. C. 1991. *Zen Dawn: Early Zen Texts from the Tun Huang.* Boston: Shambala.

Cleary, Thomas. 1998. *Book of Serenity.* Boston: Shambala.

—. 1993. *Flower Ornament Sutra: A Translation of the Avatamsaka Sutra.* Boston: Shambala.

—. 1998. *The Sutra of Hui-Neng, The Grand Master of Zen.* Boston: Shambala.

—. 1997. *The Five Houses of Zen.* Boston, MA: Shambala.

Cleary, Thomas and J. C. Cleary. 1992. *The Blue Cliff Record.* Boston: Shambala.

Cole, Alan. 2015. "Conspiracy's Truth: The Zen of Narrative Cunning in the Platform Sutra." *Asia Major*, 145-175. www.jstor.org/stable/44742489. Accessed 2020.

Conze, Edward. 1959. *Buddhist Scriptures.* New York: Penguin.

—. 2003. *Buddhism: Its Essence and Development.* Mineola: Dover (reprinted 1959 Harper).

Cook, Francis. 1977. *Hua-Yen Buddhism: The Jewel Net of Indra.* University Park: Pennsylvania State University Press.

—. 1991. *The Record of Transmitting the Light (Keisan).* Los Angeles: Center Publications.

Dalai Lama and Galen Rowell. 1995. *My Tibet.* Berkeley: University of California Press.

Dalai Lama. 2005. *How to Expand Love: Widening the Circle of Loving Relationships.* Jeffrey Hopkins, ed. New York: Atria.

Dalai Lama, Desmond Tutu, and Douglas Abrams. 2016. *The Book of Joy: Lasting Happiness in a Changing World.* New York: Avery.

Deshimaru, Taisen. 1981. *Questions to a Zen Master.* Translated by Nancy Amphoux. New York: E. P. Dutton.

—. 1983. *The Ring of the Way.* Translated by Nancy Amphoux. New York, NY: E. P. Dutton.

Dogen, Eihei. 1988. *Dogen's Manuals of Zen Meditation.* Translated by Carl Bielefeldt. Berkeley: University of California Press.

—. 1995. *Moon in a Dew Drop.* Translated by Kazuaki Tanahashi. New York: Northpoint.

—. 1958. *The Soto Approach to Zen.* Tokyo: Layman Buddhist Society Press.

—. 2010. *Treasury of the True Dharma Eye.* Kazuaki Tanahashi, ed. Boston: Shambala.

Dogen, Eihei and Kosho Uchiyama. 1985. *From the Zen Kitchen to Enlightenment.* Translated by Thomas Wright. New York: Weatherhill.

—. 1997. *The Whole Hearted Way.* Translated by Shohaku Okumura and Taigen Daniel Leighton. North Clarendon, VT: Tuttle.

Eckel, Malcolm. 1985. "Gratitude to an Empty Savior: A Study of the Concept of Gratitude in Mahayana Buddhism." *History of Religions.*

Eliot, George. 2004. *Middlemarch.* Gregory Maertz, ed. Peterborough: Broadview Press.

Eng, Tan Swee. 2020. *Differences between Theravada and Mahayana Buddhism.* http://www.buddhanet.net/e-learning/snapshot02.htm.

Feynman, Richard and Ralph Leighton. 2001. *What Do You Care What Other People Think?* New York: Norton.

Ford, James. n.d. "A Note on Dharma Transmission and the Institutions of Zen." *thezensite.* https://www.thezensite.com/ZenEssays/CriticalZen/Dharma_Transmission_Institutions.html. Accessed 2020.

Foundation for Inner Peace. 2007. *A Course in Miracles, 3rd Edition Combined Volume.* Mill Valley: Foundation for Inner Peace.

Fox, Alan. 2016. "The Huayan Metaphysics of Totality." *A Companion to Buddhist Philosophy*. Steven Emmanuel, ed. Hoboken: Wiley-Blackwell.

Fujiti, Issho. 2002 (spring). "Zazen is Not the Same as Meditation." *Insight Journal.* Barre Center for Buddhist Studies.

Goodman, Charles. 2016. *The Training Anthology of Santideva: A Translation of the Siksa-samuccaya.* Oxford: Oxford University Press.

Green, James. 1998. *Recorded Sayings Of Zen Master Joshu.* Boston: Shambala.

—. 2009. *The Sayings of Layman Pang.* Boston: Shambala.

Hamill, Sam, and J. P. Seaton, trans. 2007. *The Poetry of Zen.* Boston: Shambala.

Hanh, Thich Nhat. 2005. *Heart of Understanding.* Berkeley: Parallax Press.

—. 1992. *The Diamond That Cuts Through Illusion.* Berkeley: Parallax Press.

Henderson, Harold. 1958. *An Introduction to Haiku.* New York: Doubleday Anchor.

Hesse, Hermann. 1971. *Siddhartha.* Translated by Hilda Rosner. New York: Bantam.

Huang-Po. 1994. *Zen Teaching of Huang Po.* Translated by John Blofield. Boston: Shambala Pocket Classic.

Hui-Neng. 1969. *The Diamond Sutra and The Sutra of Hui-Neng.* Translated by A. F. Price and Wong Mou-lam. Boston: Shambala.

Jinpa, Thupten, ed. 2017. *Science and Philosophy in the Indian Buddhist Classics: The Physical World.* Translated by Ian Coghlan. Boston: Wisdom Publications.

Kapleau, Phillip. 1965. *Three Pillars of Zen.* New York: Anchor.

Katagiri, Dainin. 2007. *Each Moment is the Universe.* Andrea Martin, ed. Boston: Shambala.

—. 1988. *Returning to Silence.* Yuko Coniff and Willa Hathaway, eds. Boston: Shambala.

—. 1998. *You Have to Say Something.* Steve Hagen, ed. Boston: Shambala.

Keremidschieff, Vladimir. 2005. "Legends in Ch'an: The Northern/Southern Schools Split.". https://www.thezensite.com/ZenEssays/HistoricalZen/Legends_in_Chan.html. Accessed 2020.

Khyentse, Dzongsar. 2017. *A Celebrity Falls Sick.* 84000: Translating the Words of the Buddha. https://84000.co. Accessed 2020.

Klinkenborg, Verlyn. 2019. "The Voice of the Landscape." *New York Review of Books.*

Kramer, Hans Martin. 2013. "How 'Religion' Came to Be Translated as 'Shūkyō Shimaji Mokurai' and the Appropriation of Religion in Early Meiji Japan." *Japan Review* (25): 89-111. JSTOR, www.jstor.org/stable/41959187.

Kubo, Tsugunari, and Akira Yuyama. 2007. *Lotus Sutra.* Moraga, CA: BDK America; 2nd edition. http://www.bdk.or.jp/document/dgtl-dl/dBET_T0262_LotusSutra_2007.pdf.

Lachs, Stuart. 2011. "When the Saints Go Marching In: Modern Day Zen Hagiography." *https://www.eyeofchan.org/all-articles/articles-by-author/by-stuart-lachs/733-saintsgomarchingin.html.* Accessed 2019.

Lewis, Robert, and Zenkei Shibayama. 1996. *The Book of the Zen Grove: Phrases for Zen Practice.* Translated by Robert Lewis. Jacksonville: Zen Sangha Press.

Loori, John. 2002. *Riding the Ox Home.* Boston: Shambala.

—. 2002. *The Art of Just Sitting.* Somerville: Wisdom.

—. 1996. *The Still Point.* Mt. Tremper: Dharma Communications.

Lopez, Barry. 2013. *Arctic Dreams.* New York: Vintage Publications (Kindle edition).

Lowry, Dave. 2001. *Autumn Lightning.* Boston: Shambala.

Loy, David. 1993. "Indra's Postmodern Net." *Philosophy East and West* 43 (3): 481-510. JSTOR, www.jstor.org/stable/1399579.

Mahendra, Anagarika. 2017. *Therigathapali Book of Verses of Elder Bhikkhunis.* Roslindale: Dhamma Publishers.

Matthiessen, Peter. 1987. *The Snow Leopard.* New York: Penguin.

Mazeumi, Taizan, and Bernie Glassman. 2002. *On Zen Practice.* Somerville: Wisdom.

McRae, John. 1986. *The Northern School and the Formation of Early Ch'an*

Buddhism. Honolulu: University of Hawaii Press.

Murcott, Susan. 1991. *The First Buddhist Women.* Berkeley: Parallax Press.

Nagarjuna. 2013. *Nagarjuna's Middle Way.* Translated by Mark Siderits and Shoryu Katsura. Somerville: Wisdom Publications.

Obata, Chiura. 1967. *Sumi-e.* Berkeley: Publisher: Chiura Obata.

Pajin, Dusan. 1988. "On Faith in Mind--Translation and Analysis of the Hsin-hsin Ming." *Journal of Oriental Studies* Vol XXVI #2 270-288.

Pine, Red. 2001. *The Diamond Sutra.* Berkeley: Counterpoint.

Pye, Michael. 2002. *Skilful Means, A Concept in Mahayana Buddhism.* 2nd edition. Abingdon: Routledge.

Rahula, Walpola. 1974. *What the Buddha Taught.* New York: Grove.

Reps, Paul, and Nyogen Senzaki. 1989. *Zen Flesh, Zen Bones.* New York: Anchor.

Ross, Helen, and Cornelis Plug. 2002. *Mystery of the Moon Illusion.* Oxford: Oxford University Press.

Sahn, Seung. 1976. *Dropping Ashes on the Buddha.* Stephen Mitchell, ed. New York: Grove Press.

—. 2006. *Wanting Enlightenment is a Big Mistake.* Hyon Gak. Boston: Shambala.

Sak, D. 2015. "The Great Compassion and Fraternity in Mahayana Buddhist Traditions." *CLARITAS Journal of Dialog and Culture* 4 (2).

Sasaki, Ruth, Yoshitaka Iriya, and Dana Fraser. 1971. *The Recorded Sayings of Layman P'ang: A Ninth Century Zen Classic.* New York: Weatherhill.

Sawaki, Kodo. n.d. *To You.* Jesse Haasch and Muho, eds. http://thezenuniverse.org/kodo-sawaki-part-1/. Accessed 2020.

Schloegl, Irmgard. 1976. *The Wisdom of the Zen Masters.* New York: New Directions.

Sekida, Katsuki. 1977. *Two Zen Classics: Mumonkan and Hekiganroku.* New York: Weatherhill.

Shaku, Soyen. 1974 reprinted from 1906. *Zen for Americans, (Sermons from a Buddhist Abbot).* Translated by D.T. Suzuki. La Salle: Open Court.

Shantidiva. 1997. *The Way of the Bodhisattva.* Translated by Padmakara

Translation Group. Boston: Shambala.

Sheng-Yen. 2005. *Getting the Buddha Mind.* Berkeley: North Atlantic Books.

—. 2001. *Zen Wisdom.* Berkeley: North Atlantic Books.

Shepherd, Nan. 2011. *The Living Mountain.* Edinburgh: Canongate.

Soto Zen Buddhism International Center. 2002. *Soto Zen: An Introduction to Zazen.* San Mateo: Sotoshu Shumucho.

Stonehouse. n.d. *The Mountain Poems of Stonehouse.* Translated by Red Pine. Port Townsend, WA: Copper Canyon Press.

Suzuki, D. T. 1996. *Selected Writings of D. T. Suzuki.* William Barrett, ed. New York: Three Leaves Press.

Suzuki, Shunryu. 1999. *Branching Streams Flow in the Darkness, Zen Talks on the Sandokai.* Mel Weitsman and Michael Wenger, eds. Berkeley: University of California Press.

—. 2002. *Not Always So.* Edward Epse Brown, ed. New York: Harper Collins.

—. 1970. *Zen Mind, Beginners Mind.* Trudy Dixon, ed. New York: Weatherhill.

Ta-Hui. 1977. *Swampland Flowers.* Translated by J. C. Cleary. Boston: Shambala.

Takuan, Soho. 1986. *The Unfettered Mind.* Translated by William Scott Wilson. Tokyo: Kodansha International.

Thera, Nyanaponika et al. 2010. *Collected Wheel Publications Volume VIII: Numbers 101–115.* Kandy: Buddhist Publication Society.

Thich, Thien an. 1975. *Zen Philosophy, Zen Practice.* Cazadero: Dharma Publishing.

Thurman, Robert. 1976. *The Holy Teaching of Vimalakirti.* University Park: Pennsylvania State University Press.

Trafford, Paul. 2009. *An Analysis of the Fifth Precept as Social Protection in Contemporary Contexts with Reference to Early Buddhist Teachings.* MS Thesis, Oxford: Oxford University.

Uchiyama, Kosho. 1973. *Approach to Zen.* Translated by Thomas Wright, Stephen Yenik, and Fred Stober. Tokyo: Japan Publication.

Waley, Arthur. 1939. *Three Ways of Thought in Ancient China.* Palo Alto: Stanford University Press.

Wallis, Glenn. 2007. *Basic Teachings of the Buddha.* New York: Modern Library.

Watson, Burton. 2010. "The Diamond Sutra." *The Eastern Buddhist.* www.jstor.org/stable/26289589.

—. 1993. *The Lotus Sutra.* New York: Columbia University Press.

—. 1997. *Vimalakirti Sutra.* New York: Columbia University Press.

Watts, Alan. 1957. *The Way of Zen.* New York: Vintage/Pantheon.

Weatherspoon, C. P. 1990. "Sequoiadendron giganteum (Giant Sequoia)." In *Silvics of North America Vol 1. Conifers, Agriculture Handbook 654*, by Russell, Honkala, Barbara Burns. Washington D.C.: US Dept of Agriculture, Forest Service.

Yamada, Koun. 1979. *Gateless Gate.* Los Angeles: Center Publications.

—. 2015. *Zen: The Authentic Gate.* Translated by Paul Shepherd. Somerville: Wisdom Publications.

Yampolsky, Phillip. 1967. *The Platform Sutra of the Sixth Patriarch.* New York: Columbia University Press.

Yasutani, Hakuun. 1996. *Flowers Fall.* Translated by Paul Jaffe. Boston: Shambala.

Yun, Hsing. 2001. *Describing the Indescribable.* Translated by Tom Graham. Somerville: Wisdom Publications.

Zhuangzi. 2013. *Complete Works of Zhuangzi.* Translated by Burton Watson. New York: Columbia University Press.

Zhuhong. 1992. *Meditating with Koans.* Translated by J. C. Cleary. Berkeley: Asian Humanities Press.

Primary Sources (Pali Canon)

AN Anguttara Nikaya (The Numerical Discourses of the Buddha).

Trans. T. Bhikkhu 3.65 (1994), 5.159 (1997), 4.42 (1997), 5.148 (2004), 2.31-2.32 (2002), 148 (2004). Access to Insight.

Similar translations: Anguttara Nikaya (The Numerical Discourses of the Buddha). Trans. Bhikku Bodhi. Wisdom Publications, 2012.

MN Mihhhima Nikaya (The Middle Length Discourses of the Buddha). Trans.

T Bhikkhu 63 (1998), 86 (2003); Tera 135 (1994). Access to Insight. Bhikkhu Bodhi 147. SuttaCentral.

Similar Translations: Mihhhima Nikaya (The Middle Length Discourses of the Buddha).

Trans. Bhikkhu Nanamoli and Bhikkhu Bodhi. Wisdom Publications, 2009.

SN Samyutta Nikaya (The Connected Discourses of the Buddha). Trans. T. Bhikkhu 22.86 (2004), 12.15 (1997), 56.11 (1993), 56.11 (1993); Ireland 22.18 (2006). Access to Insight. Sujato 22.95 SuttaCentral.

Similar Translations: Samyutta Nikaya (The Connected Discourses of the Buddha).
Trans. Bhikkhu Bodhi. Wisdom Publications, 2000.

UD Udana. Trans. Ireland 1.3 (1998). Access to Insight.

ID Itivuttaka. Trans. T. Bhikku 3.11 (2001). Access to Insight.

Similar Translations at: The Udana and the Itivuttaka: Two Classics from the Pali Canon. Trans. John D. Ireland. Kandy, Sri Lanka: Buddhist Publication Society, 1997.

KN Khuddaka Nikaya (Collection of Little Texts). P. Thera Khp 1-6;9 (1999).

Similar Translations: Panca Sila. Access to Insight.

DN Digha Nikaya (The Long Discourses of the Buddha). Trans. T. Bhikku 11 (1997). Access to Insight.

Similar Translation: The Long Discourses of the Buddha: A Trans lation of the Digha Nikaya (The Teachings of the Buddha). Trans. Maurice Walshe. Wisdom, 1995.

Endnotes

Introduction

1. Francis Cook, *The Record of Transmitting the Light (Keisan)*, 33.
2. Shantidiva, "The Excellence of Bodhichitta," *The Way of the Bodhisattva,* 33 v2.
3. The online world is very dynamic. At this writing, some sites, such as 'Access to Insight' have excellent reputations for the quality of their translations. In some cases, multiple translations are available there. There are a number of similar, but less comprehensive sites, which have been referenced. In general, the internal search engines of these sites leave something to be desired and it is easier to find the sutra passage by a browser search with a site reference. Print references are also provided except for web only articles.
4. Barry Lopez, *Arctic Dreams,* Kindle loc 4476.
5. Ibid., 4481.
6. Ibid., 4537.
7. Verlyn Klinkenborg "The Voice of the Landscape," *New York Review of Books*, Sept 26, 2019, 57.
8. Arthur Waley, "The Frog in the Well." *Three Ways of Thought in Ancient China,* 57.

Chapter 1

1. Koun Yamada, *Zen: The Authentic Gate*, 179.
2. Shunryu Suzuki, *Not Always So,* 97.
3. Soho Takuan, *The Unfettered Mind,* 38.
4. Ta-Hui, *Swampland Flowers,* 37.
5. Koun Yamada, *Gateless Gate*, 210.
6. Eihei Dogen, "Recommendations for Zazen," *Treasury of the True Dharma Eye,* 907.
7. Eihei Dogen and Kosho Uchiyama, "Bendowa," *The Whole Hearted Way,* 30.
8. Eihei Dogen, "Rules for Zazen," *Treasury of the True Dharma Eye,* 580.
9. Issho Fujiti, "Zazen is Not the Same as Meditation," *Insight Journal,* Spring 2002.
10. Kosho Uchiyama, *Approach to Zen*, 34.
11. Irmgard Schoegl, "The Master Gardener."*The Wisdom of the Zen Masters,* 52.
12. Eihei Dogen, *The Poetry of Zen,* trans. Sam Hamill and J. P. Seaton, 119.

Chapter 2

1. Dave Lowry, *Autumn Lightning,* adapted from ch 3; also in Paul Reps and Nyogen Senzaki, *Zen Flesh, Zen Bones,* #91.

2. Koun Yamada, *Zen: The Authentic Gate,* 194.
3. Taisen Deshimaru, *Questions to a Zen Master,* 96.
4. Kodo Sawaki, *To You,* sec 13.
5. Yotaku Bankei, "The Ryumon Sermons," *The Unborn,* trans. Norman Waddell, 69.
6. Eihei Dogen and Kosho Uchiyama, "Bendowa," *The Whole Hearted Way,* 30.
7. Robert Lewis, trans., *The Book of the Zen Grove*, 81.
8. Koun Yamada, *Zen: The Authentic Gate,* 64 quoted.
9. Edward Conze, *Buddhism: Its Essence and Development,* (paperback), 104.
10. Charlotte Joko Beck, *Everyday Zen,* 23.
11. Ruth Fuller Sasaki, Iriya Yoshitaka, and Dana Fraser, trans., "Dialogues with Shih-Tou," *The Recorded Sayings of Layman P'ang: A Ninth Century Zen Classic,* 46.
12. Nagarjuna, *Nagarjuna's Middle Way*, ch 24, 14.
13. Hans Martin Kramer, "How 'Religion' Came to Be Translated as 'Shūkyō Shimaji Mokurai' and the Appropriation of Religion in Early Meiji Japan," *Japan Review* (25): 89-111.
14. Koun Yamada, *Zen: The Authentic Gate*, 12,174.
15. Kosho Uchiyama, *Approach to Zen*, 78.
16. Ibid., 113.
17. Taisen Deshimaru, *Questions to a Zen Master,* 62.
18. Irmgard Schoegl, *The Wisdom of the Zen Masters,* 79.
19. Bodhidharma, "Outline of Practice," *Zen Teaching of Bodhidharma,* trans. Red Pine, 3-7.
20. J. C. Cleary, *Zen Dawn: Early Zen Texts from the Tun Huang,* 34.
21. Kodo Sawaki, *To You,* sec 10, 12.

Chapter 3

1. Robert Thurman, *The Holy Teaching of Vimalakirti*, 35.
2. Dzongsar Khyentse, *A Celebrity Falls Sick,* 35.
3. Thomas Cleary, *The Five Houses of Zen*, 27.
4. Chang Chuan-Yuan, *Original Teaching of Ch'an Buddhism: Selected from The Transmission of the Lamp*, 212.
5. Michael Pye, *Skilful Means, A Concept in Mahayana Buddhism,* 2nd edition, 159.
6. Hakuyo Taizan Mazeumi and Bernard Glassman, *On Zen Practice*, 2002, 56, 58.
7. Irmgard Schoegl, *The Wisdom of the Zen Masters,* 57.
8. Kosho Uchiyama, *Approach to Zen*, (2004 edition only) xxxvii.
9. Tokusho Bassui, *Mud and Water*, 33.
10. Bodhidharma, "Breakthrough Sermon," *Zen Teaching of Bodhidharma,* trans. Red Pine, 95.

Chapter 4

1. Burton Watson, "Expedient Means," *The Lotus Sutra,* 32.

2. Michael Pye, *Skilful Means, A Concept in Mahayana Buddhism,* 2nd edition, 31.
3. Zhuangzi, *Complete Works of Zhuangzi,* trans. Burton Watson, 231.
4. Ibid., 233.
5. Katsuki Sekida, *Two Zen Classics*, 111.
6. Thanissaro Bhikkhu, *Skill in Questions: How the Buddha Taught,* 36.
7. Dainin Katagiri, *Each Moment is the Universe*, 64.
8. Tsugunari Kubo, *Lotus Sutra,* ch 7, 131.
9. Burton Watson, *The Lotus Sutra,* 135.
10. Hsing Yun, *Describing the Indescribable*, 93.
11. Thicht Nhat Hanh, *Heart of Understanding*, 45.
12. Burton Watson, "The Diamond Sutra," *The Eastern Buddhist*, 41 (1): 67-100.
13. Ibid., 73.
14. Hsing Yun, *Describing the Indescribable*, 94.
15. Alan Watts, *The Way of Zen*, 126.
16. Eihei Dogen, "Mountains and Rivers Sutra," *Treasury of the True Dharma Eye,* 164.

Chapter 5

1. Shunryu Suzuki, *Not Always So,* 87.
2. Sheng-Yen, *Zen Wisdom*, 145.
3. Seung Sahn, *Dropping Ashes on the Buddha*, 12.
4. William Bodiford, "Dharma Transmission in Theory and Practice," *Zen Ritual: Studies of Zen Theory in Practice*, 268.
5. Stuart Lachs, "When the Saints Go Marching In: Modern Day Zen Hagiography," 2011, conference paper available online.
6. James Ford, "A Note on Dharma Transmission and the Institutions of Zen," *thezensite.*
7. Francis Cook, *The Record of Transmitting the Light (Keisan)*, 91.
8. Soyen Shaku, *Zen for Americans: Sermons from a Buddhist Abbot*, 86.

Chapter 6

1. Thicht Nhat Hanh, the 2005 *Heart of Understanding* is one of many published and online translations.
2. Karen Armstrong, *The Lost Art of Scripture: Rescuing the Sacred Texts,* Kindle loc 265.
3. Tan Swee Eng, *Differences between Theravada and Mahayana Buddhism,* online table.
4. Dusan Pajin, "On Faith in Mind-Translation and Analysis of the Hsin-hsin Ming," *J. of Oriental Studies,* Vol XXVI, #2, 270.
5. Suffering and the cessation of suffering was only one aspect of the teachings.
6. Robert Bushwell, Robert Lopez, and Donald Lopez, *Dictionary of Buddhism,* dukka, 270.
7. Ṭhanissaro Bhikkhu, *Commentary on To Kaccāna Gotta Kaccānagotta*

Sutta, SN 12:15.
8. Edward Conze, *Buddhism: Its Essence and Development,* 69.
9. Paul Trafford, *An Analysis of the Fifth Precept as Social Protection in Contemporary Contexts with Reference to Early Buddhist Teaching,* MS Thesis: Oxford University, 51.
10. Reb Anderson, *Being Upright*, 137.
11. Thomas Cleary, *Hui-Neng The Grand Master of Zen,* 38.
12. Soto Zen Buddhism International Center, "Samantabhadra Sutra," *Soto Zen: An Introduction to Zazen,* 24.
13. Buddhist Text Translation Society, *Sutra in 42 Sections*, sec 15.
14. Hsing Yun, *Describing the Indescribable*, p 122, Quote: https://hsingyun.org/patience-under-insult/.
15. Shantidiva, *The Way of the Bodhisattva,* back cover.
16. Dalai Lama and Desmond Tutu, *The Book of Joy: Lasting Happiness in a Changing World,* 193.
17. Dalai Lama, *How to Expand Love: Widening the Circle of Loving Relationships,* 63.
18. Eckel, Malcolm. 1985, "Gratitude to an Empty Savior: A Study of the Concept of Gratitude in Mahayana Buddhism," *History of Religions,* 25 (1): 57-75.
19. Shantidiva, "Meditation," *The Way of the Bodhisattva*, 128 (v129-31).
20. Eihei Dogen, "Continuous Practice #2," *Treasury of the True Dharma Eye*, 365.
21. Dhammadipa Sak, "The Great Compassion and Fraternity in Mahayana Buddhist Traditions," 92.
22. Eihei Dogen, "Bendowa," *Treasury of the True Dharma Eye*, 17.
23. Sheng-Yen, *Getting the Buddha Mind*, 2005, 111.
24. Koun Yamada, *Zen: The Authentic Gate,* 160.
25. Irmgard Schoegl, *The Wisdom of the Zen Masters*, 61.
26. Stonehouse, *The Mountain Poems of Stonehouse*, 45.

Chapter 7

1. Dalai Lama and Galen Rowell, *My Tibet*, 11.
2. Dalai Lama and Desmond Tutu, *The Book of Joy: Lasting Happiness in a Changing World*, 226.
3. Eihei Dogen and Kosho Uchiyama, *From the Zen Kitchen to Enlightenment*, 64.
4. Bodhidharma, "Wake-Up Sermon," *Zen Teaching of Bodhidharma*, 75.
5. Eihei Dogen and Kosho Uchiyama, *From the Zen Kitchen to Enlightenment*, 66.
6. Bodhidharma, "Outline of Practice," *Zen Teaching of Bodhidharma*, 5.
7. Ibid., 61.
8. Seung Sahn, *Dropping Ashes on the Buddha*, 49.
9. Taisen Deshimaru, *The Ring of the Way,* 91.
10. Shunryu Suzuki, *Not Always So*, 12.
11. Ibid., 7.
12. Peter Matthiessen, *The Snow Leopard*, 246.

13. Stonehouse, *The Mountain Poems of Stonehouse*, 45.
14. Foundation for Inner Peace, *A Course in Miracles, 3rd Edition Combined*, #242.

Chapter 8

1. George Eliot, *Middlemarch,* Chapter XLII, 345.
2. Walpola Rahula, *What the Buddha Taught*, 51.
3. Huang-Po, "The Wan Ling Record," *Zen Teaching of Huang Po,* trans. John Blofield, 119, sec 3.
4. Taisen Deshimaru, *The Ring of the Way,* 66.
5. Huang-Po, "The Chun Chou Record" *Zen Teaching of Huang Po,* trans. John Blofield, 100, sec 32.
6. Ta-Hui, Swampland Flowers, trans. J. C. Cleary, 83.
7. Kosho Uchiyama, *Approach to Zen*, 57.
8. Karen Armstrong, *The Lost Art of Scripture: Rescuing the Sacred Texts,* Kindle loc 5140.
9. Yokatu Bankei, *Bankei Zen*, trans. Peter Haskel, 126.
10. Eihei Dogen, "Shusogi," *The Soto Approach to Zen*, trans. Reiho Masunaga, ch 4, 23.
11. Eihei Dogen, "Genjokoan," *Treasury of the True Dharma Eye*, 30.
12. Taisen Deshimaru, *Questions to a Zen Master,* 14, 29.
13. Richard Feynman and Robert Leighton, *What Do You Care What Other People Think?* 15.
14. Helen Ross and Cornelis Plug, *Mystery of the Moon Illusion*, 195.
15. Bodhidharma, "Wake-up Sermon," *Zen Teaching of Bodhidharma*, trans. Red Pine, 49.
16. Shunryu Suzuki, *Branching Streams Flow in the Darkness: Zen Talks on the Sandokai,* 20.
17. Koun Yamada, *Zen: The Authentic Gate*, 35.
18. Ibid., 63.
19. Kosho Uchiyama, *Approach to Zen*, 52.
20. Koun Yamada, *Zen: The Authentic Gate*, 30, 70.
21. Koun Yamada, *Gateless Gate*, 51.
22. Goodman, Charles, *The Training Anthology of Santideva: A Translation of the Siksa-samuccaya*, 230.
23.Thich Nacht Hanh, *Heart of Understanding, 3.*
24. Nan Shepherd, *The Living Mountain*, 23.
25. Ibid., 48.
26. Alan Fox, "The Huayan Metaphysics of Totality," *A Companion to Buddhist Philosophy,* 181.
27. Garma C. C. Chang, *The Buddhist Teaching of Totality: The Philosophy of Hwa Yen Buddhism*, 157.
28. David Loy, "Indra's Postmodern Net," *Philosophy East and West,* quoted 483 ref 7.
29. Thomas Cleary, *Flower Ornament Sutra A Translation of the Avatamsaka Sutra*, 891-3.
30. Francis Cook, *Hua-Yen Buddhism: The Jewel Net of Indra,* 2.

31. Alan Fox, "The Huayan Metaphysics of Totality," *A Companion to Buddhist Philosophy,*182.

Chapter 9

1. Eihei Dogen and Kosho Uchiyama, *From the Zen Kitchen to Enlightenment,* trans. Thomas Wright, 27.
2. Thupten Jinpa, *Science and Philosophy in the Indian Buddhist Classics: The Physical World,* trans. Ian Coghlan, 245.
3. Robert Bushwell, Robert Lopez, and Donald Lopez, *Dictionary of Buddhism,* 445, ksana.
4. Koun Yamada, *Gateless Gate,* 109.
5. Kodo Sawaki, *To You,* sec 10, 12, 14.
6. Nanamoli Thera, *Collected Wheel Publications,* 2010, Volume VIII: Numbers 101–11, 166.
7. Glenn Wallis, *Basic Teachings of the Buddha,* 125.
8. Thomas Cleary and J. C. Cleary, *The Blue Cliff Record,* 1.
9. Paul Reps and Nyogen Senzaki, " Zen Dialog," *Zen Flesh, Zen Bones,* 73 adapted.

Chapter 10

1. Asvaghosa, *The Awakening of Faith,* trans. Yoshito Hakeda, 2017 edition, xxix, 3.
2. Huang-Po, "The Chun Chou Record," *Zen Teaching of Huang Po,* trans. John Blofield, 47, sec 1.
3. Chang Chuan-Yuan, *Original Teaching of Ch'an Buddhism: Selected from The Transmission of the Lamp,* 88.
4. Huang-Po, "The Wan Ling Record," *Zen Teaching of Huang Po,* trans. John Blofield, 146, sec 20.
5. Asvaghosa, "Water," *The Awakening of Faith,* trans. Yoshito Hakeda, 35, part 3, ch 1.
6. Ibid., "Pottery," 11, ch 3.
7. Ibid., 11-13.
8. Irmgard Schoegl, *The Wisdom of the Zen Masters,* 79.
9. Kodo Sawaki, *To You,* sec 10, 12, 22, 33.
10. Seung Sahn, *Dropping Ashes on the Buddha,* 76, 79.
11. Dainin Katagiri, *You Have to Say Something,* 91.
12. Dainin Katagiri, *Each Moment is the Universe,* 98.
13. Eihei Dogen, "Zazenshin," *Dogen's Manuals of Zen Meditation.* trans. Carl Bielefeldt, 188.
14. Eihei Dogen, "The Point of Zazen," *Treasury of the True Dharma Eye,* 303.
15. Eitan Bolokan, "An Embracing Thought: Contemporary Soto Interpretations of Hishiryo," *J. of Contemporary Buddhism,* 25.
16. Eihei Dogen, "Fukanzazengi," *Dogen's Manuals of Zen Meditation,* trans. Carl Bielefeldt, 178.
17. Eihei Dogen, "Recommending Zazen to All People," *Treasury of the*

True Dharma Eye, 904.
18. Taisen Deshimaru, *The Ring of the Way*, 75.

Chapter 11

1. Thomas Cleary, *The Five Houses of Zen*, 72.
2. Paul Reps and Nyogen Senzaki, "A Cup of Tea," *Zen Flesh, Zen Bones*, 5.
3. Soyen Shaku, *Zen for Americans: Sermons from a Buddhist Abbot*, 165.
4. Burton Watson, "Inquiring About an Illness," *Virmalakirti Sutra,* 74.
5. Michael Pye, *Skilful Means, A Concept in Mahayana Buddhism,* 2nd edition, 86.
6. Soyen Shaku, *Zen for Americans: Sermons from a Buddhist Abbot*, 161.
7. Soho Takuan, *The Unfettered Mind*, 22.
8. Ibid., 28-30.
9. Ibid., 22.
10. Thomas Cleary, *Hui-Neng The Grand Master of Zen*, 39
11. Dainin Katagiri, *Each Moment is the Universe*, 151.
12. Hui-Neng, *The Diamond Sutra and The Sutra of Hui Neng,* trans. by A. F. Price et. al., 51.
13. Red Pine trans., *The Diamond Sutra*, 370.
14. Arthur Waley, *Three Ways of Thought in Ancient China,* 54.
15. Shantidiva, *The Way of the Bodhisattva*, 124 (Meditation v103), 169 (Dedication v49), 107 (Heroic Perseverance v63).

Chapter 12

1. C. Phillip Weatherspoon, "Sequoiadendron giganteum (Giant Sequoia)," in *Silvics of North America, Volume I. Conifers, Handbook # 654,* 552-562.
2. Over the centuries, a great body of thought has been developed so that a detailed description of karma is quite complex. The teachings describe the levels of consciousness which allow the 'energy' created by past action to be stored and manifested in the present.
3. Shantidiva, "Dedication," *The Way of the Bodhisattva*, 162 (v2).
4. Sheng-Yen, *Zen Wisdom*, 103.
5. Shantidiva, "Patience," *The Way of the Bodhisattva*, 82 (v31).

Chapter 13

1. Joshu, *Recorded Sayings Of Zen Master Joshu,* trans. James Green, 11 (#1).
2. Bodhidharma, "Bloodstream Sermon," *Zen Teaching of Bodhidharma,* trans. Red Pine, 29.
3. Ibid., "Wake-up Sermon," 59.
4. Huang-Po, "The Chun Chou Record," *Zen Teaching of Huang Po,* trans. John Blofield, 92, sec 29.
5. Ibid., 88, sec 27.
6. Ibid., "The Wan Ling Record," 140, sec 15.

7. Joshu, *Recorded Sayings Of Zen Master Joshu,* trans. James Green, 25 (#41).
8. Stephan Addiss et. al., *Zen Source Book*, 14.
9. Hakuun Yasutani, *Flowers Fall,* trans. Paul Jaffe, 9.
10. Alan Fox, "The Huayan Metaphysics of Totality," *A Companion to Buddhist Philosophy*, 189.
11. Hsing Yun, *Describing the Indescribable*, 97.
12. Mark Blum, ed., *The Nirvana Sutra: Volume 1 Bdk English Tripitaka: Taisho,* 374, 250.
13. Hakuun Yasutani, *Flowers Fall,* trans. Paul Jaffe, 66.
14. Phillip Yampolsky, *The Platform Sutra of the Sixth Patriarch.*
15. Vladimir Keremidschieff, "Legends in Ch'an: The Northern/Southern Schools Split, Hui-neng and the Platform Sutra."
16. Alan Cole, "Conspiracy's Truth: The Zen of Narrative Cunning in the Platform Sutra," *Asia Major*, 145-175.
17. John McRae, *The Northern School and the Formation of Early Ch'an Buddhism*, 10.
18. Shunryu Suzuki, *Branching Streams Flow in the Darkness, Zen Talks on the Sandokai*, 20, 40.

Chapter 14

1. William Bodiford, "Remembering Dogen: Eiheiji and Dogen Hagiography," *Journal of Japanese Studies.*
2. William Bodiford, *Studies in East Asian Buddhism and Soto Zen in Medieval Japan.*
3. Ibid., 49.
4. Hakuun Yasutani, *Flowers Fall*, 1.
5. Ibid.,10.
6. Taisen Deshimaru, *Questions to a Zen Master,* 18.
7. Eihei Dogen and Kosho Uchiyama, *From the Zen Kitchen to Enlightenment,* trans. Thomas Wright, 7, 9, 16.
8. Paul Reps and Nyogen Senzaki, "No Work, No Food," *Zen Flesh, Zen Bones*, 70.
9. Robert Thurman, "The Disciples Reluctance to Visit Vimalakirti," *The Holy Teaching of Vimalakirti,* 31.
10. Burton Watson, "The Disciples," *Virmalakirti Sutra*, 48.
11. Ibid., "Inquiring About the Illness," 65.
12. Robert Thurman, "The Consolation of the Invalid," *The Holy Teaching of Vimalakirti,* 45.
13. James Green, trans., "Subtleties of Daily Life," *The Sayings of Layman Pang*, 15.
14. Ruth Fuller Sasaki, Iriya Yoshitaka, and Dana Fraser, "Dialogues with Shih-Tou," *The Recorded Sayings of Layman P'ang: A Ninth Century Zen Classic*, 46.
15. Chang Chuan-Yuan, *Original Teaching of Ch'an Buddhism: Selected from The Transmission of the Lamp*, 145.
16. Seung Sahn, *Wanting Enlightenment is a Big Mistake,* 20.

17. Yokatu Bankei, *Bankei Zen,* trans. Peter Haskel, 125.
18. Yotaku Bankei, "The Ryumon-Ji Sermons," *The Unborn*, trans. Norman Waddell, 34, 39, 49, 52.
19. Yokatu Bankei, *Bankei Zen,* trans. Peter Haskel, 132.
20. Anagarika Mahendra, *Therigathapali Book of Verses of Elder Bhikkhunis*, 4, 119.
21. Susan Murcott, *The First Buddhist Women*, 26.
22. Ibid., 62.
22. Anagarika Mahendra, *Therigathapali Book of Verses of Elder Bhikkhunis*, 10.

Chapter 15

1. Matsuo Basho, *The Narrow Road to the Deep North,* trans. Nobuyuki Yuasa, 33.
2. Ibid., 32.
3. Chiura Obata, *Sumi-e*, 14.
4. Sam Hamill and J. P. Seaton, trans., *The Poetry of Zen*, 126.
5. Hermann Hesse, *Siddhartha,* trans. Hilda Rosner, 64.
6. Ibid., 140.

Appendix B

1. Dainin Katagiri, *Returning to Silence*, 123.
2. John Loori, *The Art of Just Sitting*, 4, 15.
3. Ibid., 13.
4. Koun Yamada, *Gateless Gate*, 67.

Made in United States
North Haven, CT
01 August 2022

22125297R00157